# The River Shannon

## A JOURNEY DOWN IRELAND'S LONGEST RIVER

Aiveen Cooper

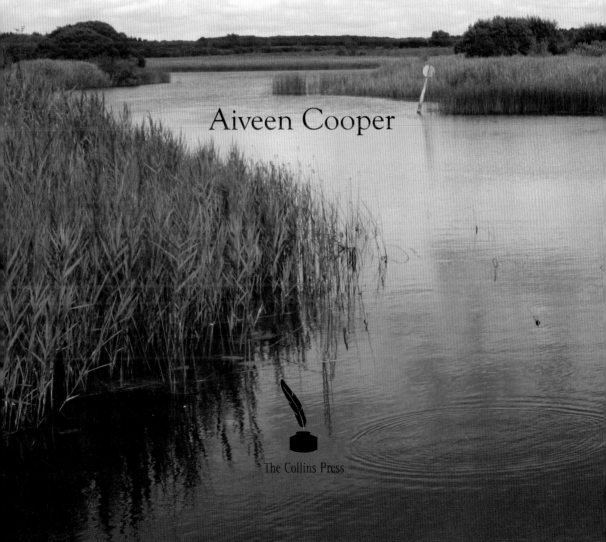

The Collins Press

FIRST PUBLISHED IN 2011 BY
The Collins Press
West Link Park
Doughcloyne
Wilton
Cork

© Aiveen Cooper

Aiveen Cooper has asserted her moral right to be identified as the author of this work.

All photographs are courtesy of the author, unless otherwise credited.

British Library Cataloguing in Publication Data
Cooper, Aiveen.
The River Shannon : a journey down Ireland's longest river.
1. Cooper, Aiveen~Travel~Ireland~Shannon River Valley.
2. Shannon River Valley (Ireland)~Description and travel.
I. Title
914.1'7'04824-dc22
ISBN-13: 9781848891074

Design and typesetting by illuminate creative consultancy
Typeset in Goudy Old Style
Printed in Dubai by Oriental Press

# Contents

# Acknowledgements

My deepest gratitude to The Collins Press for giving me the opportunity to make a lifelong dream come true, and to Juanita Browne for bringing me to their attention.

To John McGinnity and all of my colleagues in NUI Maynooth for giving me the time and flexibility I needed.

To Eric and the *Nieuwe Zorgen* for introducing me to the river, for a wonderful summer on the water, and for the beautiful drawings.

To Mum and Dad for keeping me company on numerous visits to the Shannon and for all the babysitting.

For all of the wonderful photos, thanks to Conor Cahill, Steve McKeown, Kieran Fay (RPS), Enda Thompson (Shannon RBD), Mike Brown, Tony Roche at National Monuments, Kevin Dwyer, Simon Berrow (Irish Whale and Dolphin Group), Colm Keane (Arigna Mining Experience) and Michael Clarke (Eyrecourt and District Development Company).

For advice and information, thanks to Con Manning (National Monuments), Donal Boland, Dr Ken Irvine (TCD), Dr Julian Reynolds, Ruth Delany, Kathryn Finney (BirdWatch Ireland), Colin Becker (IWAI) and John Lefroy.

For proofreading, encouragement and advice, thanks to Dr Julian Reynolds, Mairead Stack, Brendan Keenan, Dr Declan Fahy and Kay Mitchell.

And to save the best for last – to Morgan and Robin for being there for me and for putting up with me. I love you both.

'Tis, it is the Shannon's stream
Brightly glancing, brightly glancing,
See, oh, see the ruddy beam
Upon its waters dancing!
Thus returned from travel vain,
Years of exile, years of pain,
To see old Shannon's face again,
Oh, the bliss entrancing!
Hail our own majestic stream,
Flowing ever, flowing ever,
Silent in the morning beam,
Our own beloved river!

Fling thy rocky portals wide,
Western ocean, western ocean;
Bend ye hills, on either side,
In solemn, deep devotion;
While before the rising gales
On his heaving surface sails,
Half the wealth of Erin's vales,
With undulating motion.
Hail, our own beloved stream,
Flowing ever, flowing ever,
Silent in the morning beam,
Our own majestic river!

(Taken from ''Tis, it is the Shannon's Stream', by Gerald Griffin)

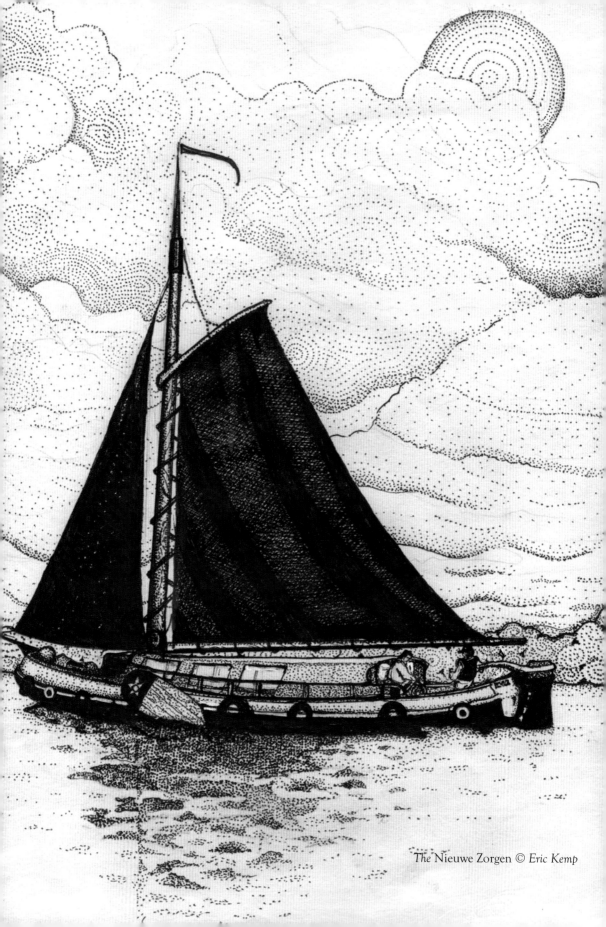

*The Nieuwe Zorgen © Eric Kemp*

# Introduction

Legend says that the River Shannon is named after Sinann, daughter of Lodan, who was son of Lear the great sea-king of the Tuatha De Danann. Sinann came to St Connla's well to gain the knowledge held by the salmon living in there. The well was surrounded by nine beautiful hazel trees, whose hazelnuts were said to hold the finest knowledge of literature, poetry and art. When the hazelnuts fell into the water, the salmon would eat them and thus gain all the knowledge they held. Sinann intended to gain that knowledge herself by catching one of the salmon from the well and eating it. However, it was forbidden for women to visit the well, and as soon as she approached, the waters rose up and burst the banks of the well, overwhelming the Lady Sinann and carrying her lifeless body away towards the river we know now as the Shannon. The well subsequently dried up, and it is not known exactly where it was located, or even who St Connla was. It is thought that the lifeless body of the unfortunate Lady Sinnan was washed up near the head of Lough Derg, close to Portumna. Another explanation is much simpler, attributing the name Shannon to the Irish for 'Old River', or Sean Abhainn.

During the second century, when the Greek geographer Ptolemy was making an atlas of the world, he marked the River Shannon as 'Senos'. But the origins of the Shannon go much further back. It is thought that the river was formed during the Neogene period over 30 million years ago, but the form and flow of the river today are mainly a result of the last glaciation in Ireland, which ended 10,000 years ago. In more recent centuries, humans have had an important role to play in determining the way the river flows. Although the river is slow flowing and naturally navigable for most of its length, in the eighteenth and nineteenth centuries major works began to improve the Shannon for navigation. These works are most obvious where locks and houses, bridges and navigation arches were constructed.

Less obvious are the works that were carried out on the river itself, from dredging and straightening to building embankments and new channels.

This work began in the 1750s, when the Dutch engineer Thomas Omer was hired by the Commissioners for Inland Navigation to improve the navigability of the river. The move stemmed from the reluctance of the Irish Parliament to send excess revenue to the English Crown. They decided instead to divert the funds to public works in the form of navigation improvements. Omer was taken on for the section between Killaloe in County Clare and Carrick-on-Shannon in County Leitrim. He started work in 1755 at Meelick in County Galway, and from there he worked his way upstream to Lanesborough in County Longford. A second engineer, William Ockenden, was hired to oversee the section of the river from Killaloe to Limerick.

In 1831, a commission was established to report on the condition of the River Shannon. Thomas Rhodes, a civil engineer who had worked on navigation and harbours in England and Scotland, was one member of the commission. Rhodes was given the task of surveying the Shannon from Limerick to the source. In Ruth Delany's book, *The Shannon Navigation*, she says that the words 'impassable' and 'dilapidated' came up very frequently in the report, even though Rhodes considered the Shannon as a river to be 'superior to any in the Empire'. Following the survey, the Shannon Commission recommended that the river be put under the auspices of a single body, with the power and resources to carry out the necessary developments to improve the navigation. A Shannon Navigation Act was passed in 1834, which appointed 'Commissioners for the Improvement of the River Shannon'. The Shannon Commissioners began work to improve the river's navigation so that it could be used by steamers, which had been introduced to the Shannon in 1826. Thomas Rhodes was appointed as principal engineer, and much of his task was to replace the earlier works of Thomas Omer. As we travel the length of the river, Omer and Rhodes are two names we will come across again and again.

The Shannon is the longest river in Ireland, flowing over 250 km to its tidal limits in Limerick from its source in the Cuilcagh Mountains, County Cavan, and 370 km in total to the mouth of the Shannon Estuary. The river drops by only 16 m for 160 km of its course. The catchment area of the Shannon is 15,000 sq. km, which makes up one-fifth of Ireland's land mass. This figure has changed in recent years as, under the aegis of the EU Water Framework Directive (WFD), Irish rivers are now being managed as River Basin Districts (RBDs). This directive compels all EU member states to maintain the 'high status' of waters where it exists, prevent any deterioration in the existing status of waters and achieve at least 'good status' in relation to all waters by 2015. In Ireland, it has been decided to divide the country into eight RBDs, and develop management plans for each in accordance with the Water Framework Directive.

The Shannon RBD covers the natural drainage basin of the River Shannon, stretching from its source, the Shannon Pot, in the Cuilcagh Mountains in County Cavan, to the tip of the Dingle Peninsula in north Kerry. It also includes coastal parts of Kerry and Clare that drain to the sea. It flows through 18 local authority areas (the largest being Limerick, Clare, North Tipperary, Offaly, Westmeath, Longford and Roscommon) and is also considered an international RBD as a small portion of County Fermanagh in Northern Ireland drains underground to the Shannon Pot. What this adds up to is a significantly larger catchment area than has been attributed to the Shannon in the past. The Shannon RBD covers around 18,000 sq. km, mostly in the lowland central area of the Republic.

The level of the Shannon was much higher just after the last ice age, and the floodplain of the river, in combination with those of the River Suck and the lower reaches of the Inny, Brosna and Little Brosna rivers, formed a 70,000 hectare body of water in the midlands known as Lough Boora. As the reeds, sedges and other plant life gradually spread into the shallows of the lake, huge swamps were formed. Eventually, these swamps became the massive areas of midland bog that restricted the Shannon to its present boundaries.

The geology of much of the Shannon catchment consists of carboniferous limestone of various ages, with a smaller amount of shales and sandstones around Lough Allen. Upper Silurian shales dominate the southern end of the catchment around Lough Derg, but a

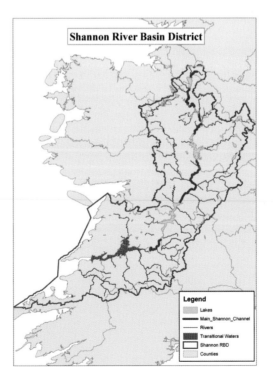

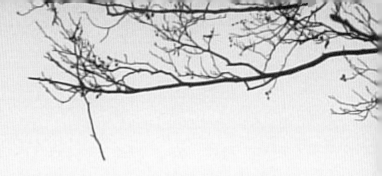

The River Shannon is a very special place in many ways. The statistics tell us that it is the longest river in Great Britain and Ireland. The history books show that many of the milestones in Irish history are mirrored by the history of the Shannon. From Viking raids on monastic settlements and military defences against Napoleon, to transportation, power generation and tourism, the Shannon has borne witness to many of Ireland's turning points throughout history.

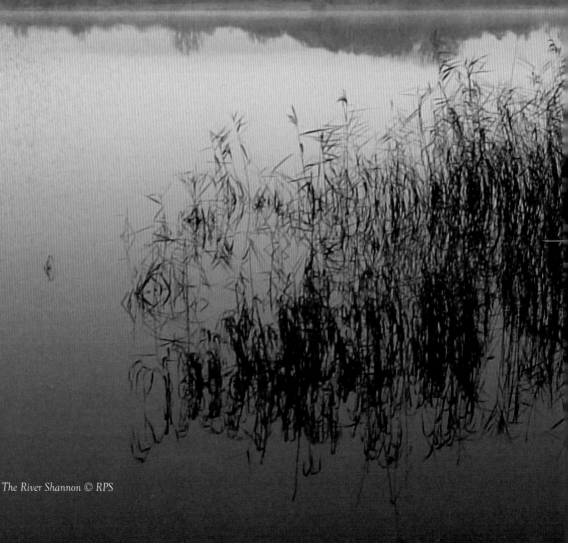

*The River Shannon © RPS*

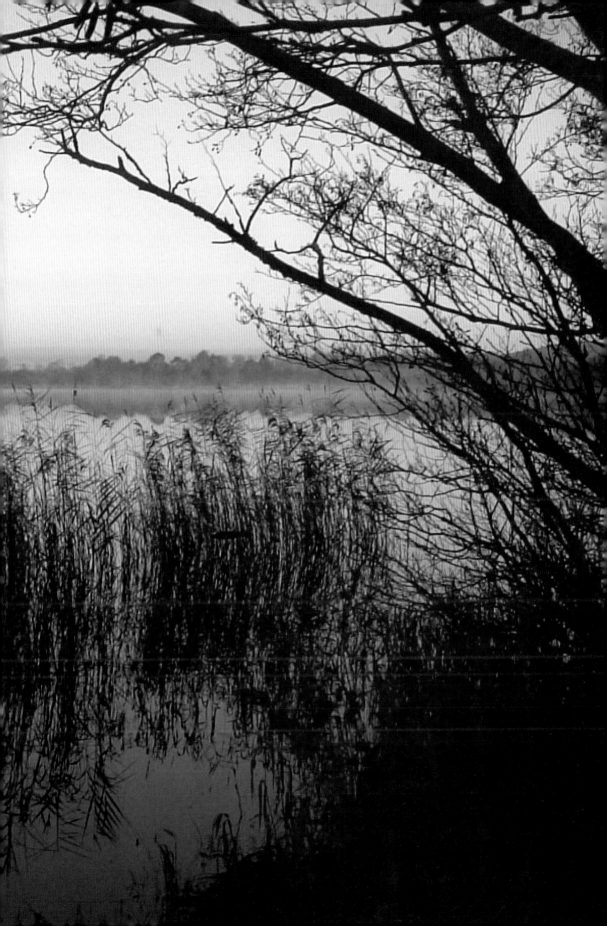

small area of Old Red Sandstone is found east of Scarriff and in the Youghal Bay area. Most of these rocks are covered by material deposited by the glaciers of the last ice age, but some areas along the east of the river are covered by bogs. The poor drainage of the glacial material facilitated the development of raised bog in the centre of the Shannon catchment.

The River Shannon is a very special place in many ways. The statistics tell us that it is the longest river in Great Britain and Ireland. The history books show that many of the milestones in Irish history are mirrored by the history of the Shannon. From Viking raids on monastic settlements and military defences against Napoleon, to transportation, power generation and tourism, the Shannon has borne witness to many of Ireland's turning points throughout history.

The Shannon is mostly shallow, slow flowing and unusually flat, with a small gradient flowing over mainly limestone rocks. Unlike most rivers, the Shannon has not eroded a distinct valley in its middle sections. It is joined by a number of tributaries along its way south, including the Rivers Inny, Suck and Brosna. The river flows through over a dozen lakes, including Lough Allen, Lough Boyle, Lough Ree and Lough Derg. Summer water levels over most of the area are only a few feet below the level of the surrounding fields, so any rise in the water level can result in extensive flooding. Thus the Shannon remains

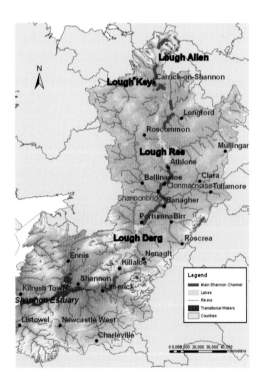

one of the largest undrained rivers in Europe. Lough Derg, the Shannon Callows and the Shannon Estuary are extremely important habitats ecologically, which is reflected in the high number of protected species found at each site. But to many people who live by and love the Shannon there is something else that makes the river special, something they feel but cannot quite put into words. Donal Boland, an underwater archaeologist who has worked and lived on the Shannon for many years, describes the river as 'Shannonland'. This term refers not just the river, but a state of mind that comes from loving the river and losing yourself on, in or near its waters.

I probably would not have understood what Donal meant when I began this project, but by the time I reached the Atlantic Ocean after my long journey from the Cuilcagh Mountains, I began to catch a glimpse. It gets under your skin, and before you realise what has happened you have fallen for the river. I have travelled the length of the river in a variety of ways. Initially I followed in the footsteps of my predecessors, reading everything I could get my hands on from authors such as Ruth Delany, Harry Rice, Maeve Henry, L. T. C. Rolt and Robert Lloyd Praeger to name just a few. Then – by foot, by car, by canoe and by boat – I made my way from the source to the sea. I have been selfish in my description of the river and passed on to you what I found interesting myself, but I hope that it is of interest to you too. At the very least, I hope that you gain some sense of the importance of Shannonland, and feel the urge to visit this magnificent river and experience it for yourself.

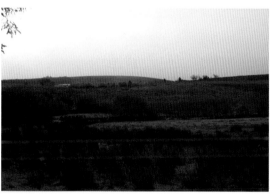
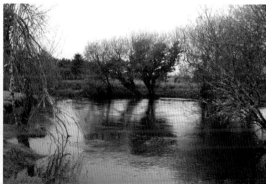

*Approaching Log na Sionna*  *The Shannon Pot*

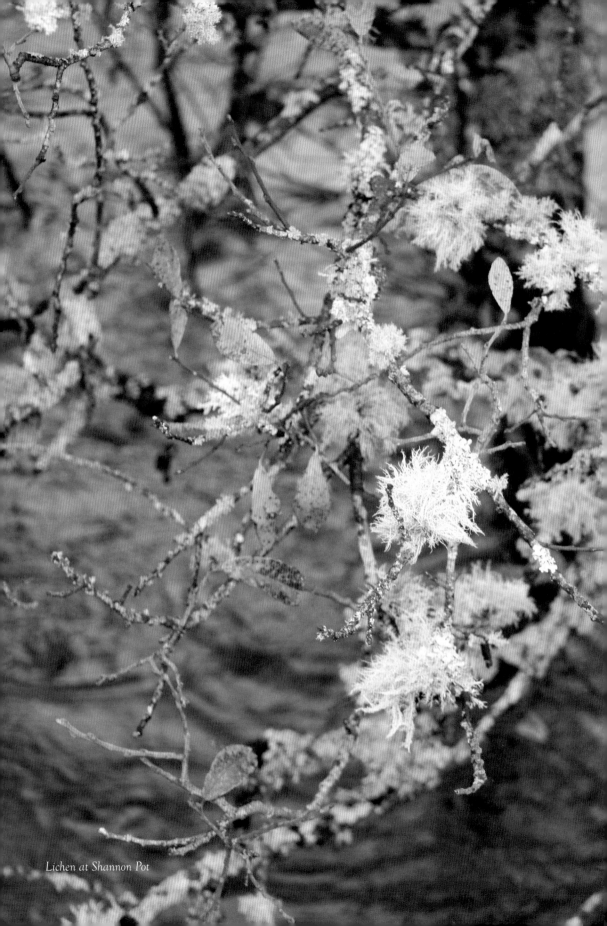

*Lichen at Shannon Pot*

# 1. The Shannon Pot to Lough Allen

My journey down the River Shannon begins on foot on a cold and blustery winter morning, at the foot of the Cuilcagh Mountains, County Cavan. Expecting a difficult walk through boggy mountain terrain, I am kitted out with the necessary rain jacket, thermal underwear, wellies and waterproof leggings. So it is with some surprise and a little disappointment that I discover a concrete path leading from the car park (with picnic benches and information signs) to Log na Sionna, the Shannon Pot. Watched closely by the curious cattle in the surrounding boggy fields, I stroll easily along the path, feeling slightly overdressed and hoping not to meet anyone else. The path leads on to a small wooden footbridge, from where I catch my first glimpse of the source of the Shannon a short distance away at the foot of Tiltinbane, one of the mountains making up the Cuilcaghs. The small brown gushing pool that is the Shannon Pot sits at 152 m above sea level. It is 16 m in diameter and 9 m deep, surrounded by a circle of willow trees. During the summer this must be a wonderfully lush and verdant place of wildflowers, ferns and rushes. But now, in November, the trees are bare except for the grey lichen that drapes their branches. The result is that I can see the pot in all its glory, gushing forth from some unseen hole beneath.

Although originally considered the source of the river, it is now thought that the water in the Shannon Pot probably comes from several different sources, flowing underground before emerging here. Water tracing experiments have shown that there are several underground streams from the Cuilcagh Mountains that flow into the Shannon Pot.

One of these streams disappears underground at Pigeon Pots, over 10 km away in County Fermanagh. From the Shannon Pot, the infant Shannon, which is little more than a stream, flows southwest and is joined by waters of the River Owenmore. The Owenmore, or Abha Mór (big river), as it is called in the Annals of Lough Cé, rises in the Bellavally Hills of the Cuilcagh Mountains and flows 5 miles to the west to meet the smaller stream of the infant Shannon. The small but rapid waters of the Black River join the now wide and fast-flowing Shannon a little farther to the west, below Derrynataun. The Shannon then continues to the small town of Dowra, its last stop before entering the first of the Shannon lakes.

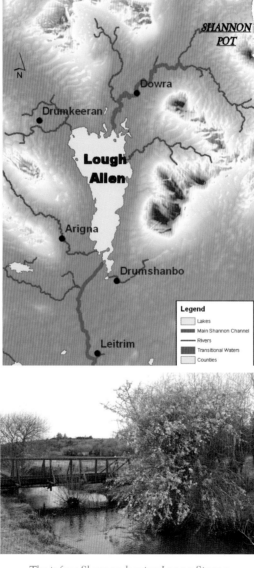

The infant Shannon leaving Log na Sionna

The River Owennyale joins the Shannon at Dowra, swelling the river further before it enters Lough Allen. For walkers, the route of the Cavan Way follows the river closely from Log na Sionna as far as Dowra, where they part ways. During this first 14 km of its journey, the infant Shannon has dropped 104 m. Lough Allen is a large triangular lake sunk into a plateau of sandstones and shales. Approximately 11 km long and 4 km wide, it is surrounded and almost enclosed by hills and mountains to the north, east and west of the lake. The first island of note sits at the northern end of the lake, not far from the entry point of the Shannon. This is Inishmagrath, home to the ruins of a church that was supposedly built by St Beog in the twelfth century.

The renowned Irish botanist Robert Lloyd Praeger described Lough Allen in his hugely influential 1937 book, *The Way That I Went*, as 'not so attractive a lake as its mountainous setting might suggest'. As much as I hate to disagree with Praeger, I feel I must. Lough Allen is beautiful in a special way. For me, it is the sense of solitude that makes Lough Allen attractive, and the mountainous setting just accentuates the beauty. From the floating jetty below the lock at Drumshanbo, at the bottom of Lough Allen, I can see Slieve Anierin hugging the eastern shore of the lake. It is actually part of the Cuilcagh Mountains, and at 585 m high it dominates the view on this side of the lake. To the west is Corry Mountain, and south of that is Kilronan Mountain, both of which have wind farms on their slopes.

The mountains that surround Lough Allen are responsible for the composition of the lake waters. Mountain streams sweep grit and broken shale down the slopes, to a lake that is lacking limestone at its base. This results in lake waters that are deficient in nutrients such as nitrogen and phosphorus, which are necessary for the development of an abundant flora and fauna. This means that the lake is not home to huge numbers of fish or visiting birds. Perhaps this is why Praeger found Lough Allen less interesting than the other Shannon lakes. But there are good stocks of pike, bream, tench and roach in the lake from May

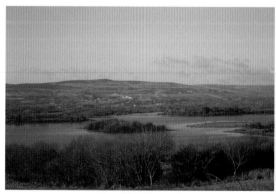

*Lough Allen from the east shore*

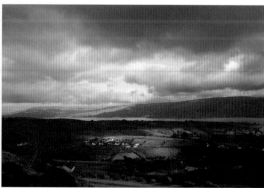

*Lough Allen from the Arigna Mining Experience*

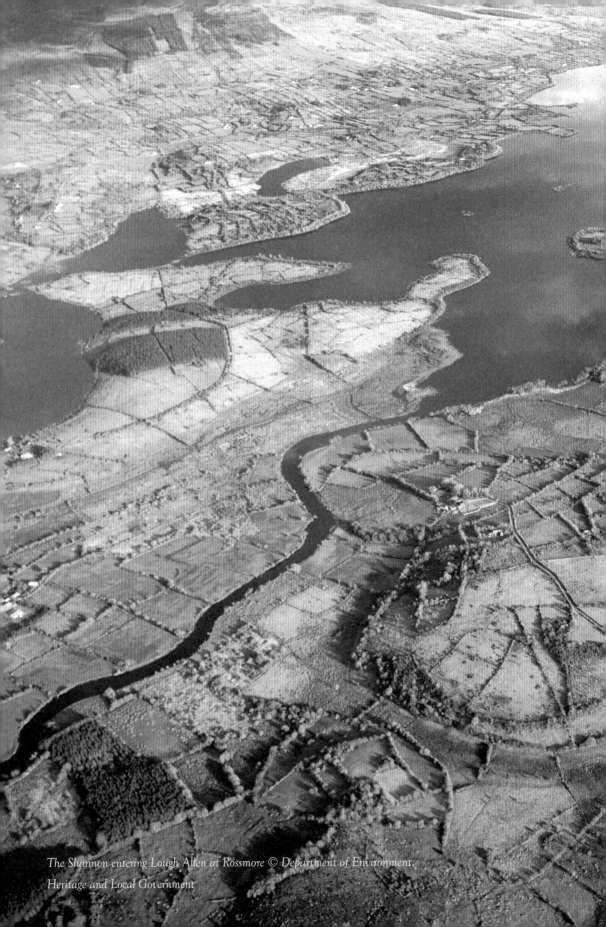

*The Shannon entering Lough Allen at Rossmore © Department of Environment, Heritage and Local Government*

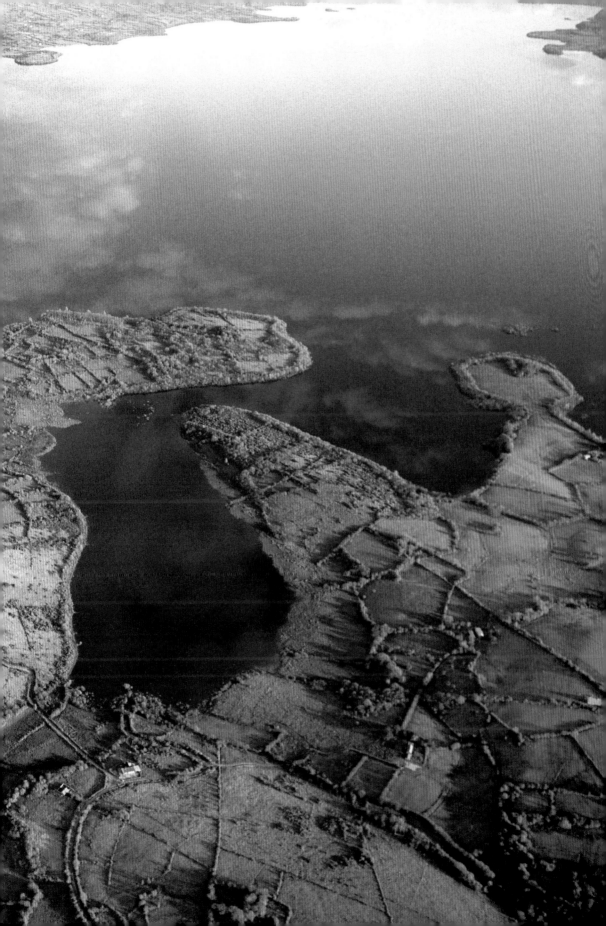

to October, and the limited mayfly hatch attracts some trout to the southern end of the lake near the mouths of the Yellow, Arigna and Stoney rivers. Slieve Anierin, the Iron Mountain, is responsible for much of the iron content in the lake, and even after mining ceased in the area, the particles and dust remain in the depths of the lake.

Kilronan Mountain, home to the Arigna mines, has a long history of coal mining that ceased only in the 1990s. The Arigna Mining Experience opened in 2003, and it is now possible to take a tour with a former miner into one of the shafts and get a sense of what it was like to work on some of the narrowest coal seams in the world. I say 'sense' because the tunnels we walk through on the tour have been widened and heightened for the comfort of us tourists.

Mining began at Arigna in the early seventeenth century with iron ore, before coal mining took over in the mid-nineteenth century. When we have watched the somewhat shaky footage in the introductory film, and drained the coffee from our mugs, we are summoned to the cave entrance to meet our tour guide. His name is Michael, and he was once a miner here. The conditions he describes sound horrific, even though he is describing life only 20 years ago. Michael began work in the mines at only 14, which he says was standard for miners, as the smaller you were the easier it was. He showed us an actual shaft where he would have lain on his side for hours on end, sometimes in a pool of freezing cold water, digging out the coal. Despite the harsh conditions and the dangers, Michael only knows of four people who were killed in the mines. However, the numbers

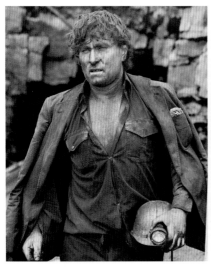 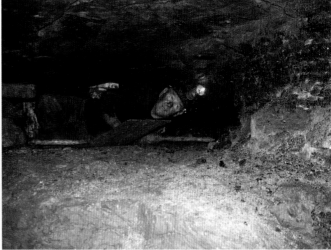

*Eugene McPartland, miner*
*at Arigna © Arigna Mining Experience*

*Maurice Cullen cutting coal*
*at Arigna © Arigna Mining Experience*

who died later as a result of breathing in dust were probably much higher. Michael, perhaps, suprisingly has fond memories of his days as a miner, and says that his fellow workers were the best men you could meet.

From the car park outside the Arigna Mining Experience there is a wonderful panorama of Lough Allen and Slieve Anierin. The shores of Lough Allen are generally rocky and interspersed by areas of peat, sand and mud. The shoreline does not have the areas of reed swamp that are common in the other Shannon lakes, with an exception at the northern end of the lake at Rossmore, where there is an area of reed bed that is very important as a refuge for the wetland birds of Lough Allen. Rossmore is also home to the protected plant species Irish Lady's Tresses (*Spiranthes romanzoffiana*), which has been recorded at two locations in Rossmore and at Dead Man's Point on the north shore of the lake. Irish Lady's Tresses is a small orchid with white flowers that occurs in damp meadows, on lakeshores, in seasonally flooded pastures and in valley bogs in Ireland. Although not a lot is known about the ecology of the Irish Lady's Tresses, it is generally considered to be a native Irish species. Known to be declining, it is protected in both Northern Ireland and in the Republic of Ireland.

In Europe, the species is found only in the western fringes of Scotland (primarily on the Hebridean Islands), a single location in England (Devon) and in the northeastern and western counties of Ireland. It was previously recorded in the southwest of Ireland, but is now absent in that region. Numbers have also declined in the Lough Neagh basin in Northern Ireland. Because little is known about the ecology of this orchid, it is hard

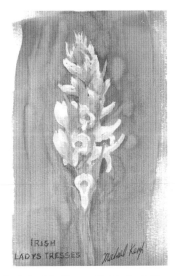

*Irish Lady's Tresses © Michael Kemp*

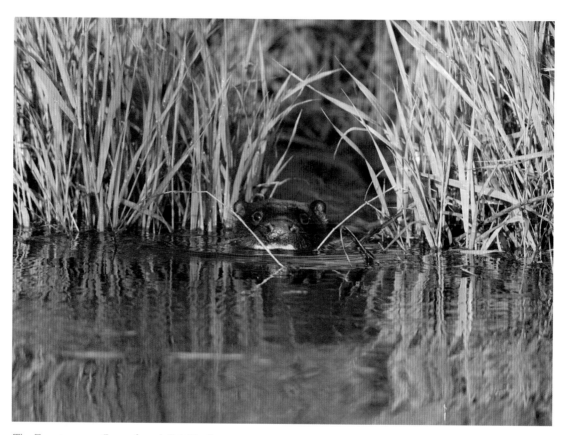

*The Eurasian otter (Lutra lutra) © Mike Brown*

to pinpoint what has caused the decline in numbers. This orchid is protected in Ireland under the Flora Protection Order because it is listed by the International Union for the Conservation of Nature (IUCN) as having 'critically low populations' in Europe.

Another ecologically important area of Lough Allen lies at the northern end of the lake at Kilgarriff, where there are a variety of important habitats such as wet grassland, poor fen and flush, quaking mire, transition bog and wet heath. Freshwater crayfish and otter have both been recorded in this area, and both are protected species under EU legislation. The Eurasian otter (*Lutra lutra*) has a few names in Irish, including Dobhar-chú, which translates as 'water-hound' ('dobor/dobur' is an old word for water and 'cú' was used to refer to any fierce dog). The Dobhar-chú is also written about in myths and legends as the King Otter. This legendary beast was described by Dáithí Ó hÓgáin in his 1990 book *Myth, Legend and Romance: an encyclopaedia of the Irish folk tradition*. Ó hÓgáin describes the King Otter as a large male, white in colour except for black-tipped ears and a black cross on his back. This creature supposedly never slept and could only be killed by a silver bullet. The Leitrim poet Katherine A. Fox wrote about the Dobhar-chú in verse:

*The story told of the dobhar-chú*
*That out from Glenade Lake*
*Had come one morning years ago*
*A woman's life to take*

The real Eurasian otter ranges from Ireland to Japan and from the Arctic to north Africa. It is widespread in Ireland in all freshwater and most coastal areas. However, there were dramatic declines in many Eurasian otter populations during the latter half of the twentieth century due to hunting and habitat loss, and otters remain threatened, declining, rare, or extinct in many European countries. This makes the Irish population of the Eurasian otter particularly important in a worldwide context.

The otter has webbed feet and a thick layer of underfur that keeps it dry by trapping air under the outer fur. It has large lungs that allow it to remain underwater for several minutes, where it can use its long whiskers to find food in murky waters. Otters are opportunistic predators that will prey on whatever is abundant locally. So in an area where freshwater crayfish are abundant, these will make up a large part of the otter's diet. The otter has two forms of shelter: an underground holt and above-ground couches. The holts can be found in the root systems of bank-side trees, among fallen rocks, in excavated tunnels in peat banks, caves and even in man-made structures like drainage pipes. The couches tend to be on islands or hidden in reed beds, scrub or brambles. These resting places are usually marked by spraints, which are otter droppings.

At the top of the village of Drumkeeran, at the northern end of Lough Allen, there is a fine view of the lake. Drumkeeran, 'the ridge of the quicken tree', is a small village of around 500 people that lies between Lough Allen and Belhavel Lough. The closest mooring point on the lake is at Spencer Harbour, and if you are planning to visit the lake by boat, Drumkeen is the only decent-sized village accessible from the water after you leave Drumshanbo travelling upstream on to the lake. As we approach Spencer Harbour it is just possible to make out the floating jetties through the morning fog. Gradually the sun emerges and burns the fog away to reveal a pretty little harbour that looks out at the tree-covered Corry Island across the lake to the Cuilcagh Mountains streaked with snow. A solitary red-brick chimney stands in the middle of a field behind the harbour. It is all that remains of a nineteenth-century ironworking site. Although there are no facilities to speak of in Spencer Harbour, it has beauty and peace to offer the boater who manages to make it this far north on the Shannon. Lough Allen is not a widely used section of the Shannon navigation, so if it is peace and quiet you are after I can highly recommend a visit.

Spencer Harbour is named after John Poyntz Spencer, the fifth Earl of Spencer and Viscount Althorp (1835–1910), also known as the 'red earl' thanks to his flowing red beard. The names Spencer and Althorp are probably ringing a bell, and that is because he is an ancestor of the late Diana, Princess of Wales, whose family home is the Althorp estate in England. The fifth Earl was Lord Lieutenant or Viceroy of Ireland twice, first for six years from 1868 and then for three years from 1882. His second term as Lord Lieutenant came about when the Chief Secretary for Ireland resigned following the release of the Irish nationalist Charles Stewart Parnell from prison. Spencer's other political duties were neglected so that he could take charge of the government's Irish policy. Spencer was a close friend of the British Prime Minister William Gladstone, and an early supporter of Irish home rule.

The southern end of Lough Allen has been proposed as a Natural Heritage Area (pNHA) by the Irish government, in recognition of the important habitats and species present. At Mountallen, where the Arigna River enters the lake, hen harrier and curlew are both found. These are species requiring special protection under EU legislation (something I will discuss further in connection with the Shannon Callows). The hen harrier (*Circus cyaneus*), or Cromán na Gearc in Irish, comes to Mountallen to feed in winter. The male and female birds are very different in appearance, with the male being extremely pale in colour (white and grey) with a white rump and black wing tips. The females and young birds are brownish, but share the male's white rump.

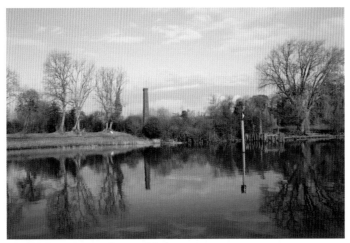

*Brickwork remains at Spencer Harbour*

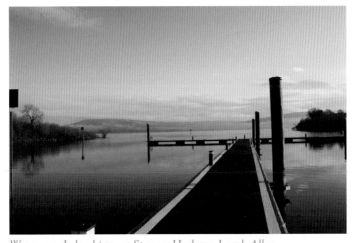

*Waterways Ireland jetty at Spencer Harbour, Lough Allen*

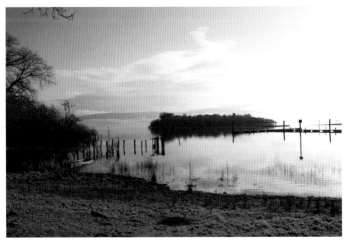

*Ruined jetty at Spencer Harbour*

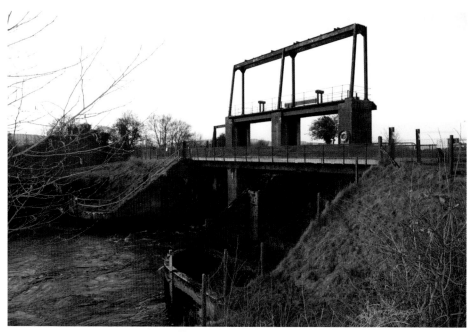

*Bellantra Bridge, Lough Allen*

Towards the bottom of the lake, not far from the town of Drumshanbo, a point of land called Inisfale Island juts out into the lake, narrowing the navigation channel just above Bellantra Bridge on the western shore. This bridge is where the River Shannon emerges from Lough Allen and enters Ireland's central plain. Bellantra Bridge is a very narrow bridge, suitable only for one car at a time. The bridge is actually part of a sluice gate controlled by the Electicty Supply Board (ESB), which manages the water levels on the lake. Before 1996 the levels were controlled for the purpose of electricity generation. Since then the lake has become more popular with boaters, and so the levels are now maintained in favour of navigation between mid-March and mid-September.

From Bellantra Bridge all the way to Killaloe in County Clare, the river will only drop by a further 12 m. On leaving Lough Allen the Shannon continues its journey with Leitrim on one bank and Roscommon on the other. Just below the Galley Bridge, where the Drumkeeran Road crosses over the Shannon, the river used to bend westwards forming a lake called Lough na gCailligh, which caused major flooding of the surrounding area. Towards the end of the nineteenth century, a new cut was added to get rid of the bend, dramatically reducing the size of the lake. Local people refer to this as the 'old Shannon'. Just below the 'old Shannon', the River Feorish joins the Shannon from the west, adding its clear limestone waters to the Shannon and increasing the current just above the five arches of Drumherriff Bridge.

Where these two rivers meet there is a large expanse of cutover bog known as the Dromore/Dereenasoo bog complex. The Dromore section of the bog is small but relatively intact, with a good cover of bog vegetation such as Ling Heather, Bog Cotton and Purple Moor Grass. The Dereenasoo part of the bog is larger, and has well-developed hummocks, hollows and lawns, typical of an intact bog. Erica Heather species, Bog Cotton and Sphagnum Mosses are the main plants found, with Bog Rosemary, Ling Heather and Cross-leaved Heath also present.

Farther down at Drumboylan, a wooden footbridge crosses the river. On the Leitrim side of the footbridge sits the island of Inis na gCon. Local legend says that St Patrick crossed the Shannon here, and that the stones he used to cross the water were removed and put on Inis na gCon when the river was dredged. Another legend says that the ill-fated O'Sullivan Beare and his followers forded the river here at the end of their 14-day trek to Leitrim from the Beara Penninsula in County Cork in 1603. We will come across O'Sullivan Beare again near Portumna in County Galway.

This is not a navigable section of the river, so boats must continue farther down Lough Allen to the Blackrock New Lock, which was built in the 1820s. This lock connects Lough Allen to Acres Lake. This small and picturesque lake lies a short distance from the town of Drumshanbo, and has floating jetties on the eastern shore of the lake. Other facilities include tennis courts, a children's playground and, for the more adventurous, an outdoor swimming pool. It is possible to walk along the canal from Lough Allen to Acres Lake. The path exits beside a modern development of houses and moorings know as Acres Cove.

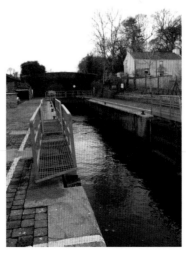

*Blackrock New Lock at Drumshanbo, Lough Allen*

*Lough Allen from Drumshanbo*

# 2. Drumshanbo
# to Carrick-on-Shannon

Drumshanbo, or Dhroim Seanbhó (bridge of the old bothy or tent), is a town of over 600 people that lies at the southern end of Lough Allen, a short distance from the mooring spots at Acres Lake. In addition to its links to the waterway, Drumshanbo has links with narrow-gauge steam trains and coal mining. You can see this by visiting the heritage centre in the market house, and through the variety of buildings in the town that are connected to the Cavan and Leitrim Railway, such as a goods store and station house. The full title of

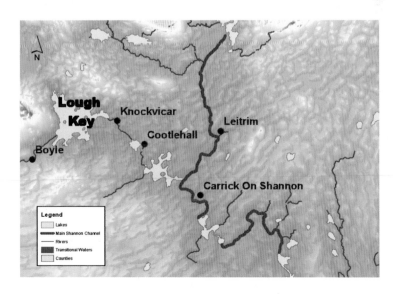

the railway, which finally closed in 1961, was the 'Cavan & Leitrim & Roscommon Light Railway and Tramway Company Limited'. The main section of the line covered 48.5 miles and passed through Ballinamore, Belturbet, Arigna, Mohill and Dromod. A branch to the Arigna coalfields opened in 1888, and a further extension to the mines in 1920.

The Lough Allen Canal connects with the natural course of the river after Battlebridge Lock at Drumhierney. It is here that the River Shannon finally becomes deep enough for navigation. In 1817 the Royal Canal connection to the upper Shannon was completed, and this encouraged the improvement of the upper Shannon navigation. One of the main reasons for this at the time was to improve the accessibility of Lough Allen and the Arigna coalfields. A canal was constructed east of the river from Battlebridge to Lough Allen, passing through Acres Lake. The canal was finished in 1820, but by then a railway with a tramway extension to the Arigna area meant there was not much demand for the canal. By the 1920s there was almost no traffic on the Lough Allen Canal, so it was decided to use Lough Allen as a reservoir controlled by sluices. As this caused large fluctuations in water levels, it became impossible to use the canal any more. Although the canal to Acres Lake was reopened in 1978, it was not until the role of Ardnacrusha as an electricity provider diminished that the ESB agreed to maintain constant water levels in Lough Allen, and in 1996 it became possible to reopen the canal to Lough Allen.

Just below Battlebridge the traffic from the Lough Allen Canal can finally get on to the River Shannon and join it on its journey south. From here the river winds its way south between two small wooded islands, before joining the Shannon–Erne Waterway, which enters the River Shannon at Leitrim. Leitrim, or Laith-dhruim (grey ridge), is a small, busy village of 258 inhabitants. Near the village lies the last remaining wall of O'Rourke's Castle, where the ill-fated O'Sullivan Beare and his followers sought refuge after their 14-day march from O'Sullivan's lands in Beara, County Cork.

The stretch of river that leads to Leitrim town was artificially straightened in the 1840s during works on the Ballinamore–Ballyconnell Canal. Now called the Shannon–Erne Waterway, it is here that our journey on the water begins in the summer of 2009. The *Nieuwe Zorgen* is on her return journey from Belleek on the Erne system. The *Zorgen* is a 100-year-old Dutch sailing tjalk, skippered by my brother Eric.

Work on the original Ballinamore–Ballyconnell Canal began in 1846, employing around 7,000 people during the Famine. With picks and shovels these 7,000 souls cut through the soggy Leitrim soil and bog, and toiled for 14 years to build a canal that was of poor quality and that became redundant after a very short period. During the 14 years of construction, the railway had come to Leitrim, making the canal system redundant. During the eight years when the canal was in operation, only nine boats travelled along it. By 1869 the Ballinamore–Ballyconnell Canal was no longer in use and fell into dereliction.

The Ballinamore–Ballyconnell Canal was renamed the Shannon–Erne Waterway in 1994, when it was reopened as part of a cross-border flagship scheme. The £30 million project involved the governments of Ireland and Britain, the Office of Public Works (OPW), the Northern Ireland Department of Agriculture, the International Fund for Ireland and the ESB. The Shannon–Erne Waterway stretches over 36 miles of remote countryside in Counties Fermanagh, Cavan and Leitrim. The waterway makes it possible to travel over 400 km from Limerick to Belleek in County Fermanagh, making it the longest leisure navigation in Europe.

The *Nieuwe Zorgen* has not had an easy journey to Leitrim. It has battled against the elements, and struggled against rising water levels to make it. The water levels rose to such a height that it was marooned on Lough Garadice for ten days, hoping the rains would ease and the water levels would drop enough for the river to become navigable again. This would be nothing compared to the floods that were to come during the winter of 2009. Although the towns along the River Shannon are no strangers to flooding, the 2009 floods were the highest recorded in ten years. Carrick-on-Shannon and Leitrim town were impassable, and over 600 residents and 250 houses were affected in a devastated Athlone. Some blamed poor planning for the floods. But for the last 200 years regular floods have been recorded along the Shannon, and some level of flooding is recorded every winter. The worst flooding is supposed to have happened in 1867, but there are not many records of this event. After the serious floods of the 1950s, a report was commissioned to investigate flood relief on

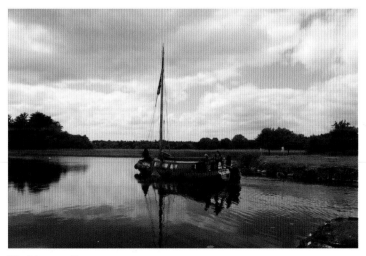

*The* Nieuwe Zorgen

the Shannon. This 1956 report, known as the Rydell Report after its author, concluded that: 'Because of the flat terrain through which the river flows, the almost imperceptible gradient of the stream within its series of lakes and connecting channels and because of the large volume of long duration of flooding, no simple or obvious solution has therefore been found – nor has the writer now found one.' The problem of Shannon flooding is still a long way from resolved, but the OPW have started work on an 'integrated multifaceted programme aimed at mitigating future flood risk and impact'.

At the other end of the spectrum, a new threat to the Shannon has emerged in the form of water extraction. In 2004 discussions began over a new water supply for nine counties in the east and midlands. There were originally ten options proposed, and the preferred option has been the cause of much contention. This controversial solution involves the extraction of 500 million litres of water per day from the north of Lough Derg, which would then be piped to storage lakes in County Offaly (Garryhinch) before being pumped to Dublin, the mid-east and midland regions. The reservoir in Garryhinch has the potential to become an important amenity site such as the Lough Boora Parkland, for fishing, boating and water sports. It would also create around 1,000 construction jobs for the area. The lakes would store enough water to supply the east for two months, meaning that the extraction of water from Lough Derg could take place during periods of high flow and the stored water would be available for use during low flow periods.

The Shannon Protection Alliance is strongly opposing the proposal on ecological, environmental, commercial, recreational and social grounds. According to the group, which was established in 2007, the amount of water that would be extracted is the same that is lost through leakages in Dublin, and if Dublin City Council were to fix the pipes then the water would not be required. The group fears that the 1.5 million people living in the Shannon region would be adversely affected by the proposal, and they have set up branches throughout the Shannon region to oppose it.

There will always be risks associated with water transfer schemes. Some independent experts have looked at the proposal and think that the risks are fairly low as long as the water is extracted from the north of Lough Derg, as per the preferred option. The proposal has to go through an Environmental Impact Statement process, before an application is made to An Bord Pleanála to determine if it will pose any threat to the ecology of the Shannon basin.

The river continues on, passing by Lough Naseer on the western bank, turning sharply to the west, before turning south again towards Hartley Bridge. This bridge is a sharp contrast to most of the Shannon bridges we will come across on our journey. It was built in 1917 from reinforced concrete. Although it might be considered unsightly, Hartley Bridge is actually an important example of a very early use of reinforced concrete. The river passes under Hartley Bridge and then widens into Lough Eidin, known as Drumharlow, and it is here that the River Boyle joins the Shannon system. Drumharlow consists of a series of coves, bays, wooded headlands and an island at the eastern end called Inishatirra. The *Nieuwe Zorgen* narrowly misses disaster as she makes her way on to Drumharlow. Momentarily distracted by two boats travelling at high speed, the skipper veers off the navigation route by accident, before correcting the boat's course to continue through Drumharlow towards Lough Key.

Drumharlow has important feeding areas for the Greenland White-fronted Goose (*Anser albifrons flavirostris*), a bird that is listed for special protection under the EU Birds Directive (something I will discuss further in relation to the Corncrake). Despite this protection, their numbers have declined seriously since the late 1990s. Other birds protected by the directive found here are Teal, Wigeon, Cormorant, Great Crested Grebe, Little Grebe, Mute and Whooper Swans. The semi-natural woodland at Hughestown lies to the southwest of the lake, and the rare Bird's Nest Orchid (*Neottia nidus-avis*) has been found there, as well as the rare fungus *Paradiacheopsis rigida*.

From Drumharlow we have two options: continue downriver to Carrick-on-Shannon, or take a detour onto the River Boyle and up to Lough Key. Our diversion to Lough Key takes us up a narrow, winding section of the River Boyle through the little village of Cootehall in County Roscommon. We pass under the three-arched stone bridge built by the Shannon Commissioners in the 1840s, en route to Oakport Lough and ultimately Lough Key. In her 1987 book, *By Shannon Shores*, Ruth Delany describes the lane that leads from Cootehall Bridge to Oakport Lough as a place of hedgerows and wild strawberries. The village of Cootehall gets its name from Colonel Chidley Coote, who was granted lands there following the Restoration in the seventeenth century. Cootehall was home to John McGahern, who

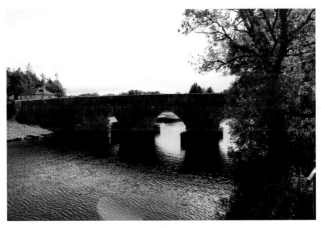

*Cootehall Bridge*

used the Garda Station here as the setting for his first book, *The Barracks*, in 1963. We are unable to find public moorings at Cootehall, due to the large number of badly moored cruisers, so continue on towards Lough Key. Just beyond Cootehall the river widens into Oakport Lough, before narrowing again in the approach to Knockvicar. Along this stretch we catch a glimpse of the mountains surrounding Lough Allen to the north, and to the south the bank is cloaked in thick vegetation. At Knockvicar the river passes under another of the 1840s bridges of the Shannon Commissioners, and emerges into a narrow channel nestled between tree-covered banks.

The town of Knockvicar developed on the site of a Franciscan monastery. Clarendon Lock, named after a Lord Lietentant of Ireland, sits 300 m upstream. It was rarely used until the 1950s and had fallen into disrepair. Thanks to the campaigning of Harry Rice and friends, the lock today is good condition and in frequent use. Entering the lock is quite difficult due to the force of water coming off the weir that lies to the left of the lock. Beyond the lock the river widens into Lough Key, which is 3 km wide and 2–3 km long. Loch Cé, as it is known in Irish, is said to be named after a woman of that name who was the daughter of Manannán Mac Lir of the Tuatha Dé Dannan. In another version, Cé is the druid of Nuada of the Silver Hand, King of the Tuatha Dé Dannan, and he was drowned when the waters of Lough Key burst from the ground.

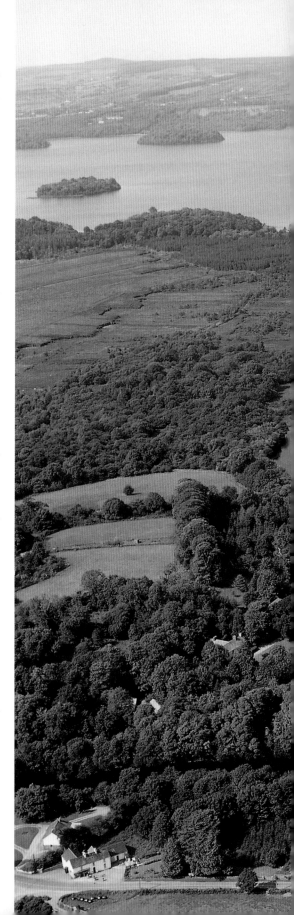

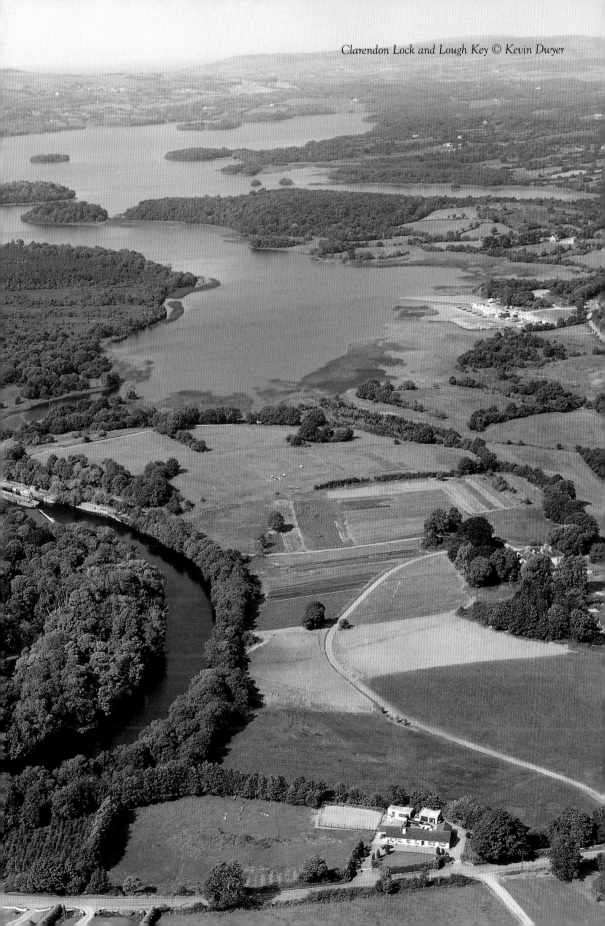

Clarendon Lock and Lough Key © Kevin Dwyer

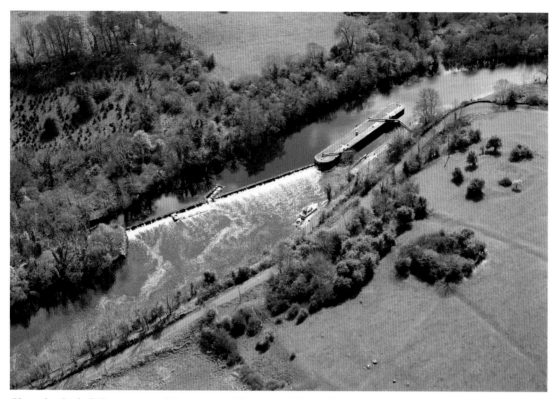

*Clarendon Lock © Department of Environment, Heritage and Local Government*

The Tuatha Dé Dannan (the people of the god whose mother is Dana) are said to have arrived in Ireland around 2000 BC, and possessed great gifts of wisdom and magic. When they arrived they defeated the small and dark people of the Fir Bolg who ruled before them. During the battle the King of the Tuatha Dé Dannan lost his hand, and because it was law that anyone with so much as a blemish could not rule, he was deposed as king. His successor was disliked so much that the craftsmen of the tribe fashioned for the deposed king a hand of silver so beautiful that it could not be considered a blemish. The king was restored and became known as 'Nuada of the Silver Hand'.

The Milesians were a tribe that supposedly came to Ireland from northern Spain around this time. They were the sons of Milesius, and were Gaelic Celts who gave our island the name Erin. The Milesians defeated the Tuatha Dé Dannan and claimed all of Erin that lay above ground. The Dé Dannan were forced to seek refuge below ground, and with their skills in metalwork and herbs, they gained the reputation of wizards and magicians with the Milesians, whose religion was druidism. In time the Milesians would view the Dé Dannan as god-like and referred to them as the 'good people', as they are still known today.

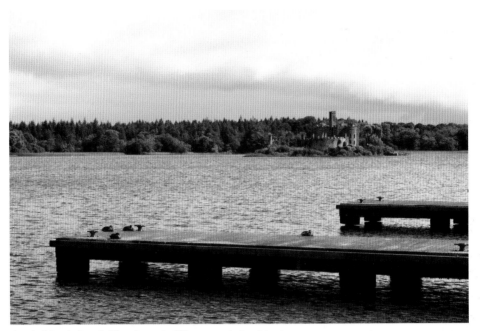

*Castle Island, Lough Key, from the Waterways Ireland jetties*

There are numerous wooded islands on Lough Key: Ash, Bingham, Bullock, Castle, Church, Green, Hermit, Lahan's, Orchard, Sally, Stag and Trinity Islands. Some of these islands are actually man-made crannógs. The name crannóg derives from the Irish words 'crann' for tree and 'óg' for young, as young trees were used to build an outer wall around a man-made island in the lake. In some cases there would have been submerged stepping stones for access.

On the southern shore of the lake, close to the Forest Park Visitor Centre, lies a small stone harbour. From here we can see the ruins of a castle on a little island just offshore. This is the aptly named Castle Island, which is recorded in the twelfth-century Annals of Loch Cé. At that time the area was called Moylurg, and it was ruled by the MacDermots, who resided on Castle Island and at the site of the Moylurg Tower until the seventeenth century. The MacDermot residence on the island was actually a fortress called 'Carraic Locha Cé' (the Rock of Lough Key). Under Cromwell, the MacDermot lands were given to an English family called the Kings, who renamed Moylurg as Rockingham. The Kings rebuilt the castle on Castle Island as a folly, which they used as guest accommodation until it was badly damaged by fire not long after the Second World War.

Lough Key Forest Park has been developed in recent years into an activity centre, consisting of the Lough Key Experience, Boda Borg and Adventure Kingdom. Part of the

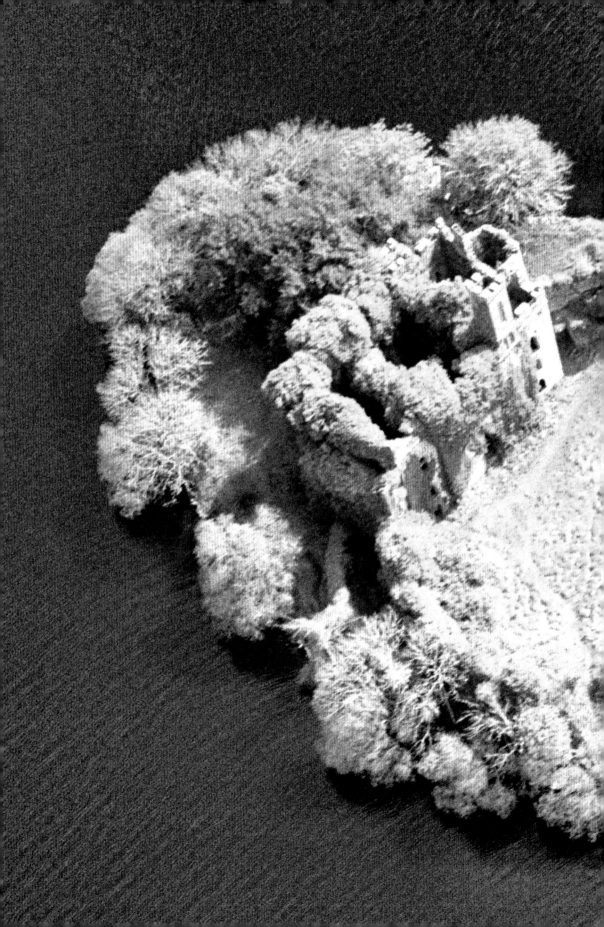

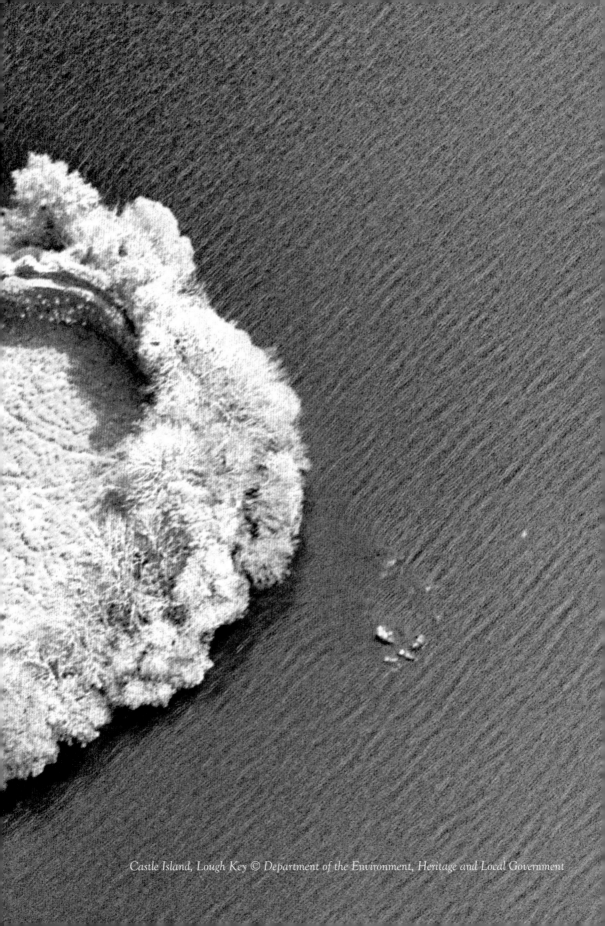

*Castle Island, Lough Key © Department of the Environment, Heritage and Local Government*

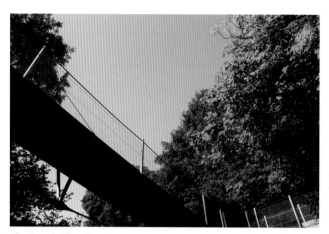

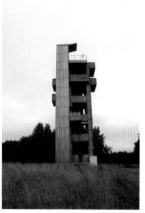

*The Lough Key Experience*

*Moylurg Viewing Tower*
*Lough Key*

Lough Key Experience is a 300 m long tree canopy walk that brings you through part of the forest. The tree-top walk, 9 m above the ground, emerges at the water's edge, just next to the Waterways Ireland mooring facilities, where there are excellent views across the lake to Castle Island. Another interesting part of the 'experience' are the nineteenth-century tunnels that lead out to the Moylurg Viewing Tower. The tower stands in the place of Rockingham House, which was designed by the architect John Nash in 1809. The house was destroyed by fire in 1957, and the surviving walls were demolished in 1971. The viewing tower was built in 1973, and although it provides some beautiful panoramas of the lake and the park, personally I find the tower quite ugly and imposing. The bottom of the tower sits in the basement area of the house, where the servants' quarters would have been, together with the underground passages that lead to the harbour and the turf quay.

The grounds of the park consist of a mix of broadleaved woodland and non-native conifer woodland. The park is home to a variety of bat species such as Brown Long-eared (*Plecotus auritus*), Soprano Pipistrelle (*Pipistrellus pygmaeus*), Leisler's (*Nyctalus leisleri*), Natterer's (*Myotis nattereri*) and Daubenton's Bats (*Myotis daubentonii*). All bats are protected in Ireland by Irish legislation and the EU Habitats Directive, but the Leisler's Bat is of particular importance, because despite being relatively common in Ireland it is rare in the rest of Europe. There are nine species of bat found in Ireland, all of which eat insects and hibernate during the winter. In late spring or early summer, the bats awaken and venture out from their roosts to hunt. Leisler's Bat is the largest of our bat species, and flies at greater heights than our other bats. It emerges from its roost in a tree hole or under the roof tiles of a house just after sunset to begin hunting over fields and water.

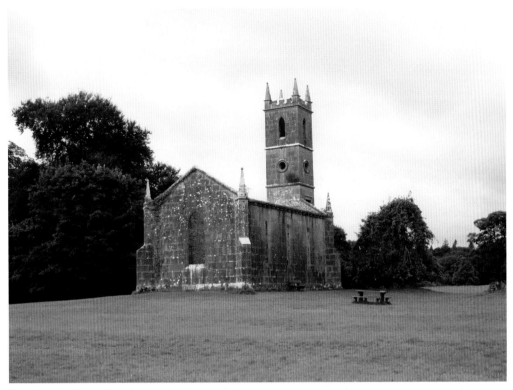

*Rockingham Estate Church*

Trinity Island lies offshore to the west of Castle Island. The MacDermot family gave the 2 acre island to the White Canons of St Francis in the thirteenth century, where they remained until the suppression of the monasteries in the seventeenth century. The White Canons belonged to the Premonstratensian Order, which was founded by St Norbert at Prémontré Abbey, near Laon in northeastern France in AD 1120. Their name stemmed from the white colour of their habits. They began construction of Holy Trinity Abbey soon after the MacDermots granted the land to them in 1220. The abbey was built from the local rocks found around Lough Key, such as the pale-grey sandstone and limestone that are found on the southern shore. The Annals of Loch Cé, which cover the period between 1014 and 1590, were written on Trinity Island. There is a tomb on the island where the body of Úna Bhán MacDermot lies. She was the daughter of the Chief Brian Óg MacDermot, who refused permission for her to marry Tomás Láidir Costello, the son of one of his enemies. She is said to have died of a broken heart, and Tomás swam across to the island every night to weep by her graveside. When Tomás died not long after Úna, her father allowed him to be buried by the side of his love.

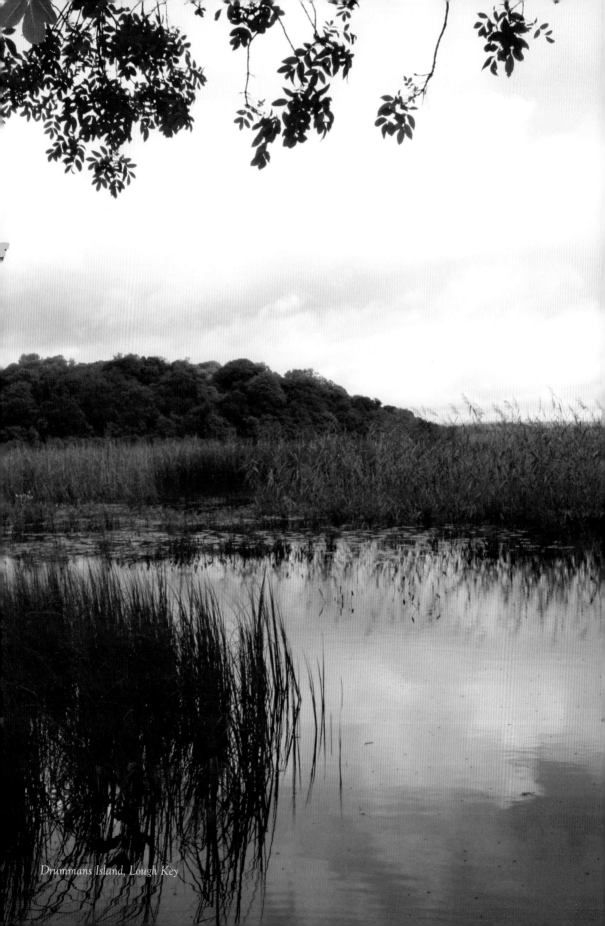

Drummans Island, Lough Key

Towards the southwest corner of the lake, beyond the site of Rockingham, the River Boyle enters the lake. It is possible to navigate up to Boyle Harbour via the Boyle Canal, which is only a short distance from the town itself. Boyle is the main town of County Roscommon, and home to the remains of the Cistercian monastery of Boyle Abbey, which was one of the most important in Connaught. Another building worth visiting in Boyle is King House, which was the eighteenth-century home of the King family. Our own journey will not bring us up to Boyle on this occasion, so we retrace our route back to the Shannon, for the journey downstream to Carrick-on-Shannon.

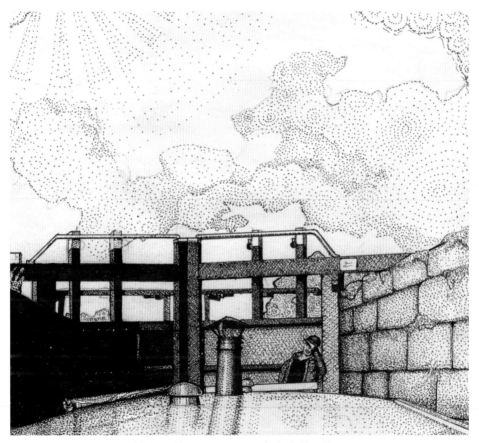

Nieuwe Zorgen *waits in a lock* © *Eric Kemp*

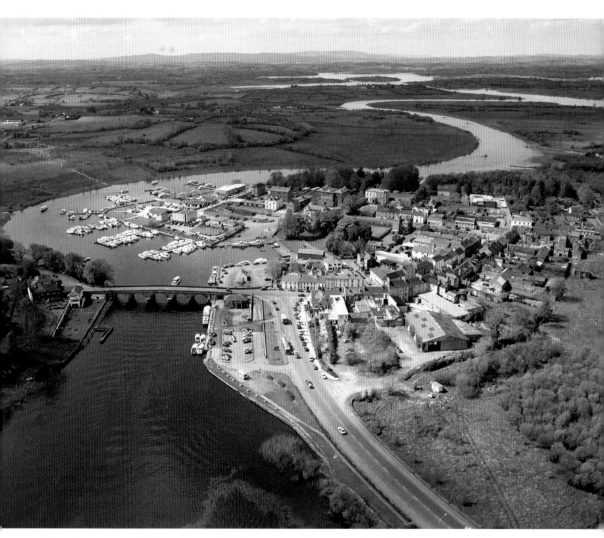

*Carrick on Shannon © Department of the Environment, Heritage and Local Government*

# 3. Carrick-on-Shannon to Roosky

The *Nieuwe Zorgen* travels back down the River Boyle through Drumharlow towards Carrick-on-Shannon, passing through a fairly flat, agricultural landscape. On the north shore of Drumharlow there is an area of seasonally flooded callows, an extremely important habitat type that we will come across again farther downstream between the bottom of Lough Ree and Banagher. As we emerge from Drumharlow, the River Boyle joins the Shannon system.

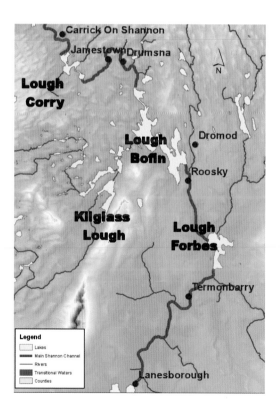

Carrick-on-Shannon, or Cora Droma Rúisc in Irish (the weir of the marshy ridge), is a large town that straddles Counties Leitrim and Roscommon. Carrick derives from the word 'carra' meaning weir, which refers to the ancient weir that was removed when the river was dredged for navigation. However, the old anglicised name for the town was Carrickdrumrusk, which translates to 'the weir of Drumrusk'. The main street of the town sits on the Leitrim side of the 1845 bridge, and is home to over 2,500 people. This 2006 census figure does not include the population on the Roscommon side of the bridge, which would bring the population nearer to 4,000 people. The town is thriving, and the figures show a population increase of 25 per cent since the previous census, giving Carrick-on-Shannon the highest growth rate of any town in Ireland. There has been a lot of development in recent years, residential, commercial and recreational. Downstream of the bridge there is a wonderful new riverside boardwalk, and mooring facilities fronting a modern but tasteful development of shops and the Landmark Hotel.

Upstream of the bridge are two large boat hire companies, Emerald Star and Carrick Craft, both with fleets of over 200 boats. Our first port of call is the tourist information office, housed in the Old Barrel Store on the quay next to the bridge. They recommend a walking tour of the town, taking in the historic points of interest along the way. We decide to start our tour by following the quay upstream towards the rowing club. This whole area is dedicated to the river, from the mooring facilities to the rowing club and boat hire companies. It used to be the site of the old jail complex, which was removed towards the end of the last century. The eighteenth-century courthouse still remains and now houses The Dock, a venue for theatre and the arts.

Before departing on our walking tour, some sustenance is required. Behind the rowing club is a small public park called Town Park, on the far side of which is a very interesting-looking building. It is Victoria Hall, which was originally a Methodist Church parochial hall built in 1887, but which has been tastefully converted into a restaurant. The current proprietor, Keith Nolan, is a professional photographer, and his work adorns the walls of the mezzanine level. It is strange to find a taste of 1960s Dublin in a Leitrim eatery, but his work is fantastic and so is the food.

Retracing our steps back to the quay, we head up towards the old courthouse, passing by a beautiful mosaic depicting river scenes of birds, animals, kayakers and fishermen. The street that leads from The Dock to the Town Clock is called St George's Terrace, after the St George family who have a long association with the town dating back to the 1600s. Hatley Manor, one of the fine buildings along the terrace, was their home from the 1830s, and that of their descendants the Whyte family.

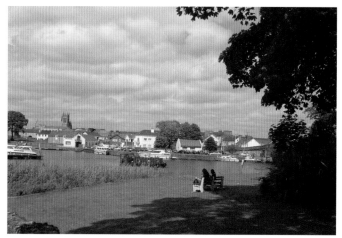

*Approaching Carrick-on-Shannon © RPS*

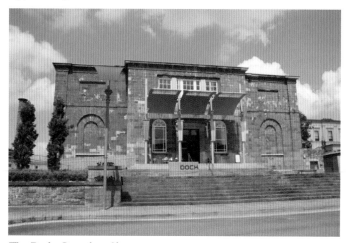

*The Dock, Carrick-on-Shannon*

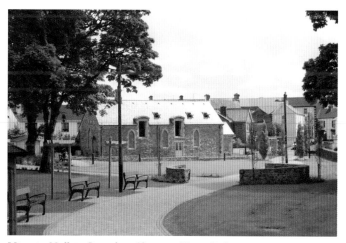

*Victoria Hall in Carrick-on-Shannon Town Park*

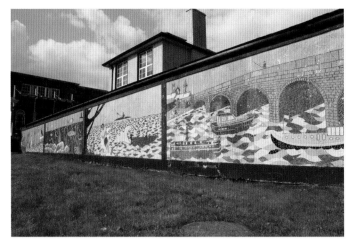

*Carrick-on-Shannon mosaic*

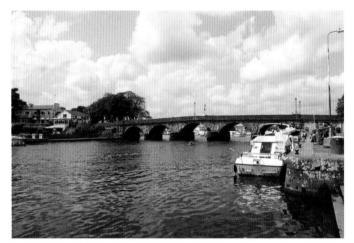

*Downstream of Carrick-on-Shannon Bridge*

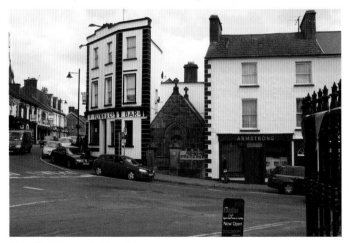

*Costello Memorial Chapel*

At the end of St George's Terrace we come to the Town Clock on the left side of the street, across from the Market Yard. The clock is actually called the McCann Memorial Monument, and commemorates Owen McCann (1851–1901), a prominent citizen of the town and first chairman of Leitrim County Council. Across the road is the Market Yard, established by Charles Manners St George in 1830 for trade in meat, butter, linen and flannel. It now houses a farmers' market and a couple of restaurants. St George's Terrace meets the main street of Carrick, which veers uphill to the right away from the river. We cross over the road, and slightly downhill come across the tiny Costello Memorial Chapel. It is the smallest chapel in Ireland, and supposedly the second smallest in the world, at 4.8 m x 3.6 m x 9 m high. Work on the chapel began in 1877 when Mary, the beloved wife of Edward Costello passed away at just 47 years of age. Edward had her body embalmed and commissioned the construction of the chapel out of stone from Bath in England. Her coffin was placed under glass, sunk into the floor of the chapel in 1879. In 1891 Edward joined his wife at rest in the tiny chapel.

We turn downhill, back towards the river, and take the steps beside the bridge back down to the water's edge. The marina area is home to the Carrick-on-Shannon Rowing Club, which claims to be the oldest rowing club in the world. There are records of a rowing 'match' in Carrick in 1854, followed by a second one in 1855 that used the title of the 'Carrick-on-Shannon Grand Annual Regatta'. The regatta continues to this day, taking place every August bank holiday.

As we move downstream of Carrick-on-Shannon to Jamestown, the river flows eastwards to Lough Corry. This area is covered in low hills and drumlins, remnants of the last ice age. Drumlins were first recognised in Ireland, and the word drumlin derives from the Irish word 'droimin', which describes a small hill formed by the movement of a glacier. These hillocks are usually between 9m and 30m high, composed of tightly compacted sand and gravel, and aligned with the direction of the ice flow. The drumlins are covered in grass and wildflowers. They occur in clusters, sometimes with streams of water flowing between them, often spreading out into pools and lakes. A broad expanse of drumlins are found across north-central Ireland, from County Down to County Mayo, and the landscape they form is often referred to as a 'basket of eggs'. We begin to see a lot more reeds alongside the river compared to farther north. This means that there are greater numbers and varieties of wildfowl along this stretch.

Before we get to Jamestown, we must leave the main river channel and turn east into the Jamestown Canal. The canal is about 2 km long, and will bring us back to the river at Lough Nanoge. A canal was first built here in the 1770s to bypass the rapids. The original canal was replaced in the 1840s by the Shannon Commissioners, who enlarged and straightened the channel by blasting through the hard surrounding rocks. There was originally a lock about halfway down the canal, but the Commissioners removed this and replaced it with the current Albert Lock which sits farther along the canal.

The village of Jamestown lies about 5 km south of Carrick. It was built in 1623 under the rule of James I, when Sir Charles Coote noticed that the area was an important strategic site, naturally defended on three sides by the fast-flowing loop of the river. He built a fortified town with a castle on the river bank. Very little of the castle remains today, but there are some ruins of a church and graveyard just inside the north gate that spans the road leading into the village. There are also ruins of a Franciscan friary in the modern graveyard in the village. The strategic importance of this location was realised long before Sir Charles Coote, however, and the evidence of this can be seen in the 'Dún of Drumsna'. The river bends northwards in a loop between Jamestown and Drumsna, forming a sort of peninsula in the river with the two towns a mile apart at the base. It was across the neck of this so-called peninsula that a huge defensive earthwork or dún was built, but when exactly is not known. The dún is possibly an Iron Age defence to protect what was a frontier between the Kingdom of Connaught and the Kingdom of Uladh to the north. The remains of the earthworks are about 6 m high and 30 m wide. They are steep on the Leitrim side, with a gentler slope on the Roscommon side.

Every year there is a marathon canoe race in the area that attracts competitors from all over Ireland and abroad. The race follows this stretch of river from Carrick-on-Shannon to Jamestown, and back via the Jamestown Canal. The race starts just downstream of the bridge in Carrick and passes through Lough Corry on the way to Jamestown, where the competitors have to jump from their boats just upstream of the weir and sprint overland carrying their canoes to the foot of the weir, where they hit the water again (this is known as a portage). The route follows the natural course of the river through Jamestown, curving around past Drumsna until reaching Albert Lock, which means another portage, lifting boats from the water and sprinting to the far side of the lock before hitting the water again in the Jamestown Canal.

In 1983 and 1987 the Canoeing Marathon World Cup took place between Boyle and Carrick-on-Shannon. This type of canoeing involves sleek and lightweight boats that are raced over long distances on the flat waters of lakes, dams or rivers. Any obstacles encountered such as canal locks or weirs are avoided by portages. Competitors from as far as New Zealand, Australia and Canada travelled to Ireland to compete in the 42 km race. This race was slightly longer than the modern one described above, as the starting point was in Lough Key.

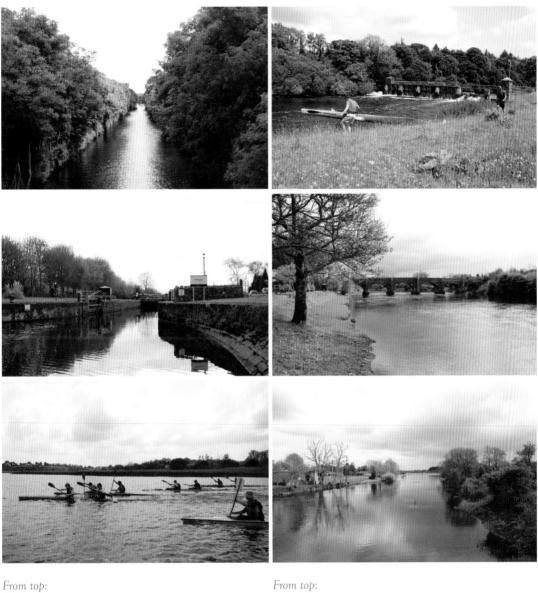

*From top:*

    *Jamestown Canal*

    *Albert Lock*

    *Carrick-on-Shannon Canoe Race 2009*

*From top:*

    *Jamestown*

    *Drumsna Bridge*

    *Downstream of Drumsna Bridge*

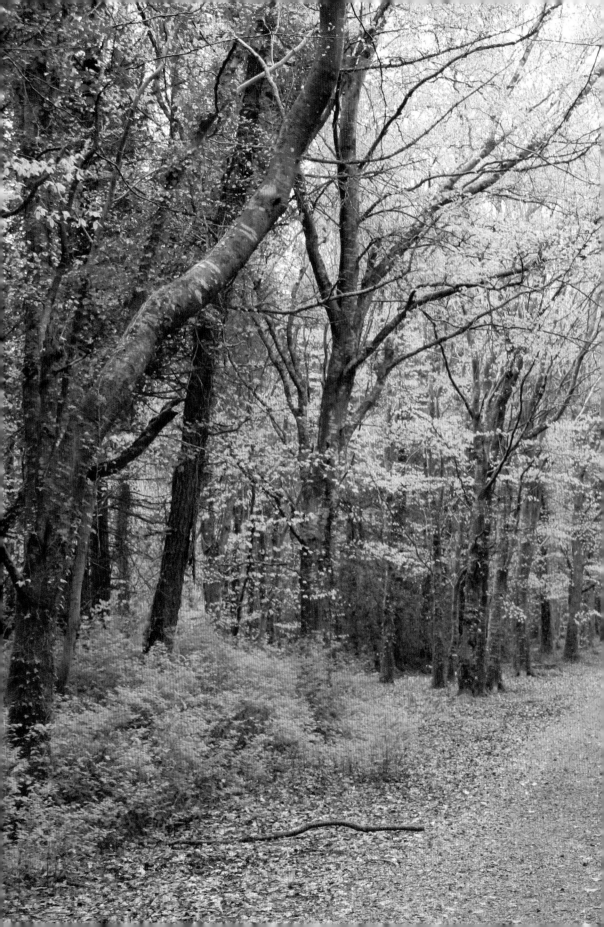

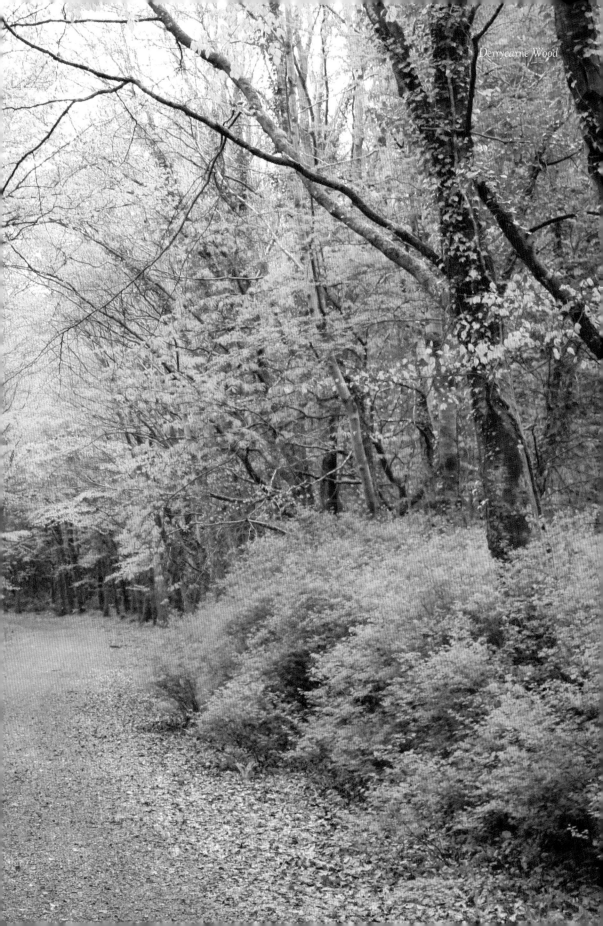

Derryearne Wood

The natural course of the river follows a 7 km long loop around to Drumsna. It is possible to navigate up to Drumsna Bridge from the end of the Jamestown Canal. This bridge is one of the few that were not replaced by the works of the Shannon Commissioners. Drumsna, or Druim-snámha (the ridge of the swimming place), sits on a hill looking out over the river. Snámh (or snave) actually refers to a deep fording point on the river, and Drumsna is located at a point where it was possible to wade or swim across depending on the time of year.

In the past Drumsna was an important port on the river and stopover for horse-drawn carriages. With the completion of the Grand Canal in 1804, Drumsna was the most northerly point on the Shannon navigation. The town had its own jail and courthouse, and was County Leitrim's most important trading town. With the construction of the Jamestown Canal in 1848, river traffic started to bypass the little town. Drumsna is also known for its association with the famous writer Anthony Trollope, who lived in the Ivy Tree Inn in the 1840s, which is now Taylor's Pub.

At the eastern end of the Jamestown Canal there is a relatively new marina located beside Albert Lock. We pass under the steel railway bridge just as the river enters Lough Tap, really just a small widening of the river channel, which soon returns to a normal width before widening again into Lough Boderg (the lake of the red cow). There is a perfect light wind, so the crew of the *Zorgen* raise the mast and hoist the main sail and jib. The lake narrows on the approach to the Derrycarne demesne. The demesne was originally part of the estate owned by Matthew Nesbitt, the High Sheriff of Leitrim in 1798. Derrycarne House was demolished in 1954 when the last owner failed to sell it and the lands passed to the Land Commissioners. There are some Douglas fir trees in the wood that would have been planted when the demesne was established, and some natural woodland along the lake shore, but most of the wood was planted in the 1960s.

The skipper of the *Zorgen* is very pleased with himself when he manages to navigate the gap at Derrycarne demesne under sail. The *Zorgen* continues southeast into Lough Bofin (the lake of the white cow) and around a wooded headland, called Inchmurrin or Rabbit Island. It is all that separates Lough Bofin from the 2 km long Lough Scannal, which sits at the northern end of Lough Bofin.

The stony shores of Boderg and Bofin are home to what is called a 'typical Shannon flora' of submerged Shoreweed, Yellow Sedge, Purple Loosestrife, Lesser Spearwort and Water Hemlock. The Greenland White-fronted Goose is found in the fields surrounding Lough Boderg, as are a variety of wildfowl such as Great Crested Grebe, Little Grebe, Mute Swan, Wigeon, Lapwing, Heron, Goldeneye, Whooper Swan, Tufted Duck, Teal,

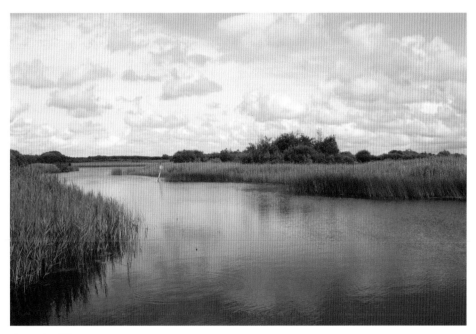

*Carnadoe Waters*

Cormorant, Mallard, Kingfisher and Moorhen. Lough Scannal is home to the Common Scoter, a bird that is Red-Listed in Ireland. This means that it is of 'high conservation concern' because they are in danger globally, or because their breeding population or range has declined by more than 50 per cent in the last 25 years, or if their breeding population has declined significantly since 1990.

The Common Scoter is one of 18 birds Red-Listed in Ireland; some of the other birds include the Chough, Corncrake, Red Grouse, Grey Partridge, Lapwing and Hen Harrier. Common Scoters (*Melanitta nigra*), or Scótar in Irish, are medium-sized ducks with dark plumage. The males have a yellow knob at the base of their bill. They spend the winter in coastal areas, but like to breed on large lakes. It is thought that their numbers have declined, in part, because of pollution killing their prey and because of mink, who are a particular threat to females incubating eggs.

On the western side of Lough Boderg, it is possible to navigate across the Carnadoe Waters. They are accessible through a narrow gap in the reeds just north of Coarse Island, which brings you under Carnadoe Bridge. A 1 km man-made stretch called Carrigeen Cut leads to Kilglass Lough, where there are the remains of two crannógs and a modern floating jetty. The jetty is not designed for barges as large as the *Nieuwe Zorgen*, so the boat is technically only half-moored.

An information board tells the story of the Ballykilcline townland south of Kilglass, which 'was the settting of one of the most extraordinary chapters in Irish history, both tragic and inspirational'. In 1834 the ownership of the Mahon Estate at Ballykilcline reverted to the English Crown, who took control and imposed exorbitant rents on the tentants. The 602 acre estate was home to over 500 people who went on strike in protest against the raised rents from 1836 to 1848. On 27 May 1847, the townlands were occupied by 60 police, 25 cavalry and 30 infantry. After the battle that followed, the homes of the farmers were 'tumbled' and the tenants evicted. Following this the Crown paid the fares to America for those tenants who would relinquish rights to their lands in an 'assisted emigration scheme'. By this time Ireland was suffering the effects of the Great Famine, and the Kilglass area was hit especially hard. The information board at Kilglass tells of 'cartloads of corpses' that were transported to Kilglass graveyard and buried in a mass grave. The 58 per cent drop in population here was one of the highest in Ireland.

Retracing our course back to the Carrigeen Cut, we make our way up to Grange Lough. The cut was made by the Shannon Commissioners in the nineteenth century, when they closed off the original channel that connected the two lakes. Just above the cut is a narrow channel that meanders through beds of reeds before it opens into the long and narrow Grange Lough. The Carnadoe Waters are renowned for their beauty, peace and tranquillity. Ruth Delany describes this 'world of narrow channels and waving reeds' as one of her favourite places on the river. At points the reeds are so tall and thick that is it not possible to see very far ahead, so other traffic is very well hidden. This adds to the sense of peace and isolation, and without the Waterways Ireland markers it would be very easy to lose your way. A visit to the Carnadoe Waters is highly recommended and worth the diversion, even just for the lovely sandwiches from the pub beside the harbour in Grange Lough.

The next stop on the river downstream of Lough Boderg, sitting on the northeast shore of Lough Bofin, is the village of Dromod, County Leitrim. Dromod, or Dromad meaning 'the ridge', is a small village of only 700 people. The harbour dates to 1829, when there was a small store and lifting crane. Today the harbour is a stopover for hire cruisers and boaters travelling the waters of the River Shannon, and the quayside has been altered and expanded to accommodate this modern traffic.

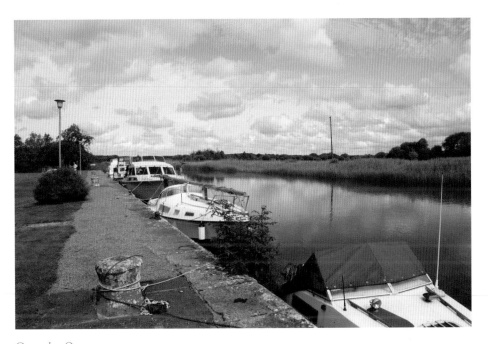

*Carnadoe Quay*

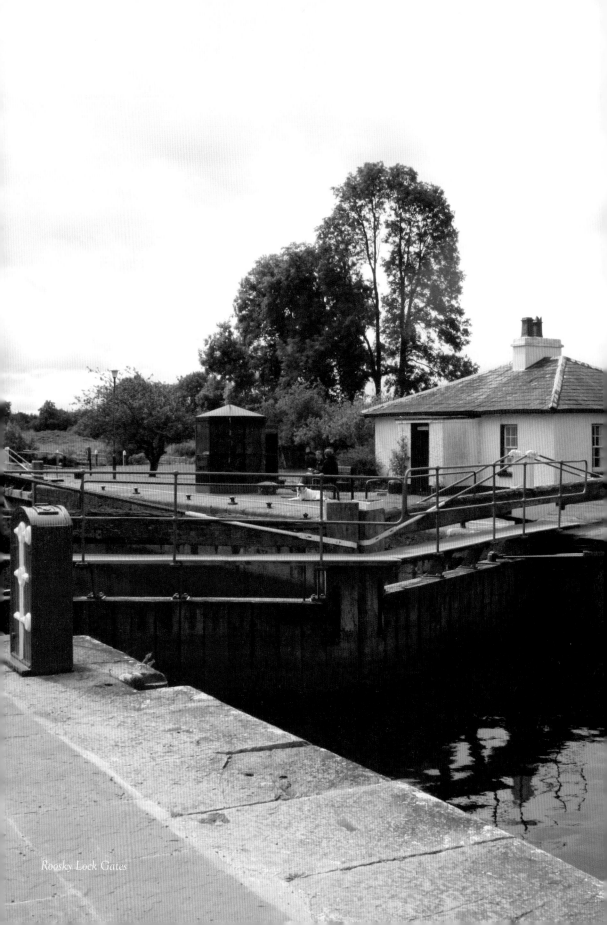

Roosky Lock Gates

# 4. Roosky to Lanesborough

Leaving Dromod behind, the lake turns to river again and we pass by Pigeon Island en route to the village of Roosky. Roosky, or Ruscagh (marshy place), is a pleasant village of just under 330 inhabitants in northeast County Roscommon, on the Roscommon–Leitrim border, nestled between Lough Boderg and Lough Forbes. We pass under the five-arched stone bridge without much headroom to spare. This section of the bridge lifts up to allow large cruisers to pass through, but with the mast of the *Zorgen* down we can pass through with relative ease. It is possible to moor just downstream of the bridge along the walls of the nineteenth-century quayside, with its original stone and iron mooring posts, which are all protected structures. The main street of the village is located on the western bank of the river in County Roscommon.

A short distance downstream of the bridge sits Roosky Lock, accessible from the town by a narrow tree-lined road that hugs the eastern bank of the river. This lock was built by the Shannon Commissioners in the 1840s, replacing the earlier 1760s' canal and lock, the overgrown remains of which can be found to the west of the river. The lock-keeper's house and the lock itself are in immaculate condition, with matching red paint on the house, bollards and edges of the lock gates. To the right of the lock are the old sluice gates and the weir, and I shiver slightly as I walk the short distance from the lock towards the weir. It was here that my husband's grandfather experienced a terrible tragedy. He was on a canoe trip down the Shannon with his friend, but when they came to the weir at Roosky, his friend was sucked into the lock and disappeared beneath the water and did not survive.

I shake these thoughts away as we pass through the lock and continue past the modern apartments and jetties on the eastern shore. The river broadens below Roosky, before

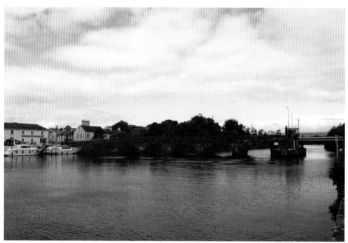

*Roosky Bridge*

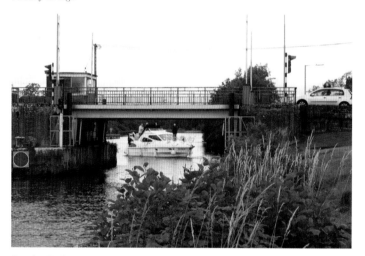

*Roosky Bridge navigation span*

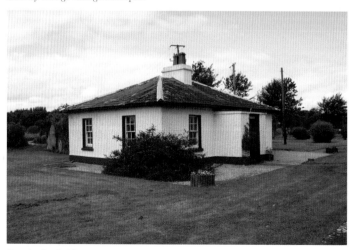

*Roosky Lock House*

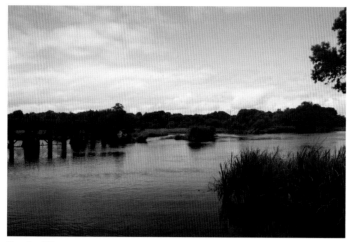

*Roosky Weir*

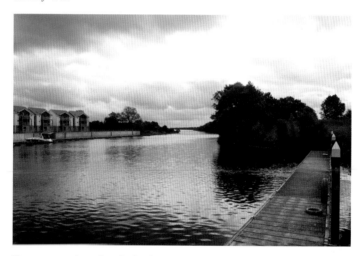

*Downstream from Roosky Lock*

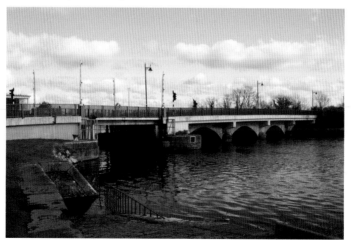

*Termonbarry Bridge*

narrowing again at Cloneen until it widens out to form the small and relatively narrow Lough Forbes. At the northern end of Lough Forbes, the River Rinn joins the Shannon system after a long journey from Lough Rinn near Mohill in County Leitrim. The eastern shore of the lake is densely forested – the Castle Forbes demense – but it does not hide the unsightly factory that looms nearby. Lough Forbes is an ecologically important site, due to the variety of habitats found in and around the lake. On the southeast shore lies an area of raised bogs called the Ballykenny–Fishertown complex, which is of international importance as these bogs are a unique example of Shannon floodplain river-edge bogs. At the southern end of the demense the River Camlin joins the Shannon after its journey down through Longford. A population of the Greenland White-fronted Goose (*Anser albifrons flavirostris*) can also be found at Lough Forbes from October to April, when they come to Ireland to feed on our peatlands.

On the eastern shore of the lake lies the demesne of Castle Forbes, a seventeenth-century castellated mansion that is the seat of the Earls of Granard (a title was first granted in 1684 to Arthur Forbes). The entrance to the castle is actually on the main street of Newtownforbes, County Longford, but it is not open to the public. This area was granted to the Forbes family during the plantations of the seventeenth century, when the area was known as Lisbrack (Lios means 'circular earthen fort' and breac usually means 'speckled'). The Forbes family changed this to the present name around 1750, but the post office still uses the original name of An Lios Breac on its stamp.

The lake narrows to become river again just below Corlehan Bay, and the fast-flowing river continues southwest towards Termonbarry in County Roscommon. Like Roosky, the seven-arched bridge in Termonbarry has a lifting section for larger boats. A small, overgrown island separates the navigable channel from the river's natural course. It is possible to moor along the west bank of the river, from where the main street of Termonbarry is accessible.

Termonbarry or Tarmonbarry is home to just over 500 people. The name of the town derives from Tearmann Berach (the Church lands of St Berach), referring to St Berach or St Barry, who established a church at Cluain Coirpthe, now know as Termonbarry. The navigation through Termonbarry Lock is slightly tricky due to the presence of a weir to the left of the lock. It is the second highest weir on the Shannon, next to Parteen. On exiting the Termonbarry Lock there is a narrow channel on the eastern side of the river, which leads to Richmond Harbour, the terminus of the Royal Canal, via the Cloondara Canal. The picturesque and stone-lined Cloondara Canal is a remnant of the original works to improve the navigation by Thomas Omer in 1760, and his lock house still stands by the bridge. A second lock leads into Richmond Harbour and the Royal Canal navigation that crosses the country to Dublin, passing through Longford, Mullingar and Maynooth. The harbour is empty now, drained as part of the works to make the Royal Canal navigable again. The navigation from the Shannon brings us as far as Cloondara Lock, but here the water disappears. Some fish have survived the drainage in little pools and puddles in the harbour floor, their small bodies perilously close to the muddy surface.

The construction of the Royal Canal, which began in 1790, took 27 years to complete. It was then officially closed to navigation in 1961. The Royal Canal Amenity Group campaigned for over 30 years for the reopening of the canal, with the aid of Inland Waterways, local authorities and the Heritage Boat Association. Works on the Royal Canal finished in September 2010, making it possible to navigate from the Shannon to Dublin.

The Shannon is wide and slow along this stretch, and we motor down towards Lanesborough at a leisurely pace, passing by a flat and wet landscape. In the distance to the west we can see the forested slopes of Slieve Bawn, which at 262 m is the highest peak in the area. We pass under a Bord na Móna railway bridge on our approach to the town, which no doubt serves the large power station that sits on the riverbank just upstream of Lanesborough. The bridge links Lanesborough, County Longford, with Ballyleague, County Roscommon, on the west bank of the river. The Irish name for this area is Béal Atha Liag (ford of the flagstones).

The population of the two towns has declined in recent years, probably partly due to the reduction of operations by the two main employers in the town, the ESB and Bord na Móna. Although the power station is probably considered an eyesore by most tourists, the fishermen might not agree. It produces a 'hot water stretch' that fish love, and so fishermen travel here from all over Europe. There are great facilities for them, such as over 60 fishing stands including some that are wheelchair friendly. The Anglo-Normans recognised how important Lanesborough was as a fording point, and occupied it in the thirteenth century with families such as the de Lacys, de Mariscos and de Verduns. The name of Lanesborough comes from Sir George Lane, to whom the land was granted during the Restoration under Charles II. Sir George is responsible for a lot of the development of these two towns, including the original bridge that connected them in 1667. The current bridge was erected by the Shannon Commissioners in the 1840s.

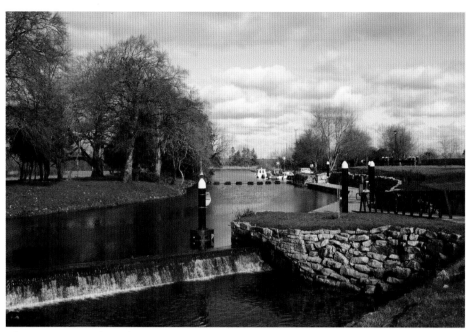

*The Moorings at Richmond Harbour*

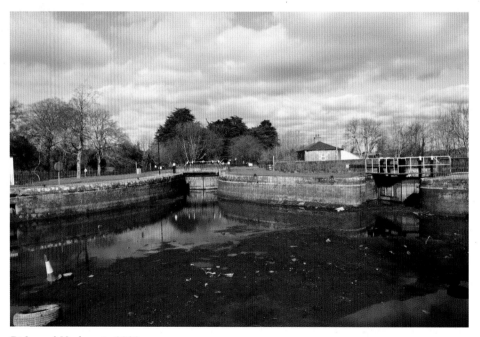

*Richmond Harbour in 2009*

The Shannon at Lanesborough

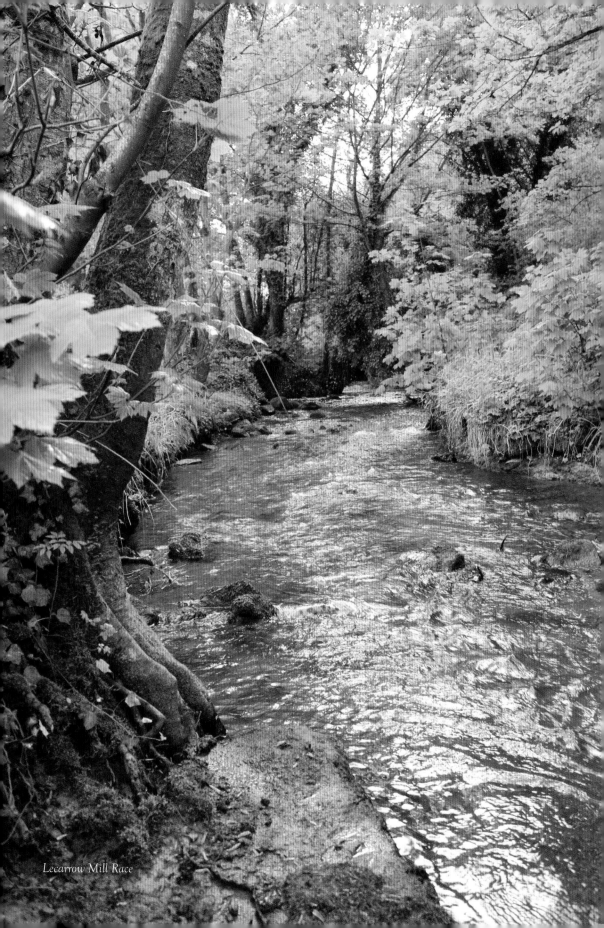

Lecarrow Mill Race

# 5. Lough Ree

As the river flows away from Lanesborough the channel widens into an almost circular area, before narrowing again as it splits around Ballyclare Island lying in the centre of the channel. The navigation route lies to the right of the island along the narrower but straighter channel. Lough Ree opens out before us, the third largest lake in the Republic of Ireland and the second largest of the Shannon lakes. It is 26 km long and varies from 1.5 km to 10 km in width. The lake lies where the counties of Longford, Westmeath and Roscommon meet. Lough Ribh is marked on Ptolemy's second-century map of Ireland, which some suggest means 'lake of the great plain (of water)'. The other school of thought is that it means 'Lake of the Kings', but who these kings were is not known. Harry Rice notes in his book, *Thanks for the Memory*, that the kings could be seven kings called John who ruled at Carlan on the Connaught shore. Most of the lake is less than 10 m deep, but there is a series of deep trenches running from north to south where the depth is up to 36 m. On the southeast shore of Lough Ree is a set of 'inner lakes' called Cleggan, Doonas, Ross, Killinure and Coosan.

At the northern end of the lake the shore is fringed with reed beds; to the east lies Commons Wood on the Longford side. We can still see the forested slopes of Slieve Bawn behind us to the north, but the land ahead on the western shore is flat and featureless. Before long we pass by the first of Lough Ree's 52 islands. The navigation markers guide us to the east of Inch McDermot, then Goat's Island, Bushy Island, Little Island, Inchenagh and Clawinch. The views to the east are more varied and interesting, with a series of small hills and ridges close to the shore. Soon the large wooded island of Inchcleraun comes into view in the centre of the lake.

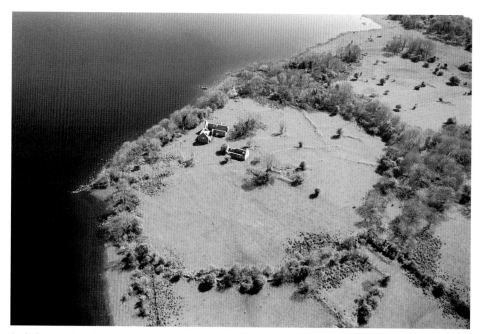

*Inchcleraun, Lough Ree © Department of Environment, Heritage and Local Government*

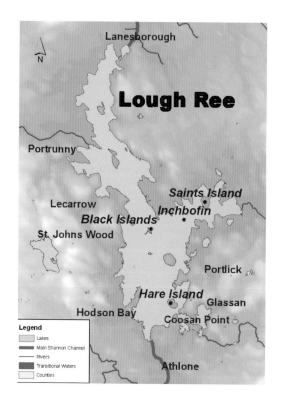

Diarmuid, son of Lugha, came to Inchcleraun in the sixth century to found a monastic settlement, and today there are remains of various ecclesiastical buildings dating from the Early Christian period right up to the sixteenth century. Many of the islands of Lough Ree were inhabited by religious communities, seeking the peace and tranquillity these islands could offer them. Such peace was short-lived, as these communities were frequently raided by Connaught and Munster tribes, and then by the Vikings between the eighth and tenth centuries. Turgesius is probably the best known of the Viking raiders on Lough Ree.

Turgesius or Thorgestr was a Norwegian Viking leader during the middle of the ninth century. He gathered a huge Viking fleet on Lough Ree, from where he attacked the major monasteries of the midlands. His wife, Ota, is supposed to have sat upon the altar at Clonmacnoise to give pagan oracles. He was eventually defeated by Maoilsheachlainn, King of Meath, whose daughter he was attracted to. Maoilsheachlainn, after a demand from Turgesius, sent his daughter to an island on Lough Owel. She was accompanied by 15 maidens Turgesius had promised to his commanders. The maidens, in fact, were beardless warriors armed with daggers. They slaughtered the commanders and captured Turgesius. Maoilsheachlainn is said to have drowned the Viking leader in the waters of Lough Owel, County Westmeath.

Inchcleraun is also known as 'Quaker Island', as it was inhabited for many years by a Quaker named Fairbrother. The name Inchcleraun supposedly derives from 'Clorina', who was the sister of the infamous Queen Maeve of the Táin Bo Cualigne (The Cattle Raid of Cooley). Following the death of her husband Ailill, King of Connaught, Maeve is said to have retired to the island. While bathing in the waters of Lough Ree off Inchcleraun, legend says, Queen Maeve was killed by her nephew Furbaide, son of Conchobar Mac Nessa, in revenge for the murder of his mother, Clothra, by Maeve. Furbaide killed her with a shot from his sling, fired from Efleet Castle across the water on the Longford shore.

It is possible to navigate around Inchcleraun to Portrunny Bay on the western shore. This is where the River Hind enters the lake, and the mouth of the river is home to many winter visiting birds including the Golden Plover and Whooper Swan. But the first creature that we encounter at the harbour in Portrunny is a sleek, dark and inquisitive mink, who poses for a photo before scampering away under the loose rocks on the side for the harbour wall. The American mink (*Mustela vison*) is a non-native or invasive species to Ireland, something we will come across in more detail at Lough Derg. Mink were brought to Ireland in the 1950s for use in fur farms, and the current population are descendants of escapees from these farms. Mink are normally found near water where they prey on waterbirds and fish, and they pose a serious threat to ground-nesting birds and native Irish species.

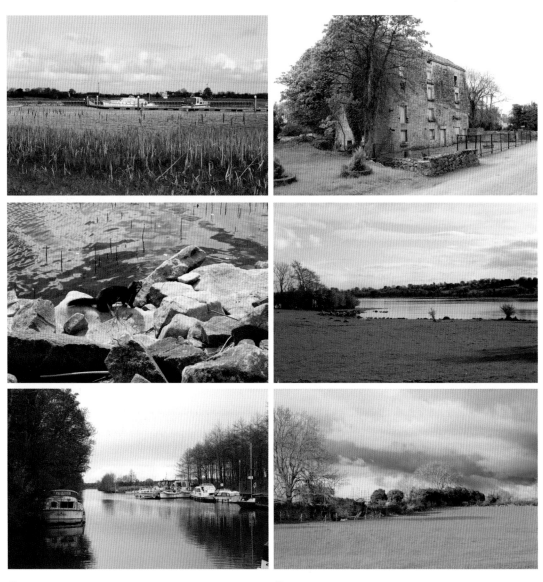

From top:

    Portrunny Bay

    The American Mink

    Lecarrow Canal

From top:

    Lecarrow Corn Mill

    Carrownure Bay Lough Ree from Rindoon

    Rindoon Defensive Wall

Lecarrow, a small town with a newly refurbished public harbour, lies down the lake from Portrunny. It is accessible via the Lecarrow Canal in Blackbrink Bay. Lecarrow, or Leth-ceathramhadh meaning 'half quarter' (of land), is a common name for townlands in Connaught. The 1.5 km stretch of canal was built in the 1840s to transport stone from a local quarry to Athlone, where it was used to construct the bridge, weir, lock and quay. After falling into disrepair, it was eventually dredged in the 1960s. Cereal cultivation used to be the main form of agriculture in this area, and there were once 12 watermills around the lake. Only four of these are still intact, including the corn mill in Lecarrow. It stands just across the road from the access road to the canal, and although it is boarded up and inaccessible on the inside, the exterior structure is fairly intact, with pale blue shutters covering the windows. The mill wheel is long gone, but it is possible to get close enough to see where it would have hung. The busy waters of the mill race pass under the road and flow down a tree-lined channel to join the Lecarrow Canal at the top of the harbour. The local community have turned the land on the banks of the mill race into a wildlife area.

It is a short journey around the shore of St John's Wood to Safe Harbour on the Rindoon Peninsula, where boaters must drop anchor and canoe or row ashore. At 330 acres, St John's Wood is the largest and most natural woodland in the midlands. Its importance lies not only in the fact that is very beautiful, but that is home to some rare and important plants. Part of the reason these species are found here is the presence of 'old woodland' – an area that has had permanent woodland cover for a very long period of time. Although the species found in the wood are described as 'typical' for this type of woodland, which lies on top of limestone, it is the exceptions such as Toothwort (*Lathraea squamaria*) and Bird's Nest Orchid (*Neottia nidus-avis*) that make St John's Wood so special. Two other species worth mentioning are the Red-listed Alder Buckthorn (*Frangula alnus*) and Bird Cherry (*Prunus padus*). This means that these two trees are in need of conservation under the terms defined

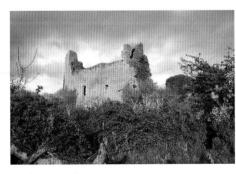

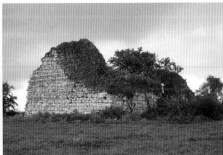

*Rindoon Castle*  *Rindoon Church*

by the International Union for the Conservation of Nature (IUCN), who set up a Red List of threatened species for the world, and encouraged each country to set one up for their own species. Ireland now has its own Red Data Book for vascular plants, which lists rare and threatened plants in Ireland.

Rindoon, or Rinn Dúin (the fort of the promontory), was once an Anglo-Norman town with a defensive wall. The name suggests that there was a pre-Norman settlement here, possibly located south of the Norman castle. It is thought that the settlement has been deserted since the thirteenth century, but there is a wonderful selection of ruins including a promontory fort, a castle, ecclesiastical remains, a church and graveyard, a windmill, four houses, a possible harbour and a field wall. The town was probably home to between 800 and 1,000 people, and was protected by a wall at the neck of the peninsula. The site is

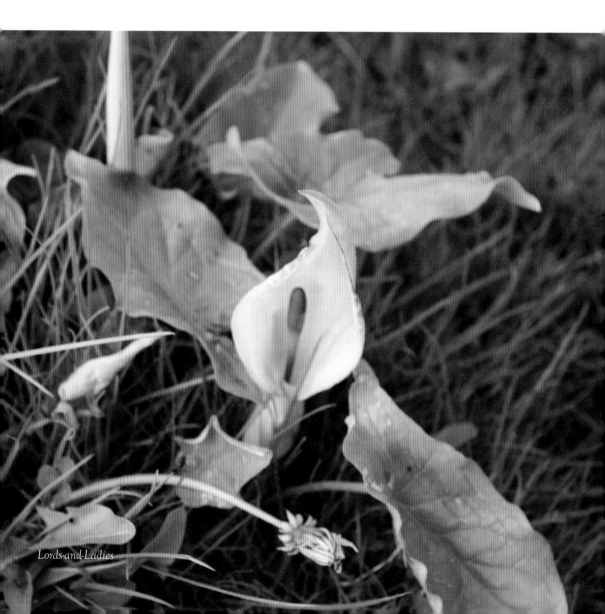

Lords-and-Ladies

accessible on the landward side from Lecarrow, and is well signposted.

The terrain is fairly rough and muddy, so come prepared. It is worth the walk to see the ruins and the beautiful views of Lough Ree from the castle, and during our visit there was an abundance of Lords-and-Ladies (*Arum maculatum*) flowering on the damp grass around the castle. Another interesting flower we came across was the Early Purple Orchid (*Orchis mascula*), a common species of woodland, grass and scrubland. The glossy, dark green leaves are spotted and the purple flowers sit atop tall spikes. From the lake it is hard to make out most of the ruins except for the castle. With rain clouds gathering rapidly we decide to call a halt to our exploration, and have to leave the search for the windmill in the woods to another day.

Back on the water the navigation route leads across to the eastern shore past the collection of small islands known as the Black Islands. These islands were populated until the 1930s, and farmers used to swim their cattle from island to island for grazing. The markers guide boats around the southern edge of these islands and between Inchturk and Inchbofin. We then continue around the tip of Saints' Island into Inny Bay on the eastern shore, where the River Owencharr, a part of the River Inny, enters the lake.

The River Inny runs through a region of Ireland known as 'Goldsmith Country'. Oliver Goldsmith was an eighteenth-century poet and dramatist born in the area. His most famous work was probably *The Vicar of Wakefield*, but his lengthy poem 'The Deserted Village' is thought to be based on the town of Auburn near Glassan in County Westmeath, where Goldsmith went to school.

> *Sweet Auburn! Loveliest village of the plain,*
> *Where health and plenty cheered the labouring swain,*
> *Where smiling spring its earliest visits paid,*
> *And parting summer's lingering blooms delayed:*
> *Dear lovely bowers of innocence and ease,*
> *Seats of my youth, where every sport could please,*
> *How often have I loitered o'er your green,*
> *Where humble happiness endeared each scene;*
> *How often have I paused on every charm,*
> *The sheltered cot, the cultivated farm,*
> *The never-failing brook, the busy mill,*
> *The decent church that topped the neighbouring hill,*
> *The Hawthorn bush, with seats beneath the shade,*
> *For talking age and whispering lovers made; ...*

*(Taken from 'The Deserted Village', by Oliver Goldsmith)*

From Auburn, Goldsmith went on to graduate with a Bachelor of Arts from Trinity College Dublin in 1750. The writer spent many years travelling, writing and working at odd jobs, but eventually he was noticed in literary circles and went on to write his celebrated works including the still-popular play, *She Stoops to Conquer* and 'The Deserted Village'. Goldsmith never forgot his youth in rural Ireland, and the excerpt I chose above does not provide the full picture of 'The Deserted Village'. The poem goes on to scorn the landlords who evicted their tenants, and to mourn the plight of the Irish forced to emigrate:

> *Sweet smiling village, loveliest o' the lawn,*
> *Thy sports are fled, and all thy charms withdrawn;*
> *Amidst thy bowers the tyrant's hand is seen.*
> *And desolation saddens all thy green:*
> *Only one master grasps the whole domain ...*
> *Far, far away, thy children leave the land.*
> *Ill fares the land, to hastening ills a prey,*
> *Where wealth accumulates, and men decay;*
> *Princes and lords may flourish, or may fade;*
> *A breath can make them, as a breath has made:*
> *But a bold peasantry, their country's pride,*
> *When once destroyed, can never be supplied.*

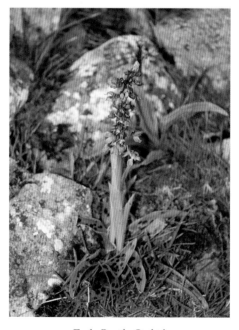

*Early Purple Orchid*

Goldsmith's likeness now guards the entrance to Trinity College Dublin, his stone sculpture sitting proudly across from that of his fellow Irishman and graduate, Edmund Burke.

The Inny joins Lough Ree at Inny Bay on the eastern shore of Lough Ree. We pass the red marker off the southern shore of Inchbofin and follow the navigation markers into the bay. Inchbofin (The Island of the White Cow) was the site of the earliest Christian settlement on Lough Ree. St Rioch, the son of St Patrick's sister Darerca, founded a monastery on the island in AD 450. Before entering Inny Bay the navigation rounds the southern tip of Saints' Island, which is joined to the mainland by a causeway. The 'island' is home to the remains of a medieval hall house, some ecclesiastical remains, a thirteenth-century Augustinian priory, a church and a graveyard. It is also an important site for birds such as the Lapwing, Golden Plover and Mute Swan. To the southeast of the tip of Saints' Island, on the eastern shore of the lake, lies a little townland with a very famous name. Bethlehem is an area inhabited by only a few families, and owes its name to the nuns of the Order of the Poor Clares.

In the seventeenth century the Roman Catholic majority of Ireland was supressed by a set of laws enforced by the British government. These Penal Laws were designed to disenfranchise the Catholic majority. During a brief lull in the enforcement of the laws, a small group of Catholic girls decided to set up the first 'House of Religion for Women in the Irish Nation'. This enclosed convent of the Order of the Poor Clares was founded on Merchants Quay in Dublin, but the presence of the convent was soon discovered and the nuns were banished. The Mother Abbess, Cecily Dillon, took the nuns west to her family land on the remote eastern shores of Lough Ree. They called their sanctuary Bethlehem. Life in Bethlehem was simple, yet harsh. The nuns did not wear shoes, and kept a strict prayer regime and vow of silence. At its peak the convent was home to 60 women, taking on the life of poverty voluntarily. The nuns finally had to flee their sanctuary in Bethlehem after the Siege of Athlone in June 1691, when marauding English troops were at large in the surrounding countryside. The nuns fled across the lake to safety, and the soldiers destroyed the convent.

Beyond Bethlehem lies the River Inny, but it is not possible to navigate up this fast-flowing and shallow waterway, so we retrace the navigation route to the red marker at Inchbofin. From here we travel south, passing the eastern shores of Inchturk and Inchmore Islands, carefully negotiating the shoals at Napper Rocks around the southern end of Inchmore and westwards into the middle of the lake.

The Napper Rocks are only one of many dangerous shoals on Lough Ree that add to the hazards of navigating such a large body of water. Such hazards are clearly marked on the navigation charts and have interesting names such as Iskeraulin, Wood, Hexagon, Godiva, Louisa and Long Shoals. There are also a variety of rocks that pose a threat to the unobservant boater, the Napper Rocks included, and not all are named or marked. The Iskeraulin shoal in the centre of the lake between St John's Wood and Efleet Bay is possibly the most treacherous. This heap of jagged stone can be submerged during flooding. The weather is another danger to the water-based traveller on Lough Ree, as it can be highly changeable with very strong winds. It is advisable for boats to travel in pairs, and to pay close heed to the markers and warnings on the charts. All of these factors combined mean that for many boaters Lough Ree is a daunting place, and a lot of them choose to cross the lake in one trip to avoid changing conditions. This is a pity because there is so much to see and so many places to explore, but the lake must be treated with respect. It has its own weather forecast and coastguard for good reason.

On the eastern shore of the mainland to our left as we pass by Inchmore, Portlick Castle sits on the Whinning Penninsula. The castle was built by the Dillon family (De Lion), under the charter of King John in 1185. The castle, which is actually a medieval tower house, is supposedly the only one in Ireland to be in continuous use as a residence. The Dillons were supporters of King James II, and when he was defeated by William of Orange during the Jacobite Wars, the castle was confiscated and granted to one of William's supporters, Thomas Keightly. Within seven years the castle had been sold to the Smyth family, in whose hands it remained until the 1950s. Portlick translates to 'bank of the flagstone', which it is suggested refers to a 'flag' on the bank that local women used for washing clothes. Another version suggests that it means 'part of the flagstone surface', referring to the geology of the underlying rocks, which are mostly limestone. Today the castle is in wonderful condition, and has been sympathetically and beautifully restored as a location for weddings and conferences.

Portlick Forest is part of the Millennium Forest project run by Coillte. Over 1,500 acres of native Irish woodland were restored and designated as 16 'Millennium Forests' under this scheme, and they are dedicated in perpetuity to the people of Ireland. Part of the restoration process involved planting a tree for every household in Ireland. In addition, damaging, invasive, non-native trees and shrubs (such as rhododendron and cherry laurel) were removed, and natural regeneration of native trees, shrubs and forest floor plants encouraged. Portlick Forest is made up of native hazel and ash woodland, with smaller amounts of oak, whitebeam, holly, alder, willow, birch and hawthorn. The forest floor is home to bluebells, primrose, violet, ivy, Lords-and-Ladies, bramble and woodrush.

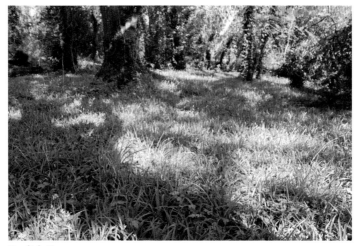

*Portlick Forest*

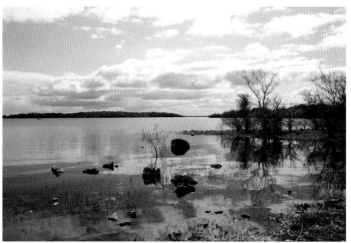

*Portlick Bay*

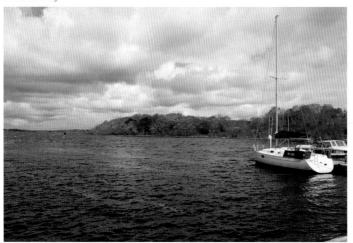

*Hare Island from Coosan Point*

From the middle of the lake, close to the Cribby Islands, the navigation map gives us a few different options. We can continue south to Hodson's Bay, or take a diversion via Hare Island to the inner lakes. Hare Island, or Inis Ainghin, lies to the north of Coosan Point, not far from Athlone and close to the entrance to Killinure Lough. St Ciaran founded a monastery here in AD 541. He came to Lough Ree at the age of 12 to be tutored by St Diarmuid on Inchcleraun. He went on to study under St Finian of Clonard and eventually St Enda of Aran. It was during his time on Aran that he had a vision that would bring him back to the River Shannon. In his vision he saw a large tree planted in the centre of Ireland, with branches spreading across the country. The birds that sat on its branches carried its fruit across the sea to other countries. St Enda interpreted the vision for Ciaran, and suggested that Ciaran himself was the tree, and he must found a church in the centre of Ireland.

After a brief stay on Scattery Island in the Shannon Estuary, Ciaran came to Inis Ainghin where he built a small oratory in the southeast corner of the island. There were mud and wicker huts for each of his followers who, as eremites, lived in seclusion. Three years and three months later, St Ciaran left the abbacy of Inis Ainghin in the hands of Enna Maccu, and departed on his journey down the Shannon, the journey that would bring him to Clonmacnoise.

Hare Island is home to the Garden Warbler (*Sylvia borin*), a rather nondescript little bird, grey-brown in colour. I mention this bird for two reasons. Firstly because of its beautiful song, and secondly because the main place it is found in Ireland is on the Shannon lakes. Another unique and interesting fact about Hare Island is that the largest Viking gold hoard in Europe was discovered here around 1802. Hare Island is only a short distance from the harbour area at Coosan, and a short jaunt in a canoe or small boat makes it possible to visit the island from the shore. Coosan itself is a lovely spot with a new and impressive children's playground, a swimming area, plenty of mooring and a pub. It is also the gateway to the 'inner lakes', which are accessed between Killinure and Coosan Point. The 'inner lakes' are called Coosan, Killinure and Ballykeeran. These lakes are enclosed to the north, east and south by hills and woodlands, which in combination with the narrow channel leading from Lough Ree makes this a safe and sheltered area.

Almost directly across from Coosan Point on the western side of Lough Ree sits Hodson Bay. From here southwards the lake narrows dramatically into river once more. Hodson Bay is well equipped with a purpose-built harbour, beach, picnic area, hotel and golf course. It is a short trip down the river to Athlone, passing by the Lough Ree Yacht Club on the way. The river is wide and the flow is strong, carrying us along towards Athlone. It passes under the first of three bridges, and the most modern of them. The 'Shannon Way' was built in 1991 to bring the motorway over the river and bypass the town in an attempt to ease congestion. It is made from concrete with a high central arch and two side arches. The next bridge we pass under was built in 1850 to carry the railway over the Shannon. It is a beautiful piece of engineering, with high white arches and massive circular piers supporting it. It is over 164m long and used to have an opening span in the centre. The iron-work for the bridge was shipped to Limerick and then brought to Athlone by barge.

The final bridge comes into view ahead, as do the domes of SS Peter and Paul's Church, and on the far side of the bridge, the castle. This is the oldest of the three bridges, and we will come to its story later. There are modern floating jetties and facilities at the marina beside the Radisson Hotel on the east of the river, but we continue on, under the navigation span on the right side of the bridge nearest the castle.

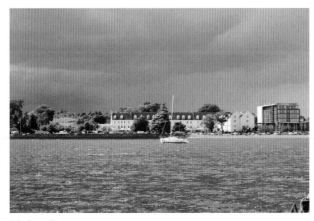

*Hodson Bay*

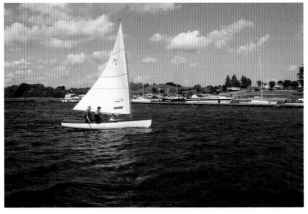

*Lough Ree Yacht Club*

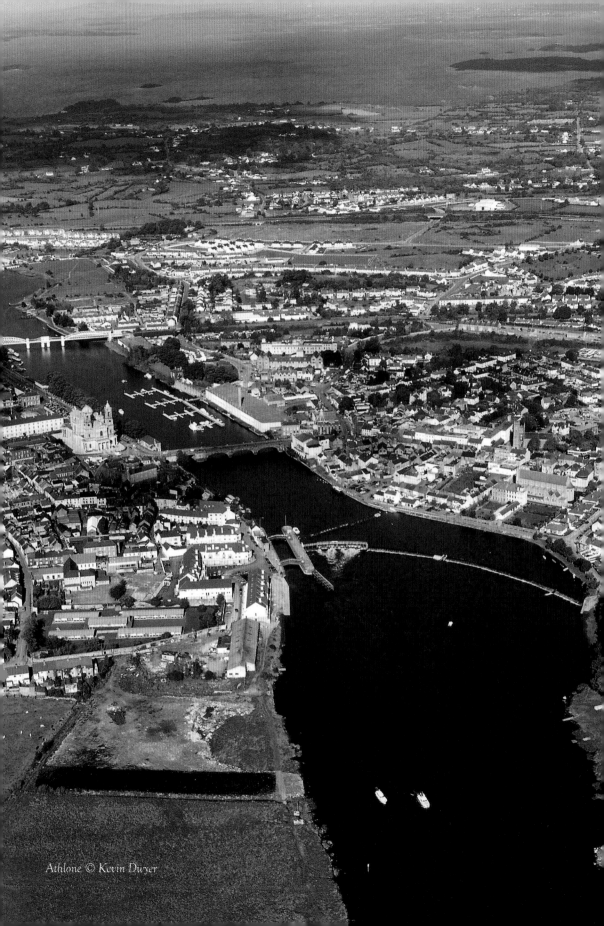

Athlone © Kevin Dwyer

# 6. Athlone

Since prehistoric times this has been a vitally important crossing place of the River Shannon, where the river breaks through an esker ridge to form a ford. In the past it was called Ath Mór (The Great Ford), but we know it better as Athlone. Ath Luain (the Ford of Luain) sits at the southern end of Lough Ree, in County Westmeath. It is thought that Luain is a man's name, but who that man was is not known. One of the stories says that Luain was Luain Mac Lughdeach (son of Lewy), who ran a hostelry close to the Great Ford and guided weary travellers with their animals and baggage across the ford. Eventually the ford came to be called after him.

Another story comes from the Táin, and attributes the name to Queen Maeve and her husband, King Ailill. An argument arose between the pair about who had the most treasure. In order to solve the quarrel, all of their possessions were gathered together, but deemed to be equal – except for the mighty 'white-horned one', a magnificent bull belonging to Ailill. Maeve was determined to find a better bull, and discovered one in Cooley, which she stole. This brown bull challenged the white bull of Ailill to battle. The ensuing combat was so terrible that the whole island trembled at the sound of their roars. The brown bull of Cooley caught the white bull on his horns, shaking him and tossing him until his body ripped to pieces. The haunch (lon) of the bull fell on the Great Ford, and thus it became known as the Ford of Luain.

My favourite version recounts the story of a pair of lovers, called Buide and Estiu. Buide and his foster-brother Luain would visit Estiu as birds, and their magical song would lull everyone to sleep, including Estiu's husband Nár, leaving the lovers in peace. Nár became suspicious about the birds, and asked a druid about them. When he realised what was happening, he travelled to a spot on the Shannon near Clonmacnoise to find the brothers. He shot the two birds with one cast from his sling, killing Buide. Luain survived long enough to fly north to Ath Mór, where he fell from the sky as he died.

Who knows which version is true, or whether the name simply means the Ford of the Moon, but what is known is that the earliest settlement of Athlone happened around the middle of the eighth century. There is also evidence of human habitation very close to Athlone during the Neolithic period between 3000–2000 BC, consisting of a portal tomb at Mihanboy, County Roscommon, just 4.5 km west of Athlone.

Recognising the strategic significance of Athlone, Turlough O'Connor (Toirrdelbach Ua Conchobair), King of Connaught, built the first bridge in AD 1120, to aid his forays into the Kingdom of Meath. Five wicker or wooden bridges succeeded this first bridge, Towards the end of the twelfth century the town of Athlone fell into Norman hands, and by 1210 it was the joint seat (with Dublin) of English administration in Ireland. Work then started on a castle on the western bank, and a new stone bridge. By 1230 the town of Athlone sat on both sides of the Shannon, and within a few years a town wall was constructed. This wall was necessary to protect the town from repeated attacks by the Irish, including a particularly successful attack by the Ó Conchobairs in 1316, when the town was burned and many Normans killed.

In 1537, under the rule of Queen Elizabeth, the Tudors revived royal authority in Ireland, and Athlone Castle was once again occupied by government forces. The construction

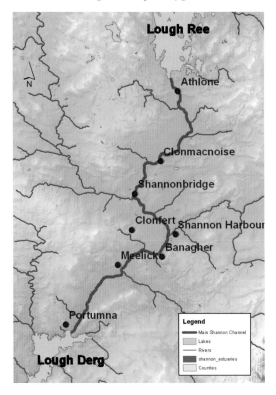

of an Elizabethan stone bridge in 1566 renewed Athlone as the focal point for east–west traffic and greatly increased the importance of the town. The bridge was 360 feet long and 14 feet wide. It had nine arches and was constructed under the direction of the Lord Deputy, Sir Henry Sidney. Corn mills were added to the bridge at a later date, utilising the fast flow of water underneath. This bridge was not replaced until 1846 under the works of the Shannon Commissioners. The current weir and lock were also constructed around this time, to replace the old canal that was needed to bypass the shallow rapids of Athlone.

By the seventeenth century a new curtain wall and bastions had been built around the eastern side of the town and earthen ramparts around the west. This was the period of the Jacobite war between King James II and William of Orange. Deposed by his daughter and her husband William, James II fled to France. Here he gained support from Louis XIV who aided his journey to Ireland to face battle with William at the now infamous Battle of the Boyne. Following the Irish defeat at the Boyne in 1690, the Jacobite forces retreated to the west of Ireland, and regrouped in Limerick to prepare the defence of the line of the Shannon. The Williamites knew that Athlone was vital to the defence of Connaught, so they attacked Athlone with a force of 10,000 under the Scottish Lieutenant General James Douglas. The aged Colonel Richard Grace defended the castle and the Williamites retreated. Grace apparently declared that he would 'defend Athlone until he had eaten his old boots', and then blow himself up rather then surrender.

The following year the Williamites returned, this time numbering 25,000 men under the command of the Dutch Godard van Reede, Baron de Ginkel. The Irish troops defended the town from the Connaught side of the river, under the command of the French General the Marquis St Ruth, and broke down several arches of the bridge so the Williamite forces could not cross over from the captured Leinster side of Athlone.

The Williamite forces bombarded the castle with grenades, stone shot and cannon-balls, and attempted to repair the damaged bridge. Sergeant Custume and his Irish men defended the bridge and dislodged the attempted repairs, but Ginkel crossed at the ford and entered the castle on 30 June 1691. His reward from William was the title of Earl of Athlone (a title that remained with his descendants until 1844) and Baron of Aughrim. The Jacobite war continued with the Battle of Aughrim and reached its climax in Limerick, where the Irish army under Patrick Sarsfield fell. Under the Treaty of Limerick they were given the choice of sailing to France to join the army of Louis XIV, or returning to their farms. Those who went to France became known as 'the wild geese'.

*Does any man dream that a Gael can fear?*
*Of a thousand deeds let him learn but one!*
*The Shannon swept onwards broad and clear,*
*Between the leaguers and broad Athlone.*

*'Break down the bridge!' – Six warriors rushed*
*Through the storm of shot and the storm of shell;*
*With late but certain victory flushed.*
*The grim Dutch gunners eyed them well.*

*They wrench'd at the planks 'mid a hail of fire;*
*They fell in death, their work half done;*
*The bridge stood fast; and nigh and nigher*
*The foe swarmed darkly, densely on.*

*'Oh, who for Erin, will strike a stroke?*
*Who hurl yon planks where the waters roar?*
*Six warriors forth from their comrades broke,*
*And flung them upon that bridge once more.*

*Again at the rocking planks they dashed;*
*And four dropped dead, and two remained;*
*The huge beams groaned, and the arch down-crashed –*
*Two stalwart swimmers the margin gained.*

*St Ruth in his stirrups stood up, and cried,*
*'I have seen no deed like that in France!'*
*With a toss of his head, Sarsfield replied,*
*'They had luck, the dogs! 'Twas a merry chance!*

*O many a year, upon Shannon's side,*
*They sang upon moor and they sang upon heath,*
*Of the twain that breasted that raging tide,*
*And the ten that shook bloody hands with Death!*

*(Taken from 'The Ballad of Athlone', by Aubrey De Vere)*

The present King John's Castle is only the most recent in a series of Athlone castles. It stands on the Connaught side of the river, next to the bridge. Bishop John de Gray of Norwich built this castle in 1210, and it began a long career of capture, betrayal and recapture over the centuries. On 30 October 1697, the castle was struck by lightning, and the subsequent explosion of the gunpowder magazine destroyed much of the town and killed many people. The castle was not reconstructed until 1827, but the original keep, curtain walls and water gate are still present.

It is in the shadow of this castle that the *Nieuwe Zorgen* moors. We are a stone's throw from the famous Seán's Bar, which holds the Guinness Book of Records title as the oldest pub in the British Isles, and maybe even the world. The pub predates the castle as the original building dates to the year AD 900, and some of the original clay and wattle this building was made from still survives in the pub today. Seán's Bar belonged to Seán Fitzsimons for over 30 years, after he bought it in 1970. Although the pub is named after a previous owner also called Seán, to the boating community it is most associated with Seán Fitzsimons and his boat *Iron Lung*. The infamous barge, now owned by Seán's nephew Andy Fitzsimons, is moored on the quay wall next to us. This 49 m vessel was built in 1928 as a Grand Canal barge and was called the *St Mary*. When the boat's working life came to an end, she was converted into a houseboat and used as accommodation for workers during the construction of Shannon Airport. The barge was bought by Seán and his friend John Connon in 1961 after they hired it for a trip to the Shannon Boat Rally.

Seán's Bar was previously known as Three Blackmoor Heads, and during the siege of 1691 it was owned by Jacob Jacques. Jaques is buried in St Mary's Church of Ireland on Church Street on the Leinster side of the bridge. The bell tower is all that remains of the church's original 1622 structure, which was replaced by the current building in the 1820s. This bell was supposedly used by General Ginkel to signal the final assault on Athlone

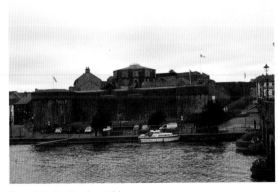

*King John's Castle, Athlone*

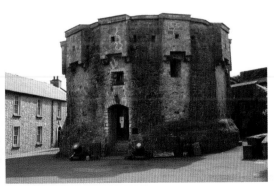

*The keep of King John's Castle*

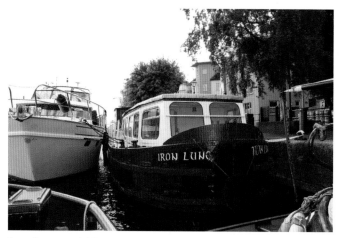

Iron Lung *in Athlone*

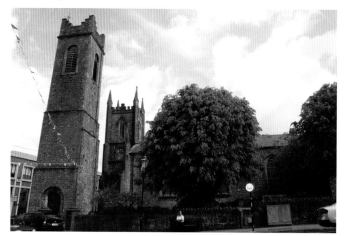

*St Mary's Church, Athlone*

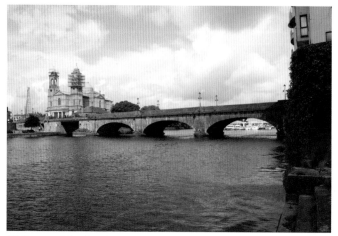

*SS Peter and Paul's Church*

during the 1691 siege. The church now houses the 'Mearing Stone', which once marked the boundary between Roscommon and Westmeath on the middle of the Elizabethan bridge.

The path to the bridge from the docks where we are moored takes us up a gentle slope between the castle and bridge to Market Square. Although the interactive tour of the castle is a little tired and frayed around the edges, it is worth it for the wealth of information and, most of all, the wonderful views of the town from the top of the castle. One of the displays in the museum is dedicated to Count John McCormack, one of Athlone's most famous sons. John Francis McCormack was born in Athlone in 1884, the fourth of 11 children. His singing career began in 1903 when he won gold at the Feis Ceoil in Dublin, and he went on to become a world-famous tenor. In 1928 he received the title of Count from Pope Pius XI to honour his work for Catholic charities. He is also remembered for many sentimental airs, and is famous for being the first singer to record 'It's a long way to Tipperary' in 1914. But the song most appropriate to us here is 'Where the River Shannon Flows'.

*There's a pretty spot in Ireland*
*I always claim for my land*
*Where the fairies and the blarney will never, never die*
*It's the land of the shillalah*
*My heart goes back there daily*
*To the girl I left behind me when we kissed and said goodbye*

*Where dear old Shannon's flowing*
*Where the three-leaved shamrock's grows*
*Where my heart is I am going to my little Irish rose*
*And the moment that I meet her*
*With a hug and kiss I'll greet her*
*For there's not a colleen sweeter where the River Shannon flows.*

*Sure no letter I'll be mailing*
*For soon will I be sailing*
*And I'll bless the ship that takes me to my dear old Erin's shore*
*There I'll settle down forever*
*I'll leave the old sod never*
*And I'll whisper to my sweetheart 'Come and take my name Asthore.'*

*Where dear old Shannon's flowing*

*Where the three-leaved shamrock grows*

*Where my heart is I am going to my little Irish rose*

*And the moment that I meet her*

*With a hug and kiss I'll greet her*

*For there's not a colleen sweeter where the River Shannon flows*

The song was written by James Russell for his sketch, *The Irish Servant Girls*, which was written for the theatre in New York in 1904. The sketch ended up being quite controversial. In America, the United Irish Society set up a working group called the Society for the Prevention of Ridiculous and Perversive Misrepresentation of the Irish Character. In the sketch James Russell and his brother John dressed up as two Irish servant girls, who blabbered, threw things and made smutty insinuations. The sketch was a big hit with the Irish immigrant population. The working group decided to target the Russell brothers' sketch, and one of their first deeds as a group was to throw a rotten egg at James while he portrayed the Irish housemaid on stage. The group targeted the sketch everywhere it played with rowdiness and various missiles including eggs and vegetables. The play suffered badly from the protests and audiences began to stay away.

To our left on the other side of the bridge sits another of the most recognisable landmarks of Athlone, the large and impressive SS Peter and Paul's Church. At 61m long it is the largest church in Athlone, and dates to 1937. From the water the most striking feature is the set of two bell towers, which rise impressively to 38 m high flanking the huge central dome. My favourite attraction of this church has to be the stained glass windows from the Harry Clarke Studios. Harry Clarke is probably Ireland's best-known stained glass artist and book illustrator. Harry died from tuberculosis in 1931 at the tragically young age of 41, but during his short career he designed over 172 stained glass pieces. Some of his best-known work includes the windows of the Honan Chapel in University College, Cork (considered by many to be his best work), and a piece that now resides in the Hugh Lane Gallery in Dublin illustrating 'The Eve of St Agnes' by John Keats. My personal favourites are the windows in Bewley's Café on Grafton Street in Dublin.

Behind the SS Peter and Paul's Church lies the oldest military barracks in Europe, the Custume Barracks. The barracks is unique in its name also, in that it is the only barracks in Europe named after a non-commissioned officer. Until the barracks were built, the Williamite troops had been housed with the civilian population, but following the great siege of 1691 much of the town lay in ruins and alternative accommodation was needed. Some of the original seventeenth-century buildings survive in the barracks today, including the Riding House with its low-pitched roof and huge chimneys dating to 1697. The group of buildings known as Pump House Square also date to the end of the seventeenth century.

The Watergate sits along Grace Road (named after Colonel Richard Grace and known locally as Accommodation Road), which runs beside the river towards the railway. This gate was built in 1850 when the military gave a strip of land to 'accommodate' the traffic to the new train station. The gate is a result of negotiations between the Railway Authority and the military who still needed access to the river. The Railway Authority agreed to provide a new cut stone wharf and a gate for access. Thus in 1852 the Watergate was built, and it is considered the best surviving example of Classical architecture in Athlone.

Our arrival into Market Square on this bright and sunny June morning coincides with an actual market. We make our way between stalls of organic fruit and vegetables, free-range meat, home-made preserves and totally irresistible cakes and buns. After stocking up for afternoon tea on board the *Zorgen* we continue our exploration of the town. The bustle and good cheer at the market follows us over the bridge towards the eastern side of Athlone. We can see the top of the weir downstream of the bridge and the lock that will take us down towards the Shannon Callows and Clonmacnoise. For now it is onwards through the rushing stream of people on the bustling streets of Athlone. Off to explore the streets and alleys for shops, cafes and pubs before we leave for the open spaces and wide still waters of the River Shannon Callows.

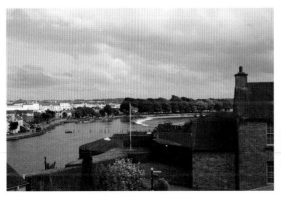

*View of the Shannon from King John's Castle*

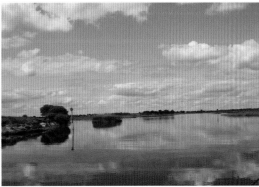

*Leaving Athlone behind*

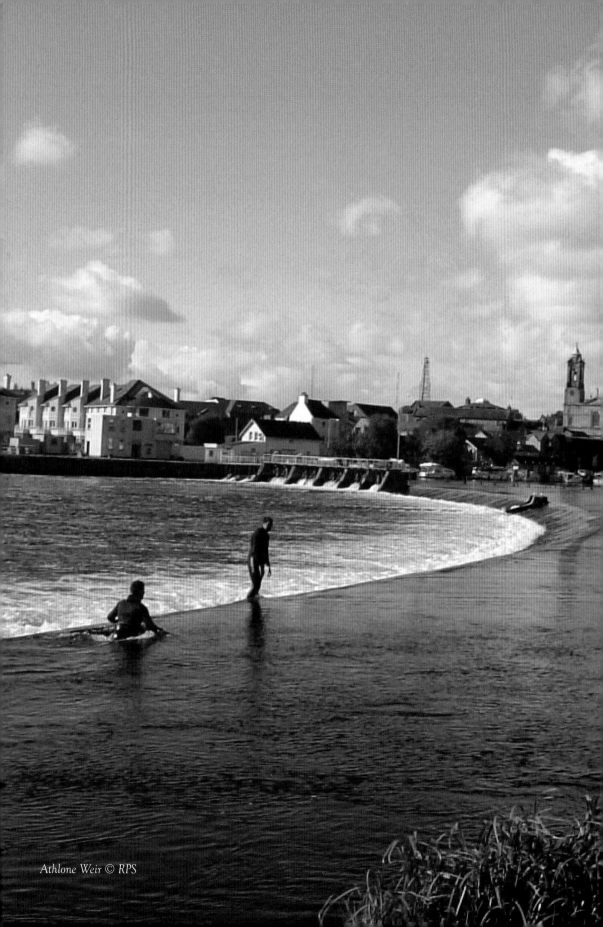

Athlone Weir © RPS

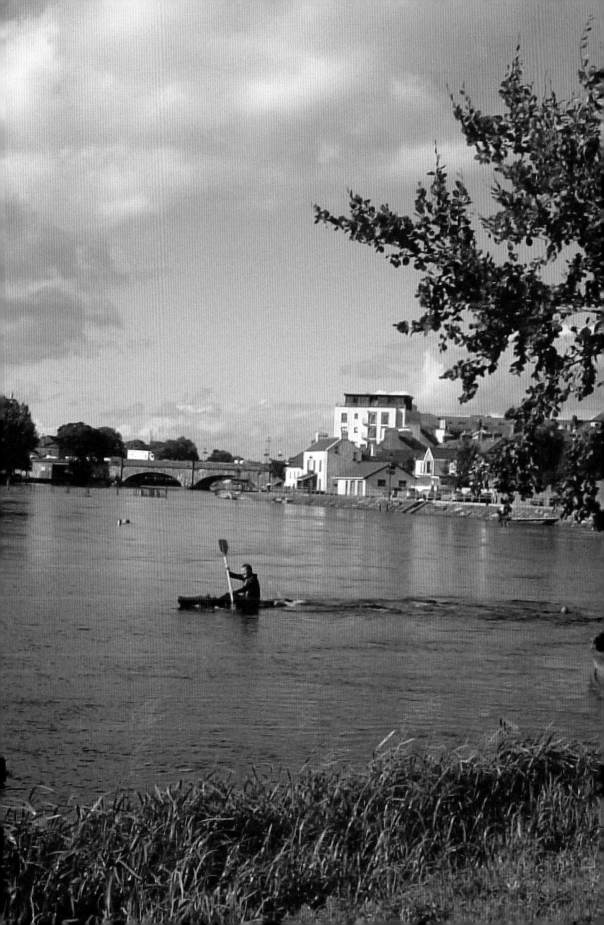

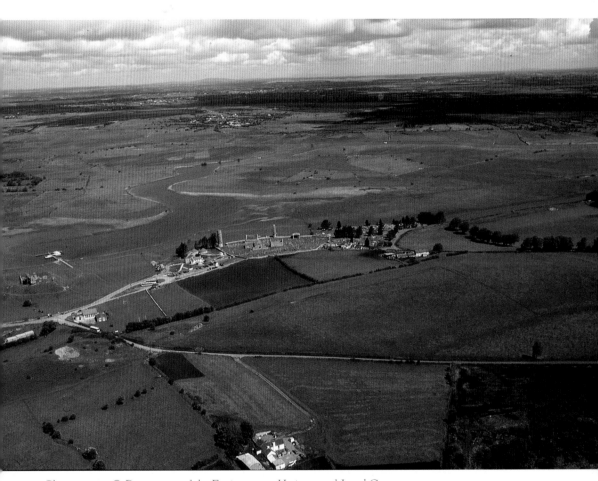

*Clonmacnoise © Department of the Environment, Heritage and Local Government*

# 7: Clonmacnoise

In a quiet watered land, a land of roses,
Stands St Kieran's city fair
And the warriors of Erin in their famous generations
Slumber there.

There beneath the dewy hillside sleep the noblest
Of the Clann Conn,
Each below his stone: his name in branching Ogham
And the sacred knot thereon.

Many and many a son of Conn the Hundred-Fighter
In the red earth lies at rest;
Many a blue eye of Clan Coleman the turf covers,
Many a swan-white breast.

(T. W. Rolleston, 'The Dead at Clonmacnoise')

I cannot help thinking about the Vikings, as the monastery comes into view again. For at least an hour now we have been catching glimpses of the round tower in the distance, then losing sight of it again. It feels like we are almost there, and then the river turns away again, and the tower disappears from view. Would the monks have noticed us already, if we were Vikings, steering our longship towards the monastery with plunder and pillage in mind?

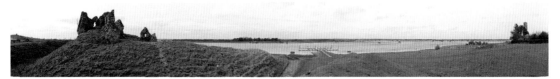

*Clonmacnoise panorama © Conor Cahill*

I can imagine the anticipation those Scandinavian seafarers might have felt, when at last the monastery came into view directly ahead, as the river makes its final bend back towards Clonmacnoise.

Sand martins swoop along the water's surface, catching flies to feed their babies. The tall and elegant Grey heron stands, graceful and statuesque, in the shallows, waiting to spear his dinner with his dagger-like yellow bill. Brilliant blue damselflies and metallic red dragonflies dart past. It is a perfect summer day. Children are jumping off the end of the jetty at Clonmacnoise, and the few other crews that are moored here are taking advantage of the weather, sipping wine and eating dinner outside. Our skipper slows down the boat in preparation for mooring.

We moor the boat on the floating jetty next to Clonmacnoise and the ruins of the thirteenth-century Norman castle beside it. Almost immediately a fellow boater approaches us, full of curiosity and questions about the *Nieuwe Zorgen*. The *Zorgen* is a change from the shoals of Shannon cruisers that frequent these waters, and this happens almost every time we moor. As our skipper happily tells the story behind the boat, I disembark and cross the field separating us from the monastery. The resident cattle are obviously used to this, as they barely glance up from drinking in the shallows of the river as I pass by. The walk up from the river towards the monastery brings you close to the precarious-looking ruins of the Norman castle on the right. Large blocks seem to hang by a thread over the edge of the mound supporting the castle remains. The castle was built in the 1200s by the Bishop of Norwich, John de Gray. The cause of the castle's current state is not known, although some suggest it was blown up, which would explain its condition.

There has been a monastery in use here for more than 1,000 years since St Ciarán established the first around AD 544. The monastic city of Clonmacnoise was renowned

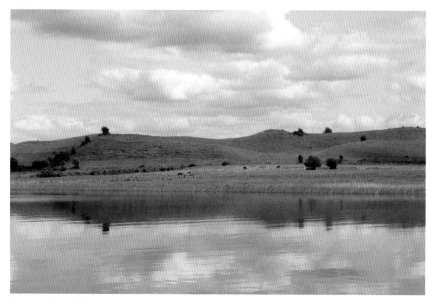

*Approaching Clonmacnoise*

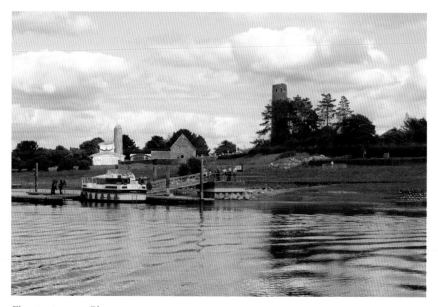

*Floating jetty at Clonmacnoise*

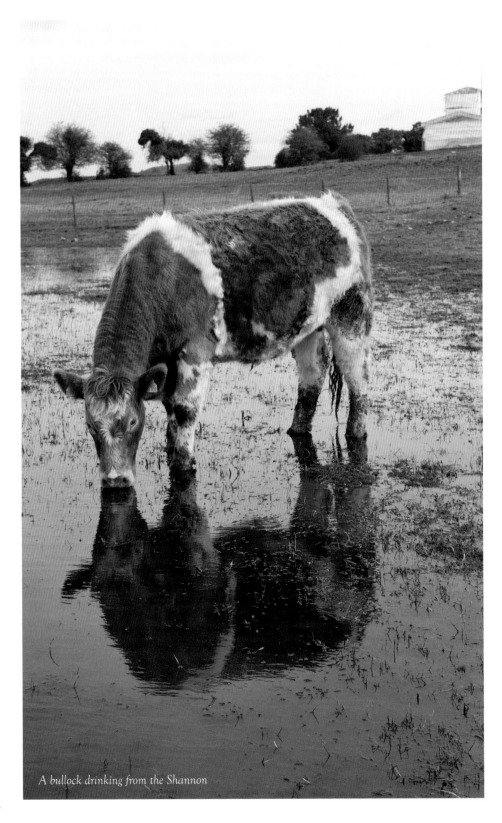

*A bullock drinking from the Shannon*

throughout the Christian world, and for a long time it was an important centre of religion, learning, craft and trade. Clonmacnoise today is probably only a fraction of its original size. Recent research has uncovered evidence of a thriving secular community surrounding the monastery. Archaeologists believe that Clonmacnoise was actually Ireland's first planned urban settlement, with streets, houses and a thriving crafts industry, based on the skills of its inhabitants. The riverbank was possibly thronged with shipbuilders and traders.

There is some speculation about the reasons why St Ciarán chose this site, but an important factor must have been location. At that time Clonmacnoise was sited where the Shannon was crossed by the 'Great Road' or 'An Slí Mhór'. The Shannon provided a natural route for travellers from north to south, and similarly the Great Road for those from east to west across the midland bogs. The Great Road ran along a series of esker ridges that are remnants of the last ice age in Ireland, which ended 10,000 years ago. Eskers are ridges of sand, gravel and boulders deposited by meltwater streams that flowed beneath the thick sheet of ice that covered the midlands, and many of the low-lying hills visible at Clonmacnoise are actually esker ridges. When the ice finally disappeared these ridges were exposed.

This series of eskers, which run east–west from Dublin through Meath, Kildare, Westmeath, Offaly, Roscommon and Galway, are known collectively as the Esker Riada. The eskers served as roads where they crossed boggy land, and early farmers utilised them for their good drainage. The name esker is Irish in origin ('eiscir' means sand or gravel hill), but has come into general use in international geology. In second-century Ireland the eskers marked the division between the two political regions of Conn and Mogha. North of the eskers was Leath Cuinn, or 'Conn's half', and south was Leath Mogha, or 'Mogha's half'.

The ruins visible at Clonmacnoise today are not those of the original monastery founded by St Ciarán. The first construction here was likely to have consisted of small, circular wooden structures. It was not until the ninth century that stone was used for construction, and the ruins seen today date from the ninth to twelfth centuries. When Ciarán arrived here with his small group of followers, he was given the land for this monastery by Diarmuid Mac Cearbaill, who then helped Ciarán to set the boundaries for the monastery. Seven months after his arrival, at just 33 years of age, St Ciarán passed away from a plague known as 'buidhe conaill'. Although he never got to see his monastery completed, one of his followers, Oenna, took over from him as abbot, and together with the rest of the followers he carried on the work St Ciarán had begun.

By the middle of the twelfth century the monastery at Clonmacnoise had been plundered and burnt over 30 times, with the first Viking attacks in the eighth century. This meant that very few valuable items have been recovered during excavations at

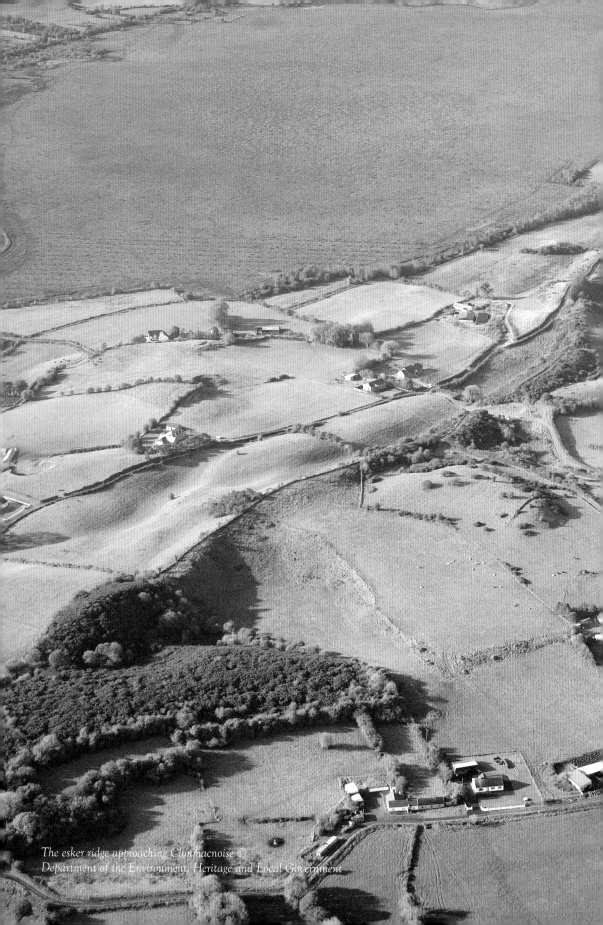

*The esker ridge approaching Clonmacnoise ©*
*Department of the Environment, Heritage and Local Government*

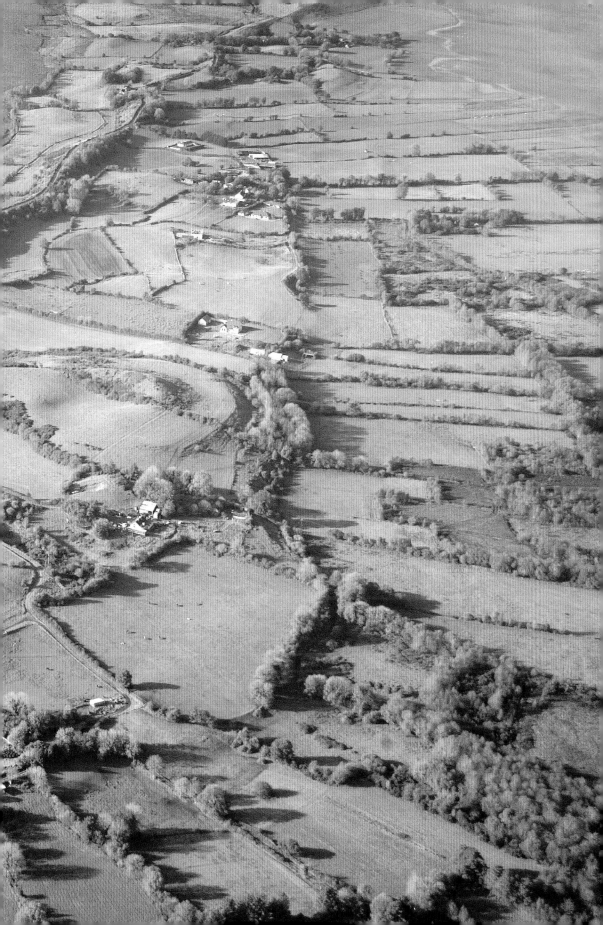

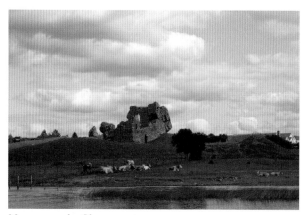

*Norman castle, Clonmacnoise*

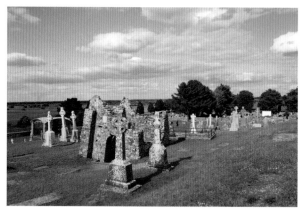

*St Ciarán's Church, Clonmacnoise*

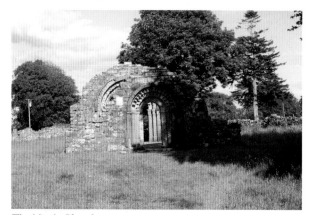

*The Nun's Church*

Clonmacnoise. However, one extremely important object was discovered in the ruins of St Ciarán's Church. The Crozier of the Abbots of Clonmacnoise is one of the finest available. It dates to the eleventh century and is now on display in the National Museum on Kildare Street in Dublin. Other items of interest discovered include a gold crown and collar, a gold torque and several bronze pins from the Nun's Church. Despite the repeated invasions, the monastery continued to flourish and the twelfth century saw the production of *The Book of the Dun Cow* (Lebor na hUidre). It is named after a sixth-century sacred relic of Clonmacnoise, the hide of the dun cow that belonged to St Ciarán. The book is the earliest surviving manuscript with literature written in Irish, and it contains the oldest versions of the Táin Bó Cuailgne, the Voyage of Bran, the Feast of Bricriú and other religious, mythical and historical material. Today the book is housed in the Royal Irish Academy on Dawson Street in Dublin.

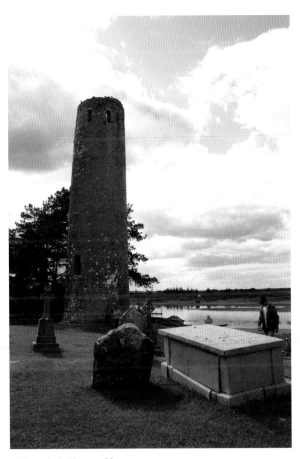

*O'Rourke's Tower, Clonmacnoise*

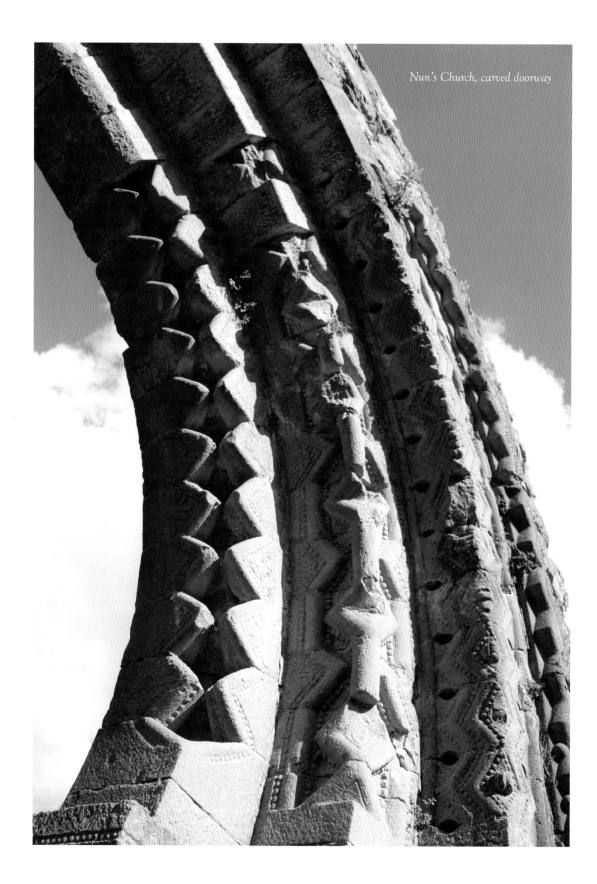

Nun's Church, carved doorway

Today there are ruins of seven churches within the walls at Clonmacnoise, and also the Nun's Church lying to the east outside the boundaries. The tower we had chased for hours on our journey here is actually one of two round towers on the site – McCarthy's Tower, which is attached to St Finian's Church, and the free-standing O'Rourke's Tower. Round towers were built as refuges for monks from attack by invaders, Scandinavians in particular. The towers were so strong that any invader found it impossible to demolish, so the monks and their treasures were well protected. The only access to the tower was from a doorway several feet up from the ground. The monks would climb up by ladder, and then pull the ladder up behind them. The towers also provided good views of the surroundings and served as watchtowers, with a window on every level all facing in different directions.

McCarthy's Tower is attached to St Finian's Church and has an intact roof, whereas O'Rourke's Tower lacks a roof. This tenth-century tower was built by Fergal O'Rourke, King of Connaught, and there is a legend connected to its construction. Supposedly a dispute erupted over costs between the stone mason and the monks. In protest, the stone mason began to remove blocks from the tower and throw them to the ground. Despite the monks agreeing to pay what he wanted if he returned to work, the stone mason refused to proceed and the tower remained incomplete.

The seven churches remaining on the site today are: Temple Connor, Temple Kelly, Temple Ciarán, Temple Hurpain, Temple Doulain, Temple Finian and the Cathedral. The Cathedral is the largest of these seven, and was probably a wooden construction originally. A short distance away along the Pilgrim's Road, you can find the ruins of the Nun's Church in a small field. To get to it, walk down through the graveyard and out onto the Pilgrim's Road. Follow the road for about five to ten minutes and the Nun's Church is in a small field on the right side of the road. It is one of the finest examples of Hiberno-Romanesque architecture remaining in Ireland and well worth the walk. The church was built in the tenth century, but the beautifully carved doorway and chancel arch were not added until 1167. These two features were added by Dearbhforgaill, the wife of Tighearnán O'Rourke, the King of Breifne.

If you continue along the Pilgrim's Road away from Clonmacnoise you will come to one of the few remaining intact raised bogs in Ireland. Mongan bog has been growing for over 3,500 years, so the intact centre of the bog is probably the same as it was during the monastic period. Mongan bog is part of a chain of raised bogs that stretches along both sides of the Shannon between Athlone and Banagher, divided at points by eskers and drumlins. It was thought that the raised bog surrounding Clonmacnoise meant the monastery was inaccessible, but research by the Irish Archaeological Wetland Unit (IAWU) has provided good evidence for the presence of gravel roads and toghers (bog roads made of wood) across the raised bogs.

Three high crosses and the largest collection of Early Christian grave slabs in western Europe are also found at Clonmacnoise. Of the three high crosses remaining (there were probably seven originally), the Cross of the Scriptures, also known as King Flann's Cross, is one of the most impressive in the country. The original cross stood outside the Cathedral until the early 1990s, when it was moved into the visitors' centre, and a replica was put in its place. This style of high cross, with a stem linked to the arms by a circle, dates from the seventh or eighth centuries, and is usually decorated with carvings of bible scenes. There are two inscriptions on the base of the Cross of the Scriptures: 'A prayer for King Flann, son of Maelsechnaill, a prayer for the king of Ireland', and 'A prayer for Colmán who made this cross for King Flann'. This cross is supposed to mark the grave of King Flann who died in AD 914. The carvings on the west face of the circle show the crucifixion, the arms at either side depict figures offering chalices, and the panels on the base of the cross on the same side show the betrayal and arrest of Christ.

In 1994 underwater archaeologists Donal Boland and Mattie Graham discovered the remains of a wooden bridge spanning the river at Clonmacnoise, which was dated to AD 804. The date was established by tree-ring analysis (dendrochronology) in Queen's University, Belfast by the researcher Mike Bailie. This means that the bridge was made before the Normans arrived in Ireland, probably by the monks from Clonmacnoise. The 120 m long bridge may be the longest wooden structure dating from the early medieval period in Ireland, and possibly the largest known from early medieval Europe. Although the river is fairly shallow here, it was never used as a fording point because of the soft nature of the river bed, which is made of alluvial clay. The bridge would have been constructed by driving two parallel lines of vertical wooden posts 3.5 m down into the clay. Boland and Graham found 17 pairs of oak posts arranged metres apart, spanning the width of the Shannon here at Clonmacnoise. They estimate that there would have originally been 25 pairs of posts.

The remains of nine dug-out boats were also discovered along the line of the bridge, two of which contained early medieval axes. A whetstone for sharpening axes was found in another of the boats. Another interesting find from the river next to this bridge was a bronze basin dating from the eighth to ninth centuries. It was badly damaged, apparently from a series of heavy blows, probably the result of one of the many raids suffered by the monastery at Clonmacnoise. At this time Clonmacnoise was under the patronage of the Kings of Connaught, so when the bridge was built it connected Clonmacnoise with the rest of Connaught, on the other side of the Shannon, thus facilitating trade. and may have been built in collaboration with the King of Connaught.

The monastery began to decline in importance from the thirteenth century on, but its significance as a place of pilgrimage has continued to this day. The invasion by the English garrison from Athlone in 1552 was probably the final nail in the coffin for Clonmacnoise. The Annals of the Four Masters record that after this invasion: 'There was not left moreover, a bell, small or large, an image, or an altar, or a book, or a gem, or even a glass in a window, from the wall of the church out, which was not carried off.'

The monastic city of Clonmacnoise and its cultural landscape has been included on a list of proposed World Heritage Sites submitted to UNESCO (the United Nations Educational, Scientific and Cultural Organisation) by the Irish government. The list includes the Burren, the Céide Fields and the Northwest Mayo Boglands, the historic City of Dublin, early medieval monastic sites (Clonmacnoise, Durrow, Glendalough, Inis Cealtra, Kells and Monasterboice), the royal sites of Ireland (Cashel, Dún Ailinne, Hill of Uisneach, Rathcroghan Complex and Tara Complex) and the western stone forts.

In a way the decline of Clonmacnoise has been a good thing, because the site now is one of great peace and tranquillity, far removed from the bustling centre of learning it was in its heyday. Even on a busy day, when the tourist coaches are lined up outside, there is a still peacefulness about the place, which for me emanates from the quiet calm of the river as it flows slowly by. Perhaps this is how St Ciarán felt when he came across the site, and that played some part in his decision to settle here at Clonmacnoise.

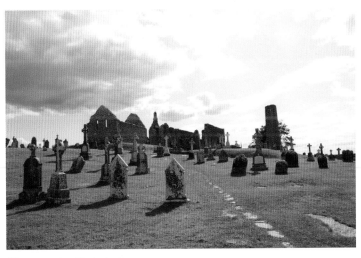

*Clonmacnoise Cathedral*

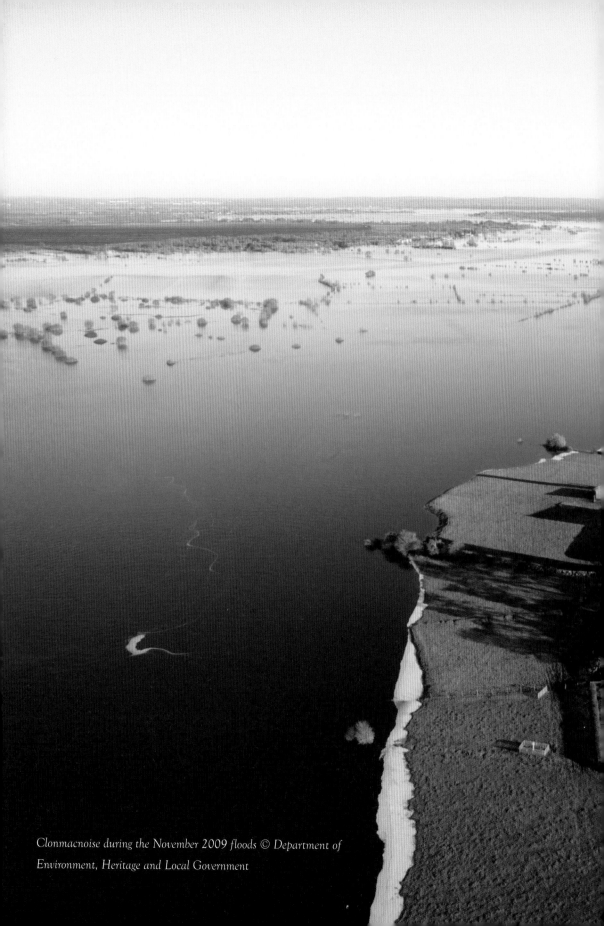

*Clonmacnoise during the November 2009 floods © Department of Environment, Heritage and Local Government*

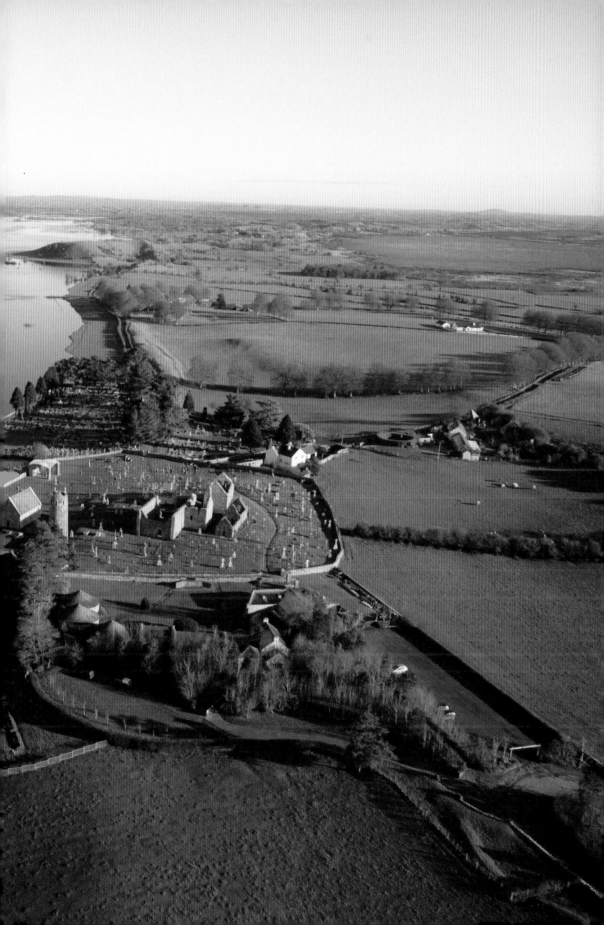

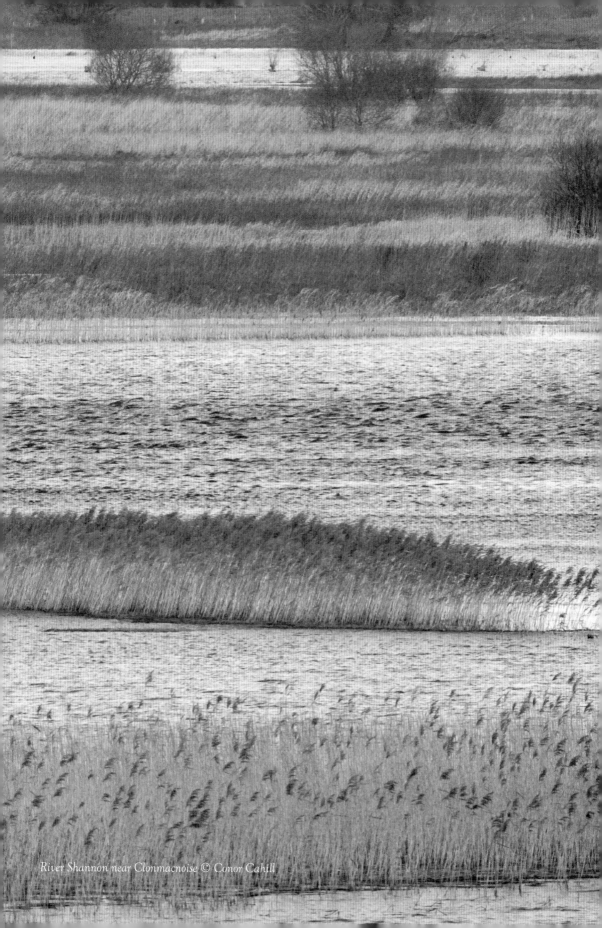

River Shannon near Clonmacnoise © Conor Cahill

# 8: The Shannon Callows

Cluain Mhic Nois, the Irish name for Clonmacnoise, translates to 'water meadow of the sons of Nós'. Clonmacnoise stands beside the river in an area known as the Shannon Callows. Callow is an anglicised version of the word 'Caladh', which means river meadow. This anglicised version was used in the early nineteenth century to describe 'lands liable to flood beside the River Shannon'. These Callows stretch for 40 km between Athlone and Portumna, where the river is broad and sluggish due to the slight gradient. During winter and spring the water level of the river rises and floods the surrounding grasslands, which dry out enough during the summer to accommodate grazing and hay production.

There are 3,500 hectares of Callows along that 40 km stretch of river, including the Callows along the Little Brosna, which enters the Shannon just below Victoria Lock, north of Portumna. The Shannon Callows are of huge importance in terms of conservation. They are home to a variety of rare and endangered plant and animal species, and an excellent example of a habitat that is becoming extremely rare throughout the world.

The grasslands of the Callows are classified as semi-natural, lowland, wet grassland. (The fact that the summer meadows are grazed and eventually cut for hay is what makes this habitat 'semi-natural'.) If there was no human intervention at all, then trees such as hazel and alder would colonise, and gradually a woodland habitat would evolve. So without agriculture, the plant and animal life currently found on the Callows would no longer exist, and the Callows grasslands would cease to be. It is a rare case of productive farming and diverse wildlife existing in harmony, and in fact the wildlife depend on the farmers to maintain their diverse and rare habitat.

The plant communities of the Callows vary with the changing habitats found as one moves away from the river, and so the plants at the edges of the river differ from those on the wet grasslands. However, the boundaries between these communities are not always clear cut, and there is a lot of overlap between habitats and species. As you move away from the water towards the surrounding peatlands, the communities found will be those typical of raised bog. Finally, in the areas not subjected to seasonal flooding, the plant communities will be those of typical dry grasslands.

The plant life on the Callows wet grasslands mainly consists of, as you might expect, species of grasses. There are other species present too, such as rushes, sedges and plants with conspicuous flowers. The most common species occurring on the Callows include the Cuckoo Flower, Marsh Marigold, Water Mint, Marsh Bedstraw, Meadowsweet, Common Sedge, Meadow Grass, Creeping Buttercup and Creeping Bentgrass. Of course there are always exceptions to the rule, so you might come across some more unusual species.

The Summer Snowflake is a rare inhabitant of the Callows, sometimes found on damp ground. It belongs to the daffodil family and so it is no surprise that it resembles a clump of daffodils, but with the typical white, bell-shaped flower of the familiar Spring Snowflake. The creamy white bells are trimmed with green, and unmistakable if you are lucky enough to find one. Two legally protected plant species occur in the Callows: Opposite-leaved Pondweed (*Groenlandia densa*) in some ditches, and Meadow Barley (*Hordeum secalinum*) in drier areas. This is one of only two known inland sites for the Meadow Barley in Ireland.

As the grassland of the Callows is flooded for most of winter and spring, the main option left to farmers is to use it for pasture in the summer months and for hay later on. The farmers leave the grassland to its own devices for the summer. They do not add fertilisers or plough the soil. The unique plant communities and habitats of the Callows are the result of a complex interaction between flooding, soil type, movement and chemistry of groundwater, and current and historical land management practices. These unique plant communities in turn determine the species of birds that utilise the Callows, be they summer breeders, winter visitors or residents. If the plant communities of the Callows were to change for any reason, the birdlife would be the first to suffer. Luckily we should be protected from this happening, thanks to two EU directives.

The Irish government has selected candidate Special Areas of Conservation (cSAC) throughout Ireland, as legally required by the EU Habitats Directive. This protects certain habitats and species that are under threat in the EU. Some of the habitats that are designated as cSAC in Ireland include raised bog, blanket bog, turloughs, lakes, rivers, estuaries and woodlands. There are 25 species of plants and animals designated too. These include otter, salmon, Bottlenose dolphin, Killarney fern and freshwater pearl mussel. Another piece of legislation relevant to the Callows, and the entire River Shannon, is the Special Protection Area (SPA) designation, which relates to the protection of rare and vulnerable bird species.

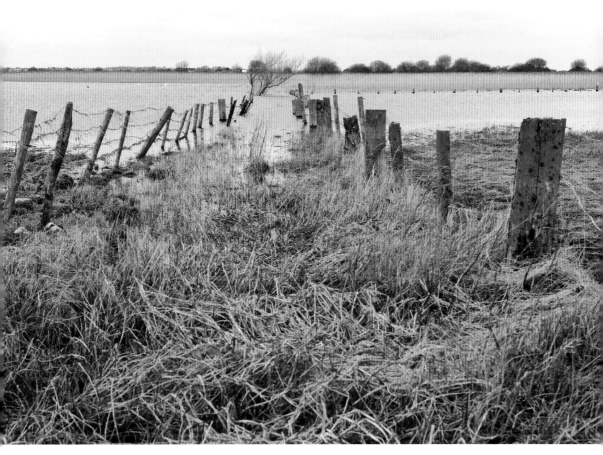

*Shannon Callows © Conor Cahill*

Many birds migrate across long distances, and it is not enough to protect them over just part of their range. The EU Birds Directive spans all EU member states to protect birds at their breeding, feeding, roosting and wintering areas. It identifies species that are rare, in danger of extinction or vulnerable to changes in habitat and that need protection. Three areas in the Callows are designated as SPAs.

The Birds Directive lists the species requiring protection in the annexes. This is why you often see a rare bird referred to an 'Annex I species'. There are 25 species on the list that occur in Ireland. The directive also requires that regularly occurring migratory species such as ducks, geese and waders are protected, as well as wetlands, and in particular wetlands of international importance, which attract large numbers of migratory birds each year. (Internationally important means that 1 per cent of the population of a species use the site, or that more than 20,000 birds regularly use the site.) I am not explaining these two directives to give you a crash course in European Law. The Corncrake is my reason. The Corncrake used to be an abundant summer visitor to Ireland, and 50 years ago the late-night mating call of the Corncrake male was a common sound. Now the Corncrake is on the list and on the brink of extinction worldwide.

The Corncrake has the Latin name *Crex crex*, which sounds like the distinctive mating call of the male bird. I have also heard the call described as the sound of a thumb being run along the teeth of a comb. The skipper of the *Nieuwe Zorgen* was lucky enough to hear it in Shannon Harbour this summer. They have been recorded on Bullock Island, which is a short walk from the 36th lock at Shannon Harbour. A group of British birdwatchers were

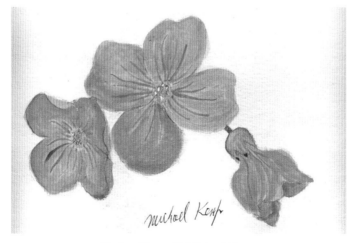

*Cuckoo Flower © Michael Kemp*

in the area hoping to hear the distinctive call. Imagine their delight at hearing it, especially when it is becoming such a rare occurrence. Our skipper confirmed for me that the 'thumb along the comb' is a pretty good description of it.

The Corncrake spends the winter in southern and eastern Africa, before returning north in April to breed, where it remains until late August or early September. In the last ten years the numbers of Corncrake in Europe have dropped by between 10 and 20 per cent. A local girl at Clonmacnoise told me that they had not heard the Corncrake at all during the summer of 2008, probably because of the wet weather which affected the juvenile birds. That is very worrying, but if the British twitchers at Shannon Harbour are right, there are courting males here this summer.

At the start of the twentieth century, the population of Corncrake was probably in the tens of thousands. By the late 1960s, the population had declined to about 4,000 singing males (fieldworkers estimate numbers by listening for the mating call of the male bird). A 1988 census of the whole island of Ireland found that the population had dropped to just over 900 singing males. A repeat census in 1993 found only 174 singing males – a decline of over 80 per cent in just five years. This survey also found that Corncrakes were now restricted to three core areas in Ireland – the Shannon Callows, north Donegal and County Mayo. By 1994 numbers had fallen to only 129.

The dramatic drop in Corncrake numbers has been attributed to changes in traditional agricultural practices on the birds' breeding grounds. The Corncrake prefers species-rich grassland as opposed to the single species of grass preferred by intensive modern farming. They like to build their nests in meadows of long diverse grasses, and lay their first clutch of eggs in late May. The eggs hatch after about three weeks, so that peak hatching is in mid-June. The females feed their fluffy black chicks for the first few days and stay with them for about ten days. The chicks cannot fly yet, but they can find food for themselves and run very quickly under the cover of the tall grasses. In fact, they are reluctant to run across open ground, which is why delayed mowing is so important. The chicks can fly five weeks later, and their mothers are free to mate again and lay a second brood that will hatch in late July.

Research has shown that, in order to maintain stable population levels, Corncrakes need to hatch two broods of chicks per year. As the peak hatching date for the second brood is in late July, Corncrakes will decline rapidly in areas where most of the mowing takes place before early August. Changes in traditional farming practices – including the drainage of damp ground, increased fertiliser applications, use of more productive grasses, increases in livestock and the use of bigger, more efficient machinery – all result in earlier mowing dates and a shorter harvest period. What this means to the Corncrake is that their preferred

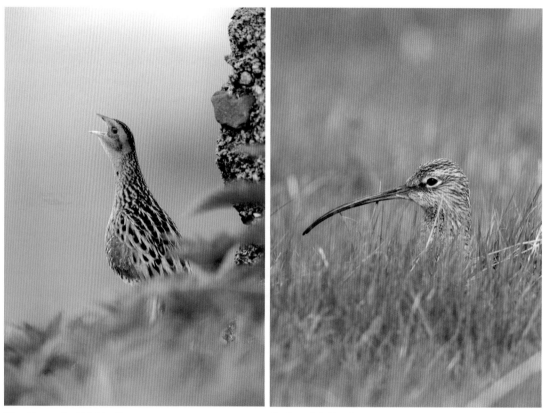

The Corncrake © Mike Brown      Curlew © Mike Brown

species-rich grassland is no longer available, and the cover they require to raise their young is removed too early. The timing of mowing is not the only thing to consider. As mentioned earlier, the chicks are reluctant to cross open ground. So if a farmer mows his field from the edges into the middle, then the chicks are left stranded in the middle of the field with no escape route. This method of mowing can kill up to 60 per cent of the chicks present.

Attempts to save the Corncrake from extinction include the establishment of a grant scheme for farmers, to encourage Corncrake-friendly farming practices. In 1991 the National Parks and Wildlife Service set up the scheme in cooperation with BirdWatch Ireland and the Royal Society for the Protection of Birds. Under the scheme farmers are encouraged to provide early cover for the birds arriving from Africa. This early cover is provided in the form of corners of fields or corridors of beds of irises, nettles, cow parsley, reeds and reed-grasses. Early cover protects the arriving birds from predators. It also gives them the cover they need to start nesting in spring when long vegetation cover is scarce in Ireland.

The Corncrake-friendly mowing method starts with delaying mowing until the chicks are large enough to avoid the mower. Ideally this would be in mid-September, but this is not always possible for the farmer. Farmers are encouraged to delay mowing until after 10 August on the Shannon Callows, and they are compensated for doing so and for modifying their mowing practices. If they can manage to delay mowing until September, a further grant is available to them. They are also encouraged to leave corridors of vegetation for any remaining chicks to use for escape.

The Curlew (*Numenius arquata*) has sadly joined the Corncrake on the endangered list. Research by Kathryn Finney of BirdWatch Ireland in 2009 has shown that numbers of Curlew on the Callows declined by 83 per cent between 1987 and 2002. This is part of a trend for wading birds in the rest of Ireland and throughout Europe, and not just with the Curlew. Redshank, Snipe and Lapwing numbers have all decreased in the same time period. These four species of bird build their nests on the ground and so are exposed to the same threats as the Corncrake. A grant scheme is available to farmers called the Breeding Wader Grant Scheme, through which agricultural practices are carefully controlled in order to protect nests and chicks.

The Callows are home to many other birds, some of which occur here in numbers of significance on an international level. The Whooper Swan (*Cygnus cygnus*) and Black-tailed Godwit (*Limosa limosa*) are two examples of this. The Whooper Swan visits Ireland from October to March to feed when the breeding season is over in Iceland. You can tell them apart from our resident Mute Swan (*Cygnus olor*) by the colour of their bills. Although the two types of swan are similar in size, the Whooper Swan has a yellow and black bill that looks triangular in profile, and the Mute Swan has an orange-red bill with a black knob at the base. It was a real pleasure to see some Whoopers at Clonmacnoise during an earlier visit in March 2009. I was there with two fellow zoologists, and none of us had seen them before. As three Whoopers flew away, a flock of Black-tailed Godwits, in their beautiful orange mating plumage, swooped by.

The Black-tailed Godwit visits from Iceland during the winter. They are a wonderful sight to behold, flying in tight formation then flashing their brilliant white wing bars and tails when they turn as one and change direction. The birds we saw in March had brilliant orange colouring in preparation for breeding on their return home. One-tenth of the Icelandic Godwit population winters in Ireland.

The Greenland White-fronted Goose (*Anser albifrons flavirostris*) is another winter visitor to Ireland, with numbers of international importance. They come here from their breeding grounds in Greenland from October to April. Although the most significant numbers winter on the Wexford Slobs (around 12,000), 500 birds are estimated to spend winter on the Callows. The Greenland White-fronted Goose is distinguished from other species of geese by its white forehead and the black bars and blotches on its breast.

I cannot stress enough the importance of the Shannon Callows to birds, from the wintering wildfowl such as the Whooper Swan, Greenland White-fronted Goose, Redshank (*Tringa totanus*), Snipe (*Gallinago gallinago*), Lapwing (*Vanellus vanellus*) and Curlew, to the summer-visiting Corncrake and Sedge Warbler (*Acrocephalus schoenobaenus*), the latter also known as the Irish Nightingale because it starts to sing before dawn. Our residents include the Great Crested Grebe (*Podiceps cristatus*), Cormorant (*Phalacrocorax carbo*), Water Rail (*Rallus aquaticus*), Coot (*Fulica atra*), Kingfisher (*Alcedo atthis*), Skylark (*Alauda arvensis*), Stonechat (*Saxicola torquata*) and Grey Heron (*Ardea cinerea*).

The farming community must be commended for their part in maintaining the Callows. By following the Corncrake-friendly and Wading Bird schemes, they are not only protecting two extremely important bird species, but also the ecological integrity of the Callows in general. By refraining from modern farming practices on the grasslands, the rich assemblage of native flora is protected, and in turn the fauna of the Callows is protected too. The Shannon Callows are a special place and should be cared for. The difficulty comes in protecting them in such a way as to accommodate all parties utilising them – nature, agriculture and tourism. Recommendations for a locally based, co-ordinated approach to conserving the Callows must be heeded. The Callows are a wonderful example of agriculture and wildlife co-existing in a positive way, and the future management of this special place should strive to strengthen that relationship.

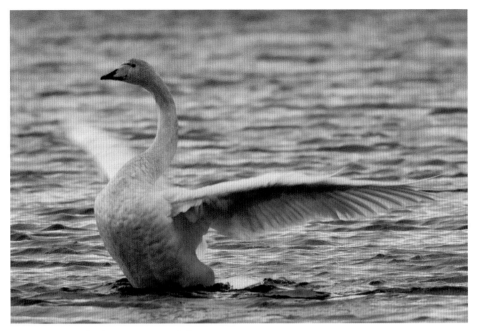

*Whooper Swan display © Conor Cahill*

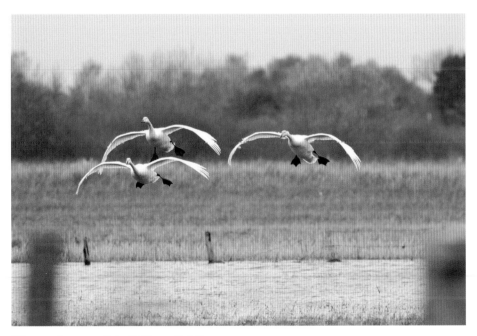

*Whooper Swans in flight © Conor Cahill*

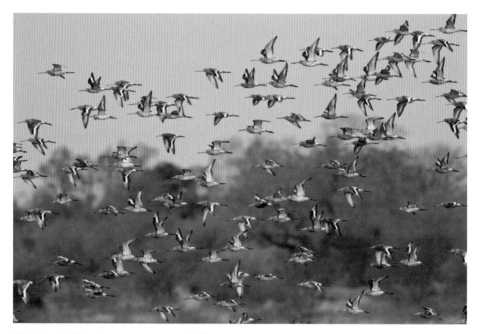

Black Tailed Godwits © Conor Cahill

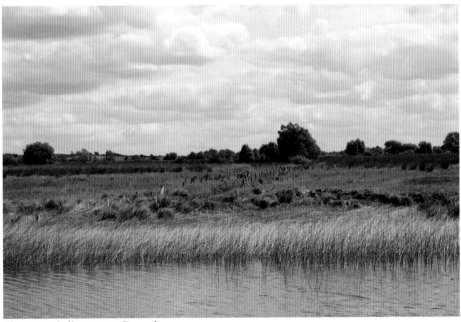

Shannon Callows near Banagher

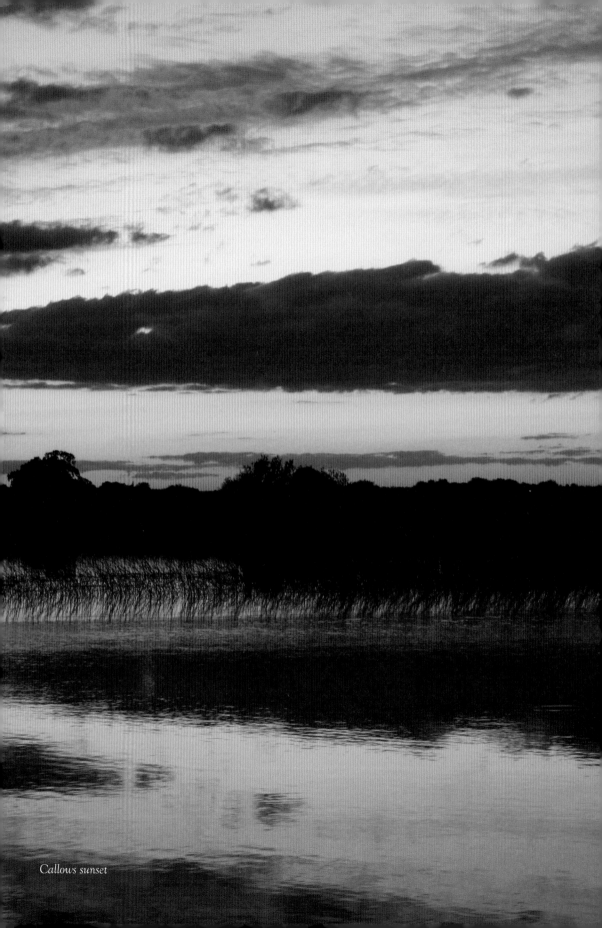

*Callows sunset*

# 9: Clonmacnoise
# to Shannonbridge

The sun sets over the Callows next to Clonmacnoise, turning the river red as it sinks behind the reed beds cloaking this stretch of the Shannon's shores. It has been a glorious day, with clear blue skies and still waters. We sit together on the *Zorgen*'s deck watching the sun sink slowly as the river laps gently against the boat, the quiet hum of conversation drifting across from the other boats moored here. But there is no conversation on our boat. We are all happy in our own thoughts and enjoying the sense of peace. It really is a magical place.

Our next move downriver is to Shannonbridge, and early the next morning we cast off and leave the tranquillity of Clonmacnoise behind. The river is wide and open and we motor along at a leisurely pace for a couple of kilometres before Devenish Island comes into view. Now the river narrows and turns south, and once again we are tower-chasing, but a very different one from the round tower of Clonmacnoise: it is the red-and-white striped tower of the Shannonbridge peat-fired power plant.

A small bit of woodland comes into view on the east side of the river not long after we pass Devenish Island. It is Clorhane Woodland, made up of hazel and yew trees. What makes this woodland unusual is that it lies on an area of limestone pavement, which is rare in the midlands and more typical of the Burren in County Clare. In fact, the limestone pavement at Clorhane is considered the best example of Crinoid limestone in Ireland, and it was used in some of the buildings at Clonmacnoise. Crinoid limestone is a type of rock that formed during the Carboniferous period around 300 million years ago. The Crinoids, also known as Sea Lilies, are related to our starfish and sea urchins; they were filter feeders that lived attached to the seabed, filtering particles from the water with their branched arms.

Pine Marten (*Martes martes*) are frequently seen here in Clorhane. They are somewhat similar to a cat and spend much of their time in the treetops, which might explain their Irish name of Cat Crainn (tree cat). The Pine Marten is becoming common again following a general decline caused by hunting, and can now be found in all types of Irish woodland, pastures, moors and coastal areas. Although the chocolate-brown body of a Pine Marten is a similar shape to the Stoat, it is larger and has a bushier tail. They are fairly solitary and nocturnal creatures and only the female ventures out in daylight when she is feeding her young, which are called kits. Their diet consists mainly of small mammals such as rats and mice, though they will occasionally catch a squirrel. They also eat insects and berries.

The journey south to Shannonbridge has been a leisurely one, drinking tea on deck, watching swallows dart across the surface of the water and the towers of the power station getting closer. I hear that the ESB has demolished the 90 m tower since our trip. This is probably a relief to some, but it is the loss of a familiar landmark to the boating community. The final approach to Shannonbridge is fairly straight, and we can see the 16 arches of the stone bridge ahead, spanning the river from County Offaly to County Roscommon. The bridge was constructed in 1759 by order of the Commissioners of Inland Navigation, who delegated their engineer Thomas Omer to make the Shannon more navigable. The town was previously known as Rachra Cluain na Fearna (the little wet meadows of the alder trees), but adopted its current name after the bridge was built. In 1835 the Shannon Commissioners took over the job of upgrading the Shannon navigation, and began works to make the river more navigable for steam boats. This involved the removal of many Shannon bridges and dredging of the river. The bridge in Shannonbridge is one of few to survive this work relatively intact.

Thomas Rhodes, the principal engineer for the Shannon Commission, removed the canal and lock put here by Thomas Omer. The lock house – also designed by Omer – remains today as the Tourist Office. In 1845 Rhodes added a cast iron swivel span to the bridge that remained until 1962, when the increased weight of vehicles made the old bridge unsafe. A bailey bridge was put in place above the swivel span, which was eventually removed in 1983 when the entire bridge was reinforced and a concrete span was added. The swivel span was placed on the quay where it still sits today, and if you look at it closely you can see the name Thomas Rhodes along the side. The quay itself and the navigation channel under the bridge are both results of the work of the Shannon Commissioners still in use today.

Our numbers have increased now with the addition of two boats to our journey. The *Peacock* is a narrow canal barge skippered by my parents, Michael and Helen, and the *Heron*

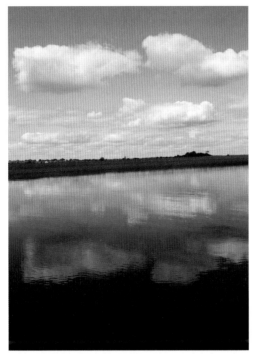

*The Shannon below Clonmacnoise*

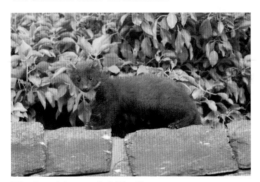

*The Pine Marten © Mike Brown*

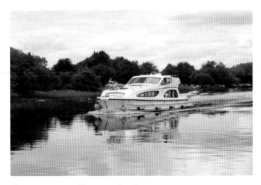

*Cruising near Shannonbridge*

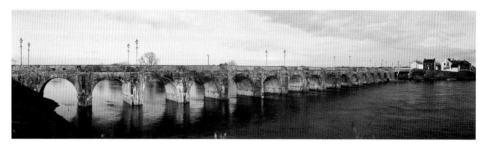

*Shannonbridge © Conor Cahill*

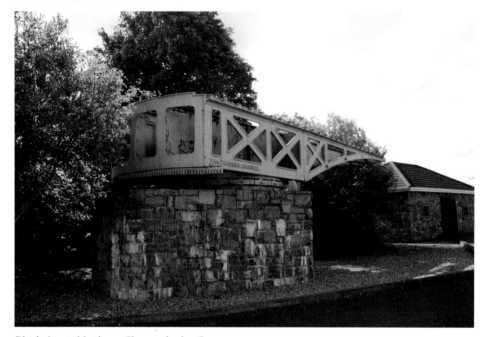

*Rhodes' swivel bridge at Shannonbridge Quay*

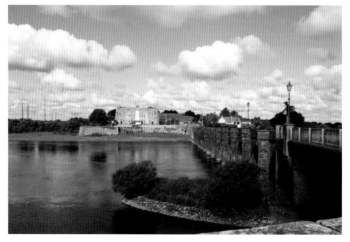

*The Old Fort, Shannonbridge*

is a wide-beam canal barge that is home to Ted Tuke. The *Peacock* is too narrow for the unpredictable waters of Lough Ree, and had to remain moored in Shannonbridge for safety.

Shannonbridge is a small town with just over 200 inhabitants, and the main street runs in an easterly direction away from the river. There are a couple of pubs and shops including Killeens, which is a lovely little spot for a pint, a coffee, dinner or a bit of shopping. We sat outside on a bench enjoying the wonderful coffee and the continuing good weather, accompanied by a little white West Highland terrier guarding the door of the pub. There is a modern floating jetty upstream of the bridge, but it is possible to moor downstream of the bridge along the quay where there are shower facilities. The Old Fort Restaurant stands majestically on the opposite bank facing the river, and its name gives a clue to the origins of the building. It is part of the Shannon fortifications that were built in the early 1800s to protect against possible Napoleonic invasion.

The British feared that Napoleon would try to invade by navigating up the Shannon and across to the east. The reasoning for the fortification of the middle stretches of the Shannon was that the French attackers would be held off until troops could be gathered from the many garrisons on the east of the river. Another reason why fortifications were only constructed at Athlone, Shannonbridge, Banagher, Keelogue and Meelick, when there were other fording places along the river, was the presence of good roads at these locations. The British knew that the French invaders would need to ford the river at points with good road access to accommodate their equipment and heavy guns. The Old Fort at Shannonbridge was originally a bombproof barracks and formed part of the tête-de-pont or bridgehead fortifications that dominate this side of the river. The tête-de-pont at Shannonbridge is considered one of the most important examples of this type of fortification in Britain and Ireland.

The road from Shannonbridge passes through the centre of these fortifications, which would have been blocked by a defended gate at the time. To the west of the bridge the long artificial slope called a glacis is still present. This glacis sloped upwards away from the river, covering the main fortification behind it – called a redoubt – and protecting it from direct artillery. The redoubt was separated from the glacis by a dry moat called a fosse. The sides of the glacis would have been stone, as was the main fortification itself. You can see this from the road if you walk up behind the Old Fort. The redoubt would have had four guns arranged along its front, and there are remains of iron pivots and a semicircular track, indicating that the guns were mounted on traversing platforms, which would have allowed the troops to fire upriver, downriver and also along the Ballinasloe road. A bombproof structure called a caponier projects out from the redoubt into the moat. It has a vaulted roof and loopholes in the sides to allow artillery fire into the sides of the moat.

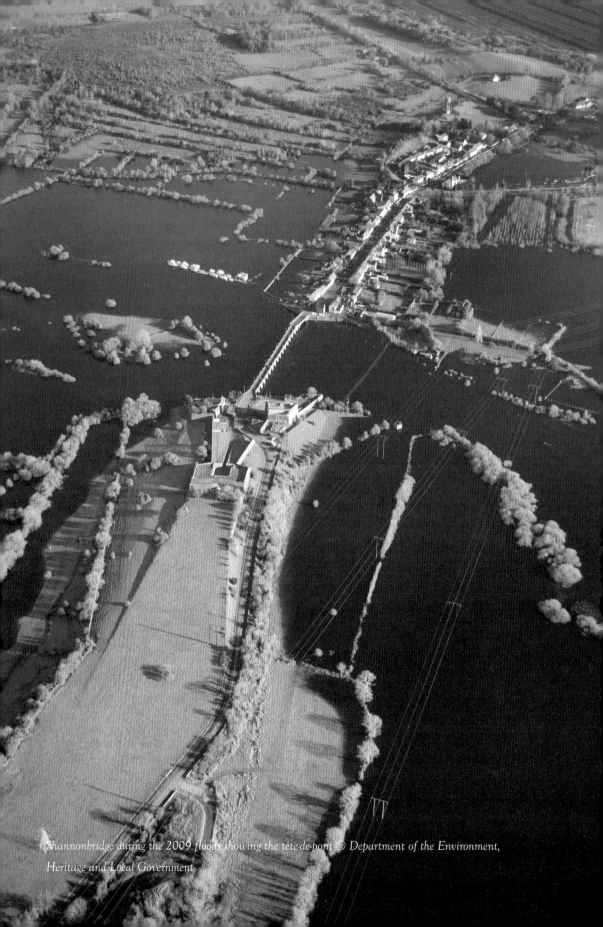

*Shannonbridge during the 2009 floods showing the tête-de-pont © Department of the Environment, Heritage and Local Government*

At the time of my visit in June 2009, it was not possible to access the area of the glacis and redoubt as the site was fenced off with barbed wire and 'No Trespassing' signs. When I spoke to the Tourist Office, they told me that the whole site was under repair, and would be open to the public later in the summer. There are similar fortifications in Banagher and Athlone, as well as two batteries at Incherky Island and a Martello tower at Meelick.

Shannonbridge power station lies to the south of the town, and although it had a damaging visual impact on the surrounding landscape, it also had advantages for some users of the river. The power station's coolant produces a stretch of hot water that is very good for coarse fishing. This stretch is noted for its large tench, who favour warmer waters to spawn and gather here from mid-May onwards. The Shannon Fishery Board has had frequent reports of specimens weighing 6–7 lb over the years.

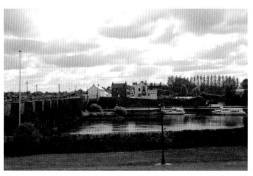

*Shannonbridge Tourist Office and Quay*

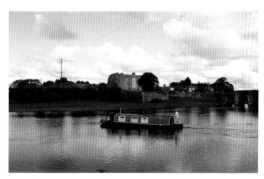

*The Peacock leaving Shannonbridge*

# 10: Shannonbridge to Shannon Harbour

The fishermen wave to us as we pass by, following the river away from Shannonbridge and the tower of the power station, not realising it is the last time we will see it. The River Suck (An tSuca) joins the Shannon from the west here, and we pass it by as we come around a bend in the river that turns us in a southeast direction, towards our destination of Banagher. It has been possible to navigate the 16 km up the Suck to Ballinasloe since 2001, bringing to an end a 40-year wait since the closure of the section of the Royal Canal in 1961. The canal, which opened here in 1828, was linked to the Dublin line by a wooden bridge over the Shannon for tracer horses. This bridge was replaced by a cable-operated ferry in the 1840s, but with the arrival of the railway in 1851, the canal gradually declined until its eventual closure in 1961. The channel of the canal is still present, apart from a filled-in section at the northern end, and you can follow its course from the Shannon to Ballinasloe. Various features have survived too, including two lock chambers and lock-keepers' houses, four bridges, four canal-related buildings and four of the original seven aqueducts.

We continue on towards Banagher, passing under the industrial railway line that crosses from the west of the river to the power station. There is a fork in the river up ahead, but we bear left, following the navigation markers. We are passing close to the tiny village of Clonfert, or Cluain Fearta (the meadow of the grave), in County Galway, home of St Brendan's Cathedral. It could be possible to access the cathedral from here with some ingenuity and bravery, involving launching the canoe off the side of the boat and paddling across to the western bank of the river. A road there leads directly up to the cathedral, but the logistics are too difficult and we decide to leave Clonfert to a later date and access it by car.

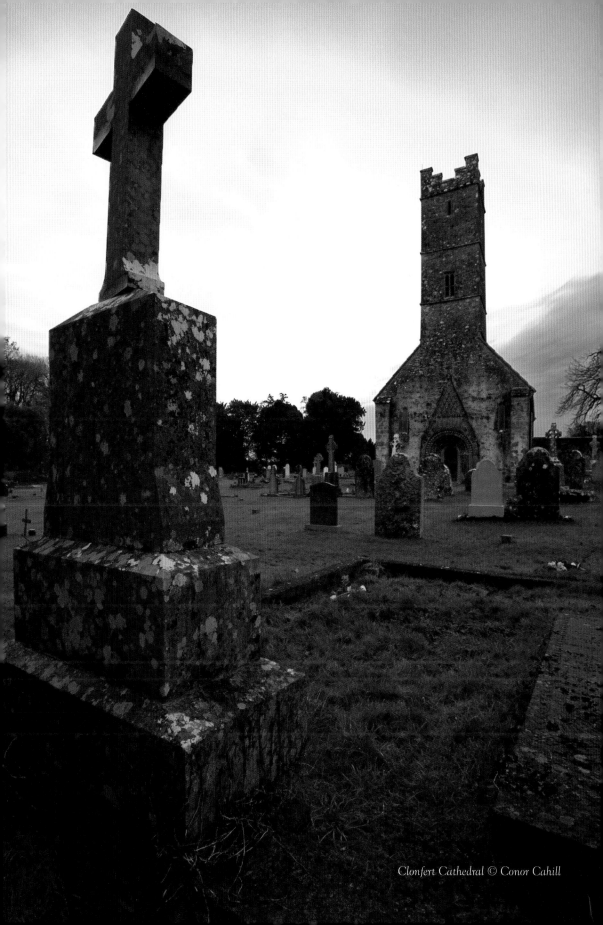

Clonfert Cathedral © Conor Cahill

St Brendan the Navigator founded a monastery here in the sixth century, but there are no remains left of the original church. That is not surprising, since the monastery was destroyed by fire in AD 744, 748 and again in 749. It was then attacked by Vikings on four different occasions in the ninth century, and reduced to ashes after one of the attacks. The fact that the monastery was located within a large sweeping bend in the river and exposed to the river on three sides meant that it was particularly vulnerable to attack. The cathedral that stands there today is only the most recent in a series of ecclesiastical buildings on that site since Early Christian times. The oldest feature to survive is the western doorway, which is the largest and most elaborate example of a Romanesque doorway in Ireland.

We continue downstream, passing green fields on one side and a sea of brown on the other where the peat is being removed, probably for the power station at Shannonbridge. As we approach the area around Shannon Harbour, we pass by the first in a series of islands that the river winds around between here and Banagher – Ash Island, Lehinch, Inshinaskeagh, Minus, Bullock, Grant's and Bird's Islands. Just after Inshinaskeagh the channel splits off to our left, up towards Shannon Harbour. This is the point where the Grand Canal ends and where many boaters begin their Shannon journey via the 36th lock, famous for being the last lock on the Grand Canal before the River Shannon.

The river is like glass as we approach the turn-off for Shannon Harbour, and only the wake of our boat causes any disturbance to the surface of the water. A pair of Mute Swans and their fluffy grey cygnets scoot into the reeds as we pass by. We have passed dozens of these little families on our journey from Shannonbridge. Shannon Harbour was designed and built as a trans-shipping centre at the terminus of the Grand Canal. We do not know it yet, but we will spend two long days here, during the hottest weather I can remember in a long time. It is midweek in early June, so many of the hundreds of boats moored here are still unoccupied and the village is quiet. The *Nieuwe Zorgen* is in dry dock for some emergency repairs. The outpipe for the sink was originally made from a gun barrel, and these do eventually corrode. Eric had carried out some temporary repairs before leaving on this trip, but these repairs had given way and the boat was taking in water. It was just luck that we checked the pipe in Shannon Harbour as the damage was sufficient to sink the boat. The boat was put into dry dock and a new outpipe fitted.

There is not a breath of air in Shannon Harbour as I walk along the canal bank, contemplating the ruins of the Grand Hotel. It is a funny kind of place; there is not much to it – a small shop at the front of a pub, a couple of houses and two other pubs that are not open. But it has a kind of charm, and standing on the bridge looking down at all the boats it is easy to imagine it in its thriving heyday. Shannon Harbour was built in 1830 in the

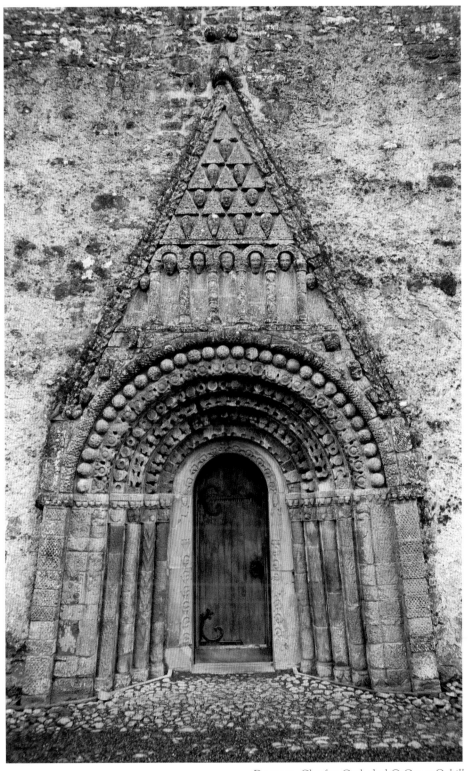

*Doorway, Clonfert Cathedral © Conor Cahill*

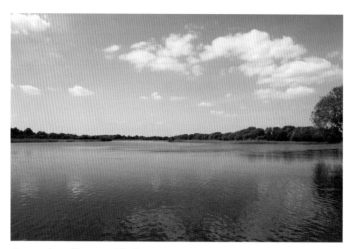

*Approaching Shannon Harbour*

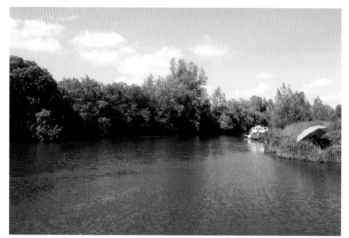

*The River Brosna joins the Shannon below Shannon Harbour*

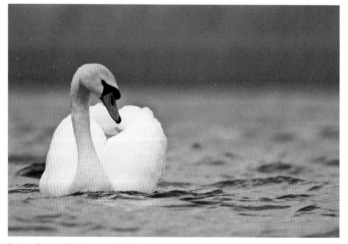

*Mute Swan © Conor Cahill*

townland of Clononeybag, or Cluain Uaine Beg in Irish. At this time over 250,000 people made use of the canal's passenger barges, and at Shannon Harbour's peak it was home to over 1,000 people. As well as the Grand Hotel there was a Harbour Master's House, a bonded warehouse, dockyards, drydocks, a Royal Irish Constabulary (RIC) barracks, a customs and excise post, livery, smithy, a small school and several taverns. After two long, sweltering days, the *Nieuwe Zorgen* is repaired and back in the water. We are all itching to get moving again, back on to the wide expanse of the river.

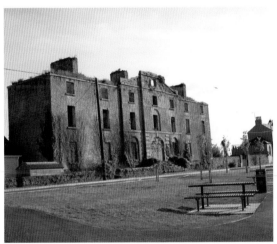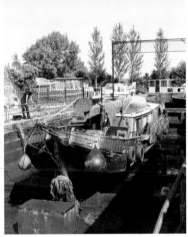

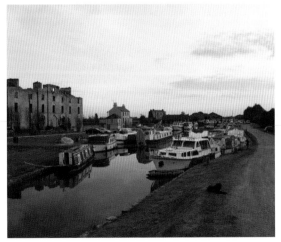

*Clockwise from top left:*
*The Grand Hotel, Shannon Harbour;*
*The* Nieuwe Zorgen *in dry dock;*
*Shannon Harbour sunset*

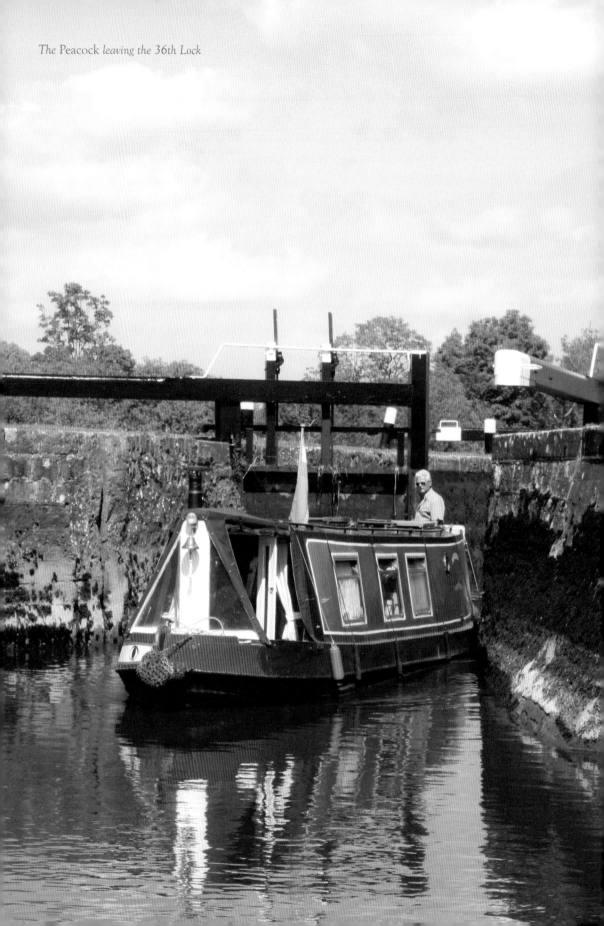

*The Peacock leaving the 36th Lock*

# 11: Banagher

It feels like a weight has been lifted from my shoulders as we exit the 36th lock, and are released from the confines of the canal onto the river again. We pass by Bullock Island almost immediately, the largest of the many islands between Shannonbridge and Banagher. The elusive Corncrake has been recorded here in the past, and if it was a Corncrake those British birdwatchers heard, then Bullock Island may well have been its location. We continue on by Grant's Island and Bird's Island, and soon the bridge at Banagher comes into view.

This seven-arched limestone bridge, which links Counties Offaly and Galway, was constructed in 1843 under the works of the Shannon Commissioners. It is not the original bridge, and there is evidence of an 18-arched bridge built here in AD 1049 by King of Connaught Roderick O'Connor. Medieval records show that a 27-arched bridge was present in 1685. When Thomas Rhodes began his work here for the Shannon Commission in the 1830s, he recorded a 17-arched bridge in poor condition, which was subsequently blown up to make way for the new bridge of 1843. An abutment of the 17-arched bridge is still visible next to Cromwell's Castle on the Galway side of the river.

We slow down our boat in preparation for mooring just before the bridge, having passed by the modern floating jetties just upstream of here. We are planning to spend the night moored along the stone wall of the harbour, but it is fairly busy already and we have to moor two of the boats side by side. It is a bit of a scramble up the side of the boat to get onto dry land, especially when one of the crew members is only 14 months old. But we soon work out a system and manage to get everyone out of the boats and up the steep wall of the harbour.

Banagher is a much larger town than Shannonbridge, with a population of approximately 1,600 people. The town is built on an esker east of the river, and this elevated location has

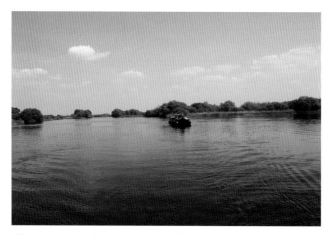

*The river approaching Banagher*

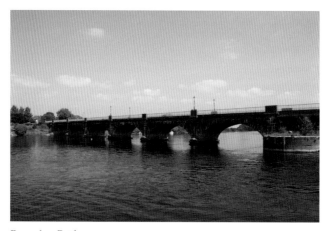

*Banagher Bridge*

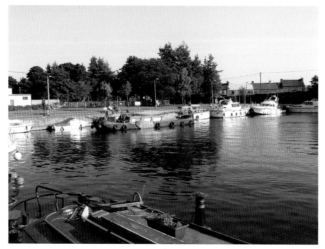

*Banagher Harbour*

protected it from the seasonal flooding of the Shannon. The town's position may also explain the origins of its name of Beannchar na Sionna (the place of the pointed rocks on the Shannon). It is thought that the first settlement was established here by St Rynagh, after whom the parish is named. Development of the town has been driven by its location at a fording point of the river. Until the seventeenth century, Banagher remained a stronghold of the Irish Mac Coghlan clan, and was the chief town of their territory of Delvin Eathra.

In 1551, after a long and difficult struggle against rival chiefs and the English, the Mac Coghlan chief finally gave up his struggle. His lands passed into English hands, to become part of the newly formed King's County (now County Offaly). Mac Coghlan received a pardon and was able to return to his lands, which were now rented from the king. In 1621, under order of King James I, Banagher was finally lost to the Mac Coghlans when the English plantation campaign began. A fort was constructed to protect the new inhabitants of Banagher from the angry disposessed natives. Sir Arthur Blundell was charged with the constuction of Fort Falkland, named after first Viscount Falkland, Lord Deputy of Ireland, which was completed in 1628. It is thought that the ruins of the nineteenth-century artillery fort visible today just below the bridge incorporate the earlier Fort Falkland. The later fort was used as a garrison from 1796 to 1815, in the period when an invasion by France was feared. It then became an RIC barracks before being destroyed by fire during the War of Independence.

Banagher now attracts over 60,000 visitors per year, and there are lots of facilities for the river user, including ample mooring space, plenty of pubs and shops and some interesting historical sites to visit. There is a modern and well-equipped playground beside the harbour, much to the delight of our smallest crew member, but despite our best efforts we cannot find anywhere to dispose of our rubbish and have to keep it on board until our next stop. The harbour itself is separated from the main river channel by a concrete pier with a stone embankment on the harbour side. Our first priority in Banagher is to replenish our food stocks, so we head for the centre of town, which is a short stroll uphill away from the river.

Very close to the harbour, on the left side of the road, is one of two protected eighteenth-century bow-fronted Georgian houses found in Banagher. This building, now called the Royal Shannon, had functioned as a hotel since the nineteenth century. Sadly it is in some disrepair now and apparently closed to business. The hotel, known previously as the Shannon Hotel, was home to the famous novelist Anthony Trollope when he came to Banagher in 1841 to work as Deputy Postal Surveyor. Trollope lived in Drumsna, County Leitrim for a short while, and it was there that he began his first novel, *The McDermotts of*

*Ballycloran*. The novel was not a great success initially, but it was the first of 47 novels he would go on to write.

Trollope is not the only literary figure with ties to Banagher. Charlotte Brontë came to honeymoon here in 1845 with her husband, Rev. Arthur Bell Nicholls, a native of Banagher who had been raised by his uncle in nearby Cuba Court. Sadly the house is now longer standing. Rev. Bell Nicholls met Charlotte in the parish of Haworth in Yorkshire, where he was curate to her father, Patrick. Charlotte and her unborn child died in 1855, and six years later, when Patrick Brontë passed away, Rev. Bell Nicholls returned to live at Hill House in Banagher. He married his cousin Mary Anna Bell, and the two are buried together in the graveyard of St Paul's Church. Hill House is now a guest house called Charlotte's Way.

The second bow-fronted house is Crank House, farther up the hill on the right side of the road. Crank House dates to 1750, and was at one stage used by William Wallers to store grain. Now painted bright yellow, Crank House has a variety of functions including hostel, tourist office, local business units and an exhibition hall. It is possible to enjoy a cup of coffee in the courtyard, courtesy of Heidi's Coffee Shop.

As in Shannonbridge, Meelick and Athlone, the importance of the town as a fording place is reflected by the presence of many fortifications, including more fine examples of Napoleonic fortifications. In preparation for a Napoleonic invasion in the nineteenth century, the old seventeenth-century Mac Coghlan Castle, now called Cromwell's Castle, was reinforced and turned into a powder magazine with a gun mounted onto the roof. The castle is visible today on the west end of the bridge, where it sits in the Shannonside Park adjacent to the swimming area on the river. On the opposite side of the road, slightly farther along, are the remains of a Martello tower, built in 1812 to house a 24-pounder cannon to fight off an invading French army, which never actually did invade. It is not possible to access it now, as it is on private property and home to someone's TV aerial.

Another relic of this era is Fort Eliza, located on the east bank of the river. At Crank House I part company with the rest of the crew in search of the fort that is roughly a ten-minute walk along Crank Road. The fort is fairly overgrown and the ground uneven, but it is definitely worth the short diversion out of town. The fort, also known as the Salt Battery, consisted of a five-sided battery protected by four guns. It also had a guardhouse and was surrounded by a moat. The section of the moat nearest to the road is now filled with Yellow Iris, and the entire ruin seems to be a haven for wild flowers. I manage to scramble up onto the outer wall, and look out over the moat towards the river. The bridge and Cromwell's Castle are clearly visible from here, and the choice of this location for the fort is obvious.

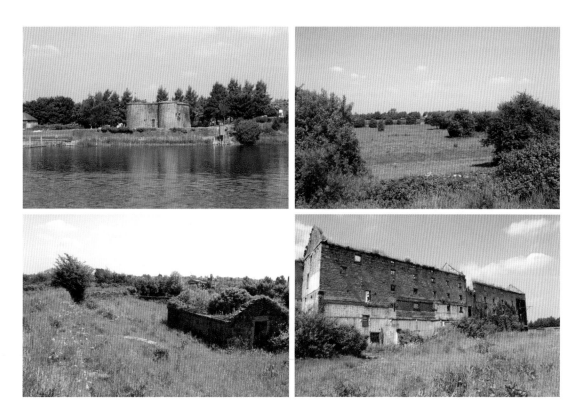

*From top:*

    *Cromwell's Castle*

    *Fort Eliza*

*From top:*

    *View towards river from Fort Eliza*

    *Waller's Quay*

I explore downstream of the bridge before returning to the boat. I follow the steps just before the bridge down towards Waller's Quay and the remains of what was originally Fort Falkland. The area is very overgrown and neglected, and there are empty beer cans littered everywhere. The now derelict F. A. Waller's Malting Works operated in Banagher from the 1880s. The builidng was originally a mill from 1853, owned by the Harton family. As you walk under the bridge away from Waller's Quay there is a handrail alond the quay's edge. This is known as the 'Duke's Rail', after the Duke of York (who was to become King George V) who made a state visit to Ireland in 1897. The duke had travelled from Portumna aboard the steamship *Countess of Mayo*, and the rail was erected so that he could disembark safely at Waller's Quay, to be greeted by Lord Rosse of Birr.

After a night to remember in J. J. Hough's pub, a favourite spot for all boaters, we cast off later than normal, and continue our journey downstream. Our plan today is to reach Portumna and spend a few days exploring Lough Derg. It is another beautiful summer's day, with clear skies and still waters, as we pass under the bridge and say our goodbyes to Banagher. I cannot spot the ruins of Fort Eliza from the river, which is probably the intention of its builders, but I do notice the landscape is changing from what we have seen between Athlone and here. The Callows are much narrower here compared to those we have seen so far, and seem to be absent from the Galway side of the river. Soon the river divides again around more islands, and from my map I can see that these are Seymour's, Esker and Inshee Islands. We follow the navigation channel on the Offaly side of Inshee Island. The river channels meet again, but only briefly, before splitting at Muckinish and the Cribbies.

The riverbank here is fringed with reeds and densely wooded. With no obvious mooring place, my next planned excursion is going to be difficult. On the opposite bank near Meelick there is a fine jetty (called Keelogue), but the fortifications I want to visit are on Incherky Island on the other side of the river. The only boat in our little fleet that can get close enough is Ted's. He brings the *Heron* as close to the *Nieuwe Zorgen* as possible, and I jump across. Ted then navigates the *Heron* as close to the shore as he can, and I jump into the shallows and wade to shore. The ruins I want to see are the final set of Napoleonic fortifications on this section of the river. I have since learned that the shore I jumped onto is actually a manmade embankment that blocks off the natural course of the river. It was constructed in the seventeenth century during the navigation works of Thomas Omer.

I squelch uphill across a field of cattle towards the fortifications on Incherky Island, soaked from the knee down after my trip ashore. From my elevated position I can see our three boats moored along the jetty on the opposite bank. The eighteenth-century defences I have come to explore are yet more of those built to defend the Shannon's fording points from

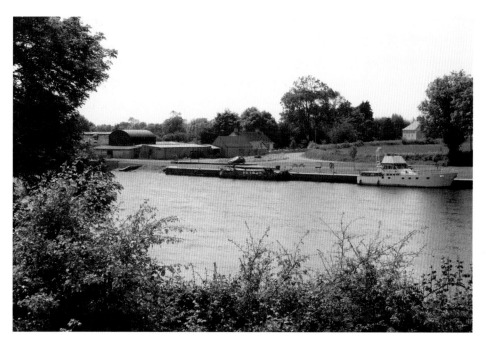

*Keelogue Jetty near Meelick*

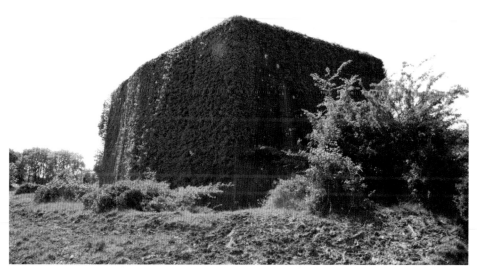

*Napoleanic fortifications near Keelogue*

Napoleanic troops. The remains of the battery and blockhouse are visible on this eastern bank from the river, and a little farther along are the remains of an earthwork battery. I circle around the remains of the battery, trying to find a way in across the moat and through the dense overgrowth. On the rear side of the site, facing away from the river, is a muddy slope leading into the ruins, which looks like it is a regular route for the cattle grazing alongside. This battery would have been a strong, six-sided, stone building surrounded by a moat and protected by seven guns mounted on traversing platforms and two howitzers on the roof of the blockhouse. A wooden door is still visible on the blockhouse, but most of the site is covered in thick brambles. I retrace my steps back down the river and wait for the *Heron* to cross the river from Keelogue to collect me. I decide to stay on board with Ted until we reach Victoria Lock, where we will make our descent to Lough Derg.

This beautiful stretch of river at Meelick and Lusmagh is one of my favourites, so it was very suprising for me to learn just how much this area has been altered from its natural state. Donal Boland is an underwater archaeologist who has worked and lived on the Shannon for many years. I was lucky enough to hear him speak about his work on a cold clear night in the local pub in Meelick. The Shop, as the pub is called, is a real taste of what Ireland used to be. Here the word 'community' still means something, and it is wonderful to see that community coming together on a Friday night to listen to Donal, and later on, to sing some traditional Irish songs.

Donal tells us about the modifications and alterations that the river has undergone at Meelick over the centuries. By closely studying the surveys that were carried out, Donal reckons that the stretch of river below the weir at Meelick is the only remaining ancient river bed on this stretch. Every other bit has been dredged, straightened or diverted to become the river we see today.

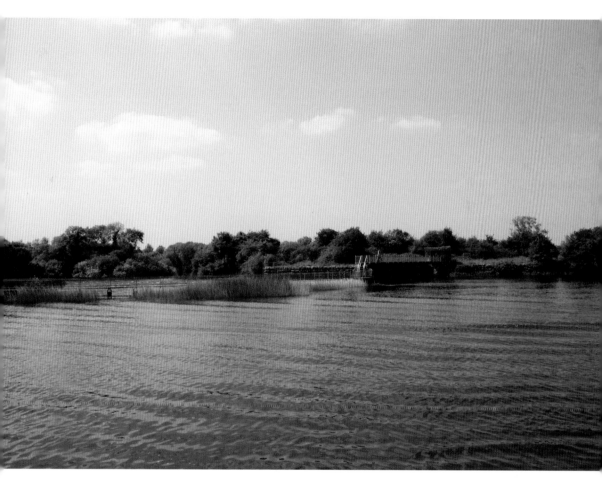

*Meelick*

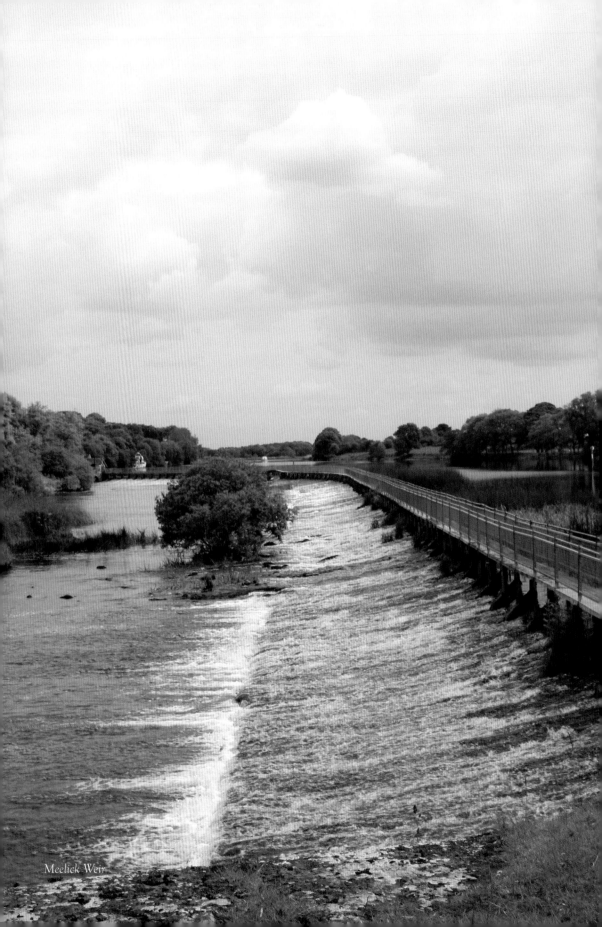

Meelick Weir

# 12: Victoria Lock

Just above Victoria Lock the river channel splits again. Its natural course spills down over the weir to our right, but we follow the man-made channel to the left. This channel is separated from the river by an island on which the Meelick Martello tower is marked. The tower is a cam-shaped tower, similar to the nineteenth-century towers of the east coast of England. The roof of this tower was supported by a large central pillar shaped like a mushroom, which helped to support the mountings for a 24-pounder gun and two howitzers on traversing carriages. I plan to pop across the lock gate for a brief detour to have a look at it.

This was not always an island. When Thomas Rhodes decided to build a new canal here in the 1840s, he cut through the headland, isolating the tower on this newly formed island. From the map I can see that the river had also split earlier, just below the Cribbies. By blocking off the natural channel there were later problems with flooding (exacerbated by the fact that the weir had no sluice gates), so a drainage commission was set up in the 1880s to make alterations to reduce the floods. They designed a drainage channel called the 'new cut', and added sluice gates to the weir. This channel flows parallel to Victoria Lock and exits below the weir, and its water level is controlled by Shaughnessy's Gates farther upstream. Finally there is the Clonahenogue Canal, parallel to the new cut, and farthest away from Meelick. This canal was built by Thomas Omer in 1755.

I must make a confession here. Despite having an Ordnance Survey map, and knowing that there is a Martello tower on the island, after one hour of exploration I still could not find it. My crewmates and I eagerly set off down the towpath towards the weir, with plans of working our way back down the island. This is mistake number one. The sorrowful braying

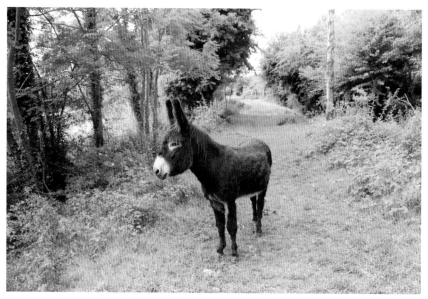

*Meelick donkey*

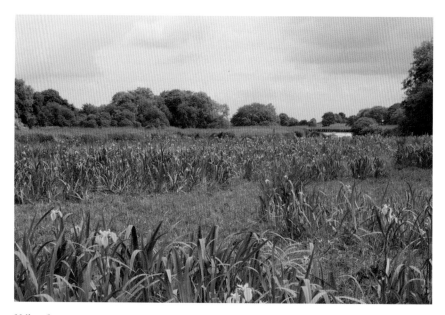

*Yellow Irises*

of a little black donkey accompanies us along the path, as does the donkey himself. There is a large hotel barge in the lock, with a group of American tourists on board who are highly amused by the donkey's serenade. Mistake number two is inappropriate attire. My shorts and sandals are no match for the slippery ditches and thorny brambles, and I take a very ungraceful tumble onto my bum as I try to jump across a ditch. I still have a small scar on my calf to prove it. The tower, I now know, is at the opposite end of the island away from the weir, but I do recommend the walk in summertime just to see the Yellow Irises and the view of the weir.

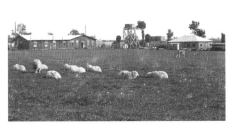

Siemens Camp, Meelick © Hanlon collection courtesy of Eyrecourt and District Development Company

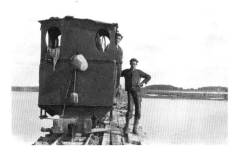

Workers on the Shannon Scheme embankment at Meelick © Hanlon collection courtesy of Eyrecourt and District Development Company

Another interesting feature of the Meelick area is the embankment along the Galway side of the river. This embankment runs from the top of Meelick Weir all the way to Portumna at the entrance to Lough Derg. It was built in the 1920s as part of the Ardnacrusha hydroelectric scheme and is possibly the longest earthen embankment in the country. We will talk more about the Shannon Scheme when we get to Ardnacrusha, but it is worth mentioning it here at Meelick because of the scale of work that went into constructing this embankment. The German company Siemens built the power station, and in 1928 a team of German engineers and workers came to Meelick and set up a work camp. A light railway was built, and the German team shipped work trains and steam excavators by water from Limerick. I have been fortunate enough to get permission from the Eyrecourt and District Development Company to reproduce some photos of these works here. The photos were taken by a native of Liverpool called George Hanlon, who came to the area to work as a farm labourer after he was discharged from the British army following an injury.

We admit defeat in our search for the Martello tower and cross over the lock gate back towards the boats, which are moored along the floating jetty, waiting to enter Victoria Lock. I have one final exploration to make before we depart for Portumna. I want to see Thomas Omer's Hamilton Lock, and the remains of his canal. He decided to build a lateral canal, Clonahenogue Canal, to bypass the shallows at Meelick and Keelogue. The original Hamilton Lock was replaced by a smaller one in the 1800s by the Grand Canal Company, and it is the remains of this lock and canal that I am looking for today.

This exploration turns out to be much simpler than the search for the Martello tower. I follow the narrow road along the bank and over a metal bridge spanning a fast-flowing stretch of water – this is the 'new cut' mentioned earlier. From the far side of the bridge, it is a short walk to Hamilton Lock and the original lock-keeper's cottage designed by Thomas Omer in 1755. The current keeper of Victoria Lock lives here now, and it is a beautiful, tranquil spot. In front of the house are the remains of the lock, which is remarkably well preserved considering how old it is. The stone walls are intact, as is the frame of the lock gates. The lock itself is empty, and only a puddle of water remains. To the left of the lock gates, a muddy slope and the remnants of some stone steps lead down to what would have been the bed of the Clonahenogue Canal, and you can see into Hamilton Lock from here. It is definitely worth the short detour.

I retrace my steps back along the narrow road and over the metal bridge to the boats. My explorations have delayed us, and now we must hurry to make the 5.30 p.m. opening of the swing bridge at Portumna or we will have to wait two hours for the next – and last – opening of the night. But first we must pass through the impressive Victoria Lock. Victoria Lock at Meelick. It is a massive structure, 43 m long and 12 m wide, built from limestone blocks to accommodate the large Shannon steamboats that carried passengers on the river from 1820. It was designed by Thomas Rhodes in the 1840s under the Shannon Commission. Victoria Lock is one of the two biggest locks on the Shannon navigation system (Athlone being the other one). Metal chains hang down the stone walls into the lock, and we cling tightly to them from the decks of our boats to keep them steady as the lock empties to bring us down the level of the river downstream.

We exit Victoria Lock to another beautiful stretch of the river that weaves peacefully around small wooded islands and surrounding callow lands. The only disturbance, braying donkeys aside, is the hum of our engine and the haunting sound of a low whistle floating back from the front deck of the *Nieuwe Zorgen* (as well as historian and artist, our skipper is a musician too). We pass by the Little Brosna, which joins the Shannon just below Victoria Lock. The Little Brosna callows are used by a variety of internationally important birds such as Whooper Swan, Teal, Greenland White-fronted goose, Wigeon and Black-tailed Godwit. The Little Brosna Callows are an integral part of the whole Shannon Callows system.

The river splits at points along this section, meandering around a series of islands – Srubby's Island, Friar's Island, Big Island, Long Island and Portland Island. There are small patches of broadleaved trees along this stretch and on the islands, with wet broadleaved semi-natural woodland dominated by both birch (*Betula pubescens*) and alder (*Alnus glutinosa*), and dry broadleaved woodland dominated by hazel (*Corylus avellana*). It is so peaceful and beautiful here, but we cannot linger if we want to make it to Portumna for the night. At Long Island we pass by the point where Donal Cam, Chief of the O'Sullivan Beare clan, crossed the river on his legendary march from Cork to Leitrim.

In 1602 the armies of Queen Elizabeth I had defeated the Irish and Spanish at the Battle of Kinsale. They then advanced into the territory of Donal Cam O'Sullivan Beare in west Cork. After losing his castles at Dursey and Dunboy to the English, O'Sullivan Beare and his supporters withdrew to the Coomerkane Valley, near Glengarriff, and launched guerrilla attacks on their enemies. The English captured their herds, and by the end of 1602 the group was effectively starved out of hiding. They left Cork for the 14-day march north to their ally, O'Rourke of Breifne in County Leitrim. Faced with much opposition from their fellow Irish, terrible conditions and constant hunger, the group of 1,000 men, women and children struggled north to the Shannon. By the time they reached the river their numbers had been almost halved.

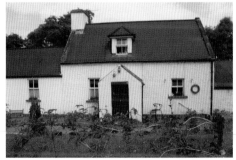
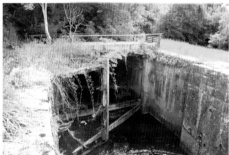

*Lock-keeper's house, Hamilton Lock*    *Hamilton Lock*

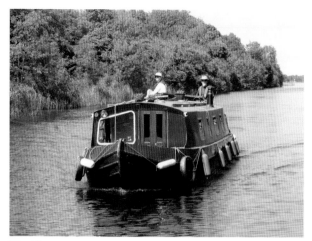

*The* Heron

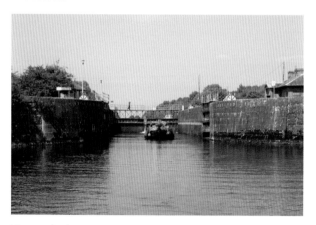

*Victoria Lock*

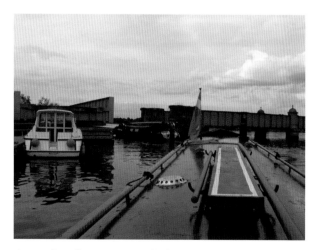

*Approaching Portumna swing bridge*

When they arrived at the Shannon near Redwood Castle, O'Sullivan Beare ordered the group to kill their horses and use their skins to make rafts to cross the river. This is the reason behind the name of the area where they crossed: Gort na gCapall (the field of the horses). The O'Sullivan Beare group were attacked by the MacEgans of Redwood Castle when only halfway across the river, and many of them were killed. The survivors continued on the march north towards Leitrim, but only 35 of the original 1,000 people survived.

The Heritage Council is co-ordinating a massive project called the Beara–Breifne Way, which when finished will be a walking and cycling route following the epic march of O'Sullivan Beare and his clan from Beara in Cork, to Breifne in Leitrim. The completed route will pass through counties Cork, Kerry, Limerick, Tipperary, Offaly, Galway, Roscommon, Mayo, Sligo and Leitrim. The main route will be divided into smaller local routes with loops and spurs along the way when there are points of interest. Two such local routes are already in place at the Beara Way and the Ballyhoura Way.

Our little fleet races along at full throttle. Luckily there are a few other boats waiting patiently to go through the swing bridge at Portumna, so we make the 5.30 p.m. opening. The river is divided at the bridge by Hayes Island, with County Tipperary on one side and County Galway on the other. To the right of the island is the swivel section of the bridge, which we pass through as the road traffic waits above. In 1796 the river had to be crossed by means of a wooden toll bridge, built by Lemuel Cox. This wooden structure was erected in two halves, with Hayes Island in the middle and a drawbridge to the west. The current bridge dates to 1911, and replaced the earlier 1834 one built by the Shannon Commissioners. The operator's house from the 1834 bridge is still intact. Prior to this the river was crossed by ferry. This is one of the busiest sections on the river, for road traffic and river traffic. From here it is a short jaunt down the river to the top of Lough Derg.

Immediately north of the bridge, we passed by two harbours that are remnants of the Shannon steamboat era. Connaught Harbour, which lies on the west bank of the river, is a small stone harbour, now used as a hire craft marina. On the opposite bank is Munster Harbour, built around 1828. These harbours are part of the infrastructure of the steamboat companies, who were responsible for many of the quays and harbours on the Shannon and Lough Derg in the 1820s. We will find out more about them in Killaloe where the Inland Steam Navigation Company had its headquarters. The steamboat quays and harbours on Lough Derg are the harbour at Williamstown near Whitegate, and the quays at Mountshannon, Scarriff, Kilgarvan, Mota, Castle Bawn, Scarriff Bay Dromineer, Derrycastle and Garrykennedy.

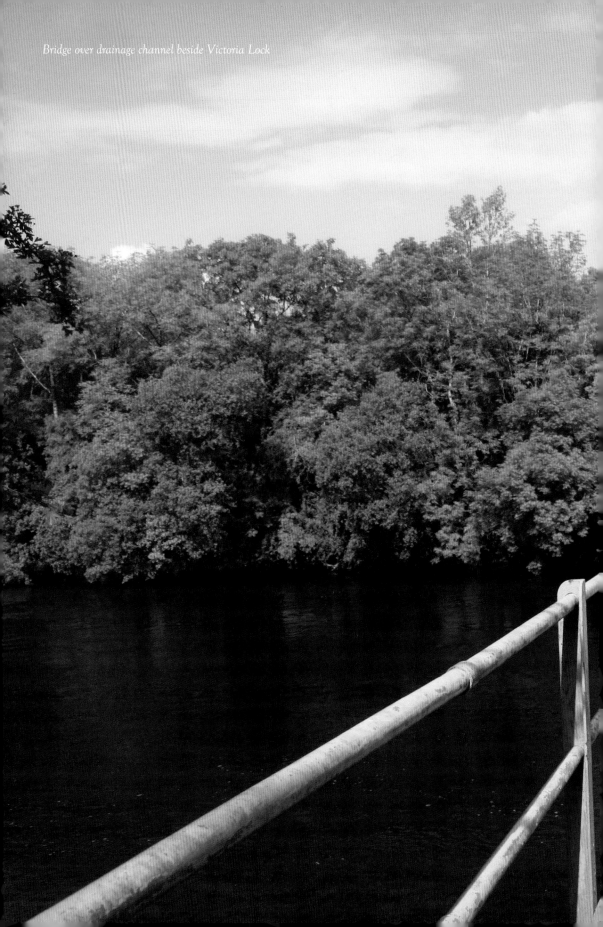

Bridge over drainage channel beside Victoria Lock

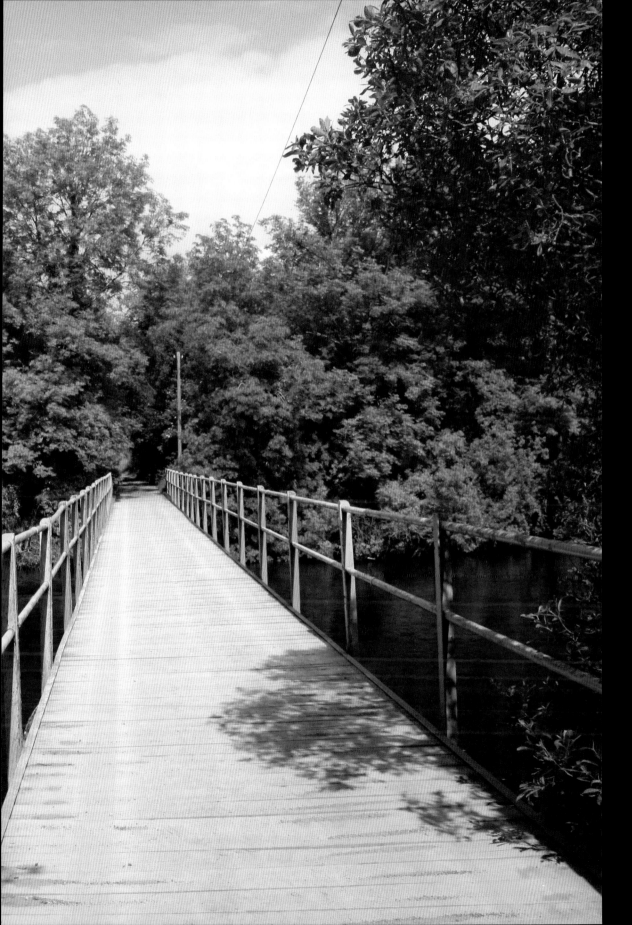

*The river widens approaching Lough Derg*

# 13: Lough Derg – Portumna

The river disappears as a broad expanse of water opens up before us. We have arrived onto the largest of the Shannon lakes: at 118 sq. km in area and 41 km in length, Lough Derg is also the third largest lake in Ireland. Here at the northern end, the lake is broad and shallow (only around 6 m deep), with an indented shoreline of wide bays and wooded headlands. At the southern end of Lough Derg, the lake narrows and becomes deeper, with the maximum depth of around 43 m. The lower lake is extremely picturesque and enclosed by the Slieve Aughty and Bearnagh Mountains to the west and the Arra Mountains to the east. Our boats follow the markers guiding us across this top section of lake, toward the harbour at Portumna. A Great-crested Grebe is diving for fish just outside the harbour, and we can see Cormorants in the distance, near the small islands just off the shore, where I know there is a large colony.

The name Lough Derg derives from the Irish Loch Dergdherc (lake of the bloody eye). The legend goes that the one-eyed King of South Connaught and Thomond, Eochy Mac Luchta, was visited by the famous bard Ahirny. Bards were very powerful and could make or break a reputation. So the tradition was, in order to keep the bard sweet, you would grant him anything he wished for after meeting him. Ahirny apparently took a dislike to King Eochy, and so he decided to ask for the king's remaining eye. Surprisingly, the king agreed and plucked out his good eye for the nasty bard. A servant of the blinded king led him to the lake's edge where he washed out the empty socket ('dearc'), turning the lake waters red ('dearg') with his blood. King Eochy proclaimed that the lake would forever be known as the lake of the bloody eye.

The pretty Georgian town of Portumna is called Port Omna in Irish, which means 'the landing place of the oak'. The town is actually located a mile west of the river in County Galway, near a historically important crossing point of the Shannon between Counties Tipperary and Galway. The town is easily accessible from Lough Derg via Portumna Harbour, also known as Castle Harbour due to its proximity to Portumna Castle. It is also called the 'new' harbour as it was built in 1978. The arrival of the *Nieuwe Zorgen* into the harbour causes quite a stir, and the crews of most of the boats moored here gather on the harbour wall to watch the approach of our unusual craft. Yet again we leave our skipper to answer the questions of a variety of water users from a retired English couple, a German father and son, three American fishermen and a family from Dublin. As I step off the boat the first thing I hear is the distinctive call of a Cuckoo, coming from the direction of the forest park, which lies just behind the harbour.

I think the Meadow Pipit (*Anthus pratensis*) deserves a special mention here. It is not a particularly striking bird – small, brown and streaked with a longish tail. But this poor unfortunate is not only the dinner of choice for the Merlin (*Falco columbarius*); it is also the

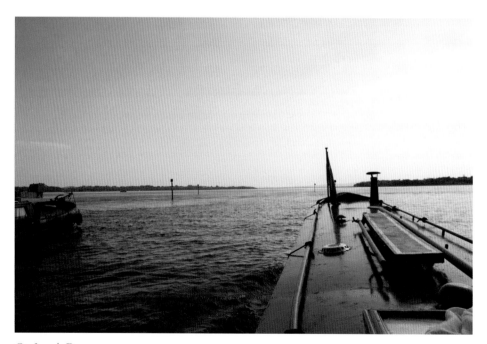

*On Lough Derg*

Cuckoo's songbird of choice when selecting a nest for her eggs. In late April after mating, the female Cuckoo (*Cuculus canorus*) removes one of the Meadow Pipit eggs from the nest and lays her own in its place. When the Cuckoo chick hatches, it shoves the Meadow Pipit eggs out of the nest. The unknowing foster parents slave to feed this enormous offspring, totally unaware that it is not one of their own. Meanwhile, the Cuckoo's real parents have departed for South Africa, leaving the young to find their way there in July or August.

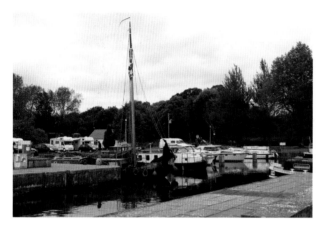

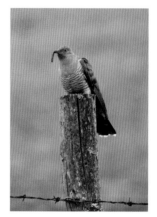

*Castle Harbour, Portumna*                                          *Cuckoo © Mike Brown*

Leaving the exploration of the forest park for now, we decide to head for Portumna town instead, and take the path to the right of the harbour that leads towards the castle entrance and the town. Almost immediately behind the harbour is the back of Portumna Castle, visible across a field to the left of the road. The castle was built before 1618 by Richard de Burgo, fourth Earl of Clanricarde, and it remained the seat of the Clanricarde earls until 1826, when the castle was destroyed by an accidental fire that reduced it to a roofless shell. The castle is a fine example of a semi-fortified or strong house, which is a style of Irish architecture dating to the late sixteenth and seventeenth centuries. It is a transitional style between the vertical tower house, such as Derryhiveny Castle in County Galway (one of the latest tower houses to be built in Ireland), and the later manor house. This castle was built by the fourth earl to consolidate his claim to the medieval de Burgo Lordship of Connaught. The de Burgos, also known as de Burgh, Bourke and Burke, were a Norman-French family, with William de Burgo the first of the family to arrive in Ireland with Prince John in 1185.

A short distance along the road we come across the ruins of a medieval Dominican priory. A church was originally built on the site in the thirteenth century by the Cistercians, but they later granted permission to the Dominicans to build the priory there in the

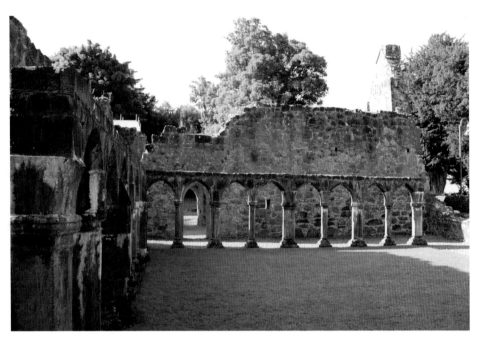

*Dominican Priory, Portumna*

fifteenth century. Across the narrow road are the stables and outbuildings, which became home to the de Burgo family after the 1826 fire. Work began on a new castle in the 1860s, between the priory and the lake, but this was also destroyed by fire in 1922 and there is no trace of it today. The original castle was inherited by the great-nephew of the last Marquis of Clanricarde in 1916, who was Viscount Lascelles and would become the sixth Earl of Harewood in Yorkshire. Although he had great plans for the restoration of Portumna Castle, none of them came to pass. Deteriorating Anglo-Irish relations, the Second World War and estate taxes conspired to make the sale of Portumna a necessity. In 1948, 1,400 acres of Portumna Castle became the property of the Irish Land Commission and subsequently the Board of Works. The castle has been undergoing a very slow restoration since 1968. It has been re-roofed, the massive chimney stacks have been put in place again and the ground floor is open to the public.

Just as we pass the priory there is a loud cracking and rustling, and acting on instinct I jump into the hedge and swing my camera around in preparation. My instincts prove to be spot on, when two young Fallow deer leap from the trees onto the road ahead of me. They take one look in my direction and are gone again as quickly as they appeared. I am delighted but not all that surprised. There is a herd of Fallow deer (*Dama dama*) in the forest park, and seeing these two as well as hearing the Cuckoo earlier makes me determined to visit

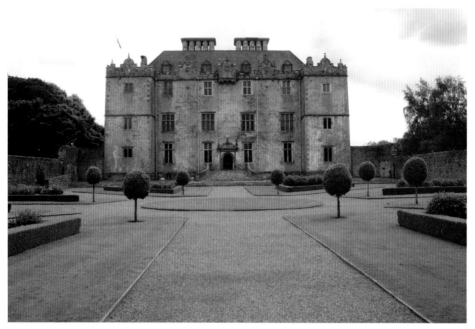

*Portumna Castle*

the forest park properly as soon as my exploration of the town is over. Fallow deer are the most widespread deer in Ireland, and were brought here by the Normans in the thirteenth century.

Around the final bend I see the first of three sets of gates that lead to the castle. The first gates are 'Adams Gates', and the remains of two nineteenth-century gate lodges are at either side. The first avenue is lined with cherry trees. It leads to the second set of gates where the lodges have been restored to house the information centre. There is a lovely kitchen garden to the left of the information centre, and if you time your visit when the gardener is there, you might be able to buy some of her fruit and vegetables. The third and final gate is the Tuscan Gate, which brings you to the castle by the rose garden. Be sure to come when the roses are in bloom.

Leaving the castle behind and continuing towards the town, I pass by a small gate lodge and gateway that leads me out to Castle Avenue. Looking left I can see the spire of Christ Church, the 1832 Neo-Gothic-style Church of Ireland place of worship. Straight ahead is Abbey Street with its typical Georgian style of two-storey stone frontages. The remains of a Norman earthwork or motte, visible just off Patrick Street in the grounds of 'The Nunnery', may be the site of the original Norman dwelling from which Portumna arose. The Normans chose this spot for its strategic location at a crossing point of the River Shannon.

There are lots of buildings of note in the town, but probably the most important is the post-Famine workhouse on the Ballinasloe Road. The workhouse was built in 1852 under the Poor Laws of 1838, which divided Ireland into Poor Law Unions, with a workhouse in each union. Up until the 1920s the workhouses took in men, women and children and housed them in separate wards. A project is currently under way to restore the workhouse and use it for Enterprise and Community space, holiday accommodation, independent living units for the elderly and heritage areas. To date a bat survey has been carried out, ivy has been removed, conservation work has been carried out on some of the windows and three of the buildings have been re-roofed. There is a master plan for the site that has received input from the local community and a wide number of organisations.

Our good luck with the weather has finally come to an end, and we quickly make our way back to the harbour as the rain clouds gather. My exploration of the forest park will have to wait. We make it back just in time, and spend the next day trapped on board trying to keep our smallest crew member entertained. When the rain finally stops, the crew of the *Nieuwe Zorgen* gently manoeuvre the boat out of the harbour and on to Lough Derg. The conditions are good for hoisting the sails, and they are planning a short trip across the lake to Terryglass, which lies on the northeastern shore of the lake in County Tipperary. As they set off onto the lake, I travel on foot into the forest park.

Portumna Forest Park covers about 1,500 acres of mainly coniferous woodland, with Scots Pine and Norway Spruce in abundance. In some areas the coniferous trees have been

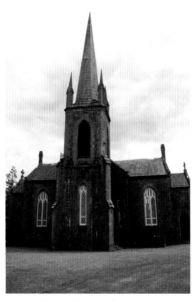

*Christ Church, Portumna*

felled by Coillte, the body which owns and commercially manages Ireland's forests. It has planted native oak, ash and hazel woodland in these areas as part of the Native Woodland Scheme, which aims to conserve and expand native Irish woodlands as part of our national forest policy, and grants are provided by Teagasc to conserve, restore and expand native woodlands. There are naturally occurring areas of native woodland in the forest park too, made up mainly of ash, beech and Silver birch. Along the lakeshore yew and juniper occur in open woodland.

There are four looped trails in the park ranging from a multi-access trail suitable for all visitors, of approximately 1 km length, to a longer multi-use trail of over 10 km for walkers and cyclists. I decide to take the trail from the harbour to Rinmaher Point, which takes me past one of the native woodland restoration areas, marked by a wooden sign amongst the

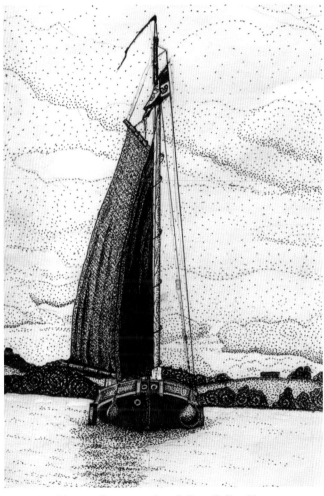

Nieuwe Zorgen on *Lough Derg* © *Eric Kemp*

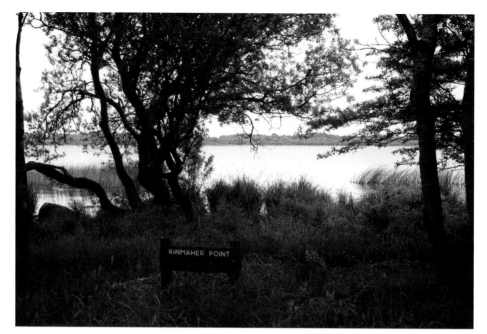

RINMAHER POINT

*Rinmaher Point*

trees. After a very pleasant and easy walk I emerge from the trees to the lakeshore. From here I can see the *Nieuwe Zorgen* with her sails hoisted, but the wind has died down and she is making very slow progress. As I look to my right along the shore from Rinmaher Point I can see the small island that is home to a Cormorant colony. The Cormorant (*Phalacrocorax carbo*) is a familiar sight on this journey. We have passed many of them along the river, perched on marker signs waiting to catch a passing fish or two. It is a large, dark seabird with a long hooked beak and is often spotted with its wings outstretched to dry. The inland birds tend to nest in trees, whereas the coastal birds nest on cliffs.

The park and the castle grounds are also home to our elusive native Red squirrel, and as I head off into the park, it is in hope of seeing one or two of them. The Red squirrel (*Sciurus vulgaris*) is now one of the most threatened mammals in Ireland. This is not the first time the Red has been under threat. They have probably become extinct here in the past a number of times, since they arrived in Ireland before the last ice age. The last reintroduction happened in the nineteenth century with squirrels from Great Britain. The numbers of Red squirrel in Ireland have declined since the middle of the twentieth century, and there are probably only 40,000 left. A 2007 survey found no records of Red squirrels in Meath or Westmeath, and only handfuls were recorded in Louth, Carlow and Kilkenny combined.

The decline in numbers of Reds has been attributed to the introduction of the North American Grey squirrel (*Sciurus carolinensis*). A number of Greys were released in Castle Forbes, County Longford, in 1911, and they are now present in 20 counties in the republic, east of the Shannon. It is not known exactly how the presence of the Grey affects the Red, but zoologists believe that the Greys out-compete Reds for food because they are larger and have a wider dietary range. For example, they can eat unripe acorns, which the Reds cannot, thus depleting one of the main food sources of the Red. Another factor is that the Grey may carry a horrible disease called Squirrel Pox Virus (SQPV), which does not affect the Grey but is fatal to the Red, killing them in a horrific manner. Luckily the virus has yet to kill any Reds in Ireland as far as we know.

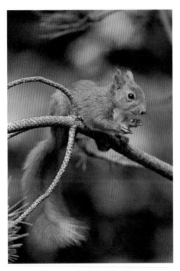

*Red squirrel* © *Mike Brown*

The Grey squirrel is only one of many non-native or invasive species causing problems in Ireland. These non-natives often have a competitive advantage over our native species and can out-compete them for food and space. This leads to a massive expansion of the non-native at the expense of native species. Non-native or invasive species such as the Giant Hogweed, Japanese Knotweed, Rhododendron and American mink are among the greatest threats to Irish biodiversity.

The whole of Lough Derg, its shoreline and islands, are of huge ecological importance. This is reflected in the designations of candidate Special Area of Conservation (cSAC), proposed Natural Heritage Area (pNHA) and Special Protection Area (SPA) to the entire lake. These designations are there to protect the variety of important habitats and species found in and around the lake. But a little shellfish with a big name is threatening the ecology of Lough Derg. The Zebra Mussel (*Dreissena polymorpha*) is a native of the Black Sea and the Aral-Caspian Sea. This small, striped mussel was introduced to the lower Shannon in 1994, attached to the bottoms of secondhand boats imported from Britain and the Netherlands.

Once the mussels were established in the river, they began to attach themselves to leisure craft, so that by 1996 they had been carried north to the major Shannon lakes of Loughs Derg, Ree and Key.

Worldwide the massive loss of biodiversity caused by invasive species introduced by humans is a silent holocaust, second only to the impact of complete habitat destruction. Once an invasive species is introduced, it is virtually impossible to eradicate. Preventing establishment of invaders in the first place is the only successful strategy. Zebra Mussels attach to hard surfaces in the lake, which can mean anything from the lake bed, the bottom of a boat or the inside of a pipe. This in turn causes problems for boat owners, water treatment plants, power plants, fish hatcheries and industry. They can also attach themselves to the shells of our native Freshwater Mussels (*Anodonta anatina, Anodonta cygnea*), and consequently numbers of both these species have declined in the Shannon and Boyle system.

Any threat to our biodiversity has to be taken very seriously. Here in Lough Derg the threats posed by non-native species are of particular concern, as Lough Derg is home to some very important species of fish. The Pollan (*Coregonus autumnalis*) is Ireland's only whitefish species, and is threatened with extinction globally. Pollan is not found anywhere else in Europe except Loughs Derg, Ree, Allen, Lower Erne and Neagh. It is thought that the numbers of Pollan in the Shannon lakes are only in the hundreds or very low thousands.

The Pollan likes to spawn on rocky or gravelly areas of the lake, but because the Zebra

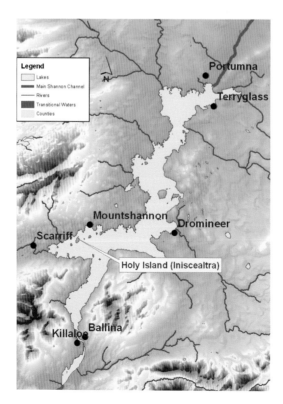

Mussel attaches to any hard surface available, potential Pollan spawning sites are covered by the mussel. But the Zebra Mussel is not the only non-native species causing problems for Pollan. The introduction of the Roach fish, and the subsequent growth of their numbers, coincides with a fall in numbers of Pollan on the Shannon lakes. The Roach (*Rutilus rutilus*) was introduced to Ireland by humans in the 1800s to be used as live bait in pike fishing. The Roach competes with other fish species for zooplankton (animal plankton) to eat, and can quickly become the dominant fish species in a lake. It is thought to be one significant factor for the decline in numbers of Atlantic salmon and Brown trout too.

The presence of the Zebra Mussel has, however, improved the clarity of the waters of Lough Derg. This might seem a good thing. But the improved clarity is partly a result of the Zebra Mussel's diet. They are filter feeders, and filter the microscopic organisms that make up the lake's plankton. Each mussel can filter up to one litre of water a day, and any plankton they do not digest is ejected as 'pseudo-faeces'. This 'pseudo-faeces' covers the lake bottom, depleting the lower end of the food chain, which has a knock-on effect on larger organisms including game fish. The improved clarity of the water also results in excessive weed growth. This has a serious impact on the lake's recreational value, which in combination with reduced game fish could mean serious problems for Lough Derg.

If nothing is done to halt the spread of invasive species in Lough Derg, the fisheries, navigation and amenity value of the lake will face severe consequences in an area increasingly reliant on tourism. But we must not forget the threat to our native biodiversity, which we are morally and legally obliged to protect. Sadly the usual threats to water quality are still a problem here in Lough Derg – that is, pollution in the form of nutrient enrichment of nitrogen and phosphorus from agriculture, septic tanks, sewage disposal and industrial effluent. It is worth noting that once these sources of pollution are removed the lake can eventually recover, but the ecological changes brought about by the Zebra Mussel are irreversible.

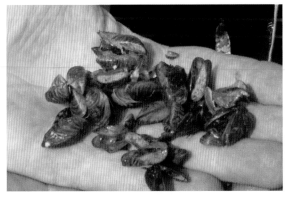

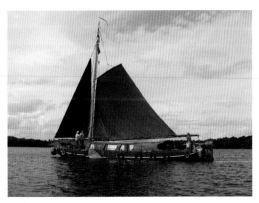

*Zebra Mussel*

Nieuwe Zorgen *in sail*

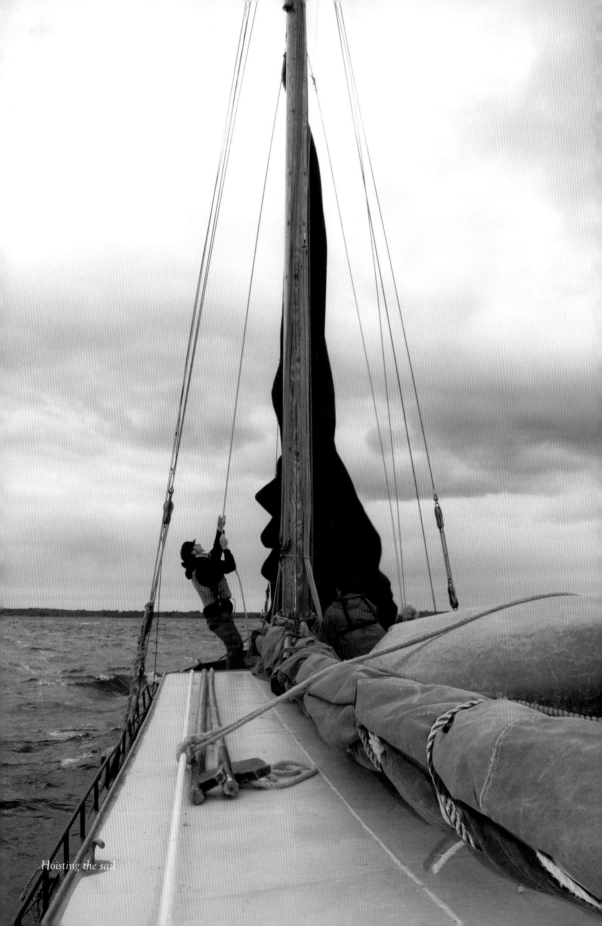

*Hoisting the sail*

# 14: Lough Derg – Terryglass

The conditions are perfect for sailing, so the skipper decides to hoist the jib for a second short trip across the north of the lake from Portumna to Terryglass. The skipper mans the tiller while Mick and Ted hoist the jib. The wind is too strong for the mainsail, and the journey is too short to warrant hoisting it anyway. It is wonderful to lose the noise of the engine and listen to the wind catching the sail instead, and the sound of the boat cutting through the waters of Lough Derg. It is not long before the harbour at Terryglass comes into sight, and the crew starts letting the sail down in preparation for mooring. The engine is turned on again for the final approach to the marina where the only space big enough to accommodate us is along the outside of the wall.

I step off the quay onto dry land and the first thing I see is the bronze bust of a man. It is John Weaving, a legend of the river, who passed away in 1987. His friends and admirers erected this bust in his memory, and also a white cairn at the top of the lake just before the entrance to the river leading to Portumna. Weaving was a familiar sight on the Shannon for over 20 years. John Lefroy of Killaloe, a close friend, described him as a 'scrupulously honest person'. John Weaving's father, T. H. Weaving, was the organist in Christ Church Cathedral, Dublin, in the 1920s, and was also the conductor for the famous Rathmines & Rathgar Musical Society. John had small parts in some of the productions in his youth.

John Weaving was involved in dinghy sailing from a young age, and was the National Dinghy Racing Champion. He worked as an agent for the Bank of Ireland, but found the work too restrictive and soon became disenchanted. He moved on to selling commercial

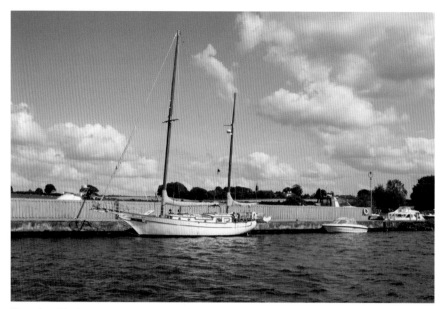

*Terryglass Harbour*

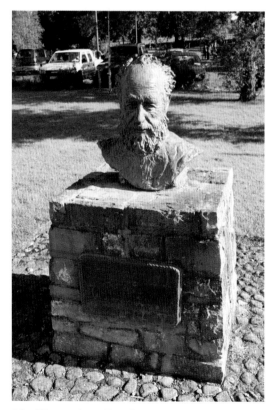

*John Weaving bust, Terryglass*

stands for exhibitions and shows. His partner in that enterprise had an interest in boat hire long before it became a popular pursuit. In the late 1950s the pair had a small fleet of three or four boats for hire on the Shannon. John would spend his weekends on the river arranging the turnaround from one hirer to the next.

In the 1960s Bord Fáilte commissioned a survey of the Shannon to determine the works required to make the river more user-friendly. George O'Brien Kennedy, from Jamestown, hired John as a subcontractor for this work, and obtained a barge for John that he would go on to buy. John was now living on the river full time, on board his 125 B barge that he called *The Talisman*. Many people familiar with John would know this boat as the *Peter Farrell* – Peter was the previous owner and had his name put on the side of the boat. The conditions on board were fairly basic. John lived in a 2.4 m x 3 m cabin that he built on to the back of the boat. He shared a foam mattress with his dogs, warmed himself by a stove, and stored his collection of maps and documents in an old bathtub. The conditions that he lived in would probably seem like squalor to most, but to him it was paradise. If he spent too long away from his boat and his beloved river, he would be itching to return. He was extremely knowledgeable about the birds of the Shannon, and co-authored the chapter on birds in the *Shell Guide to the River Shannon* with Gerrit van Gelderen.

I leave John behind and follow a shady path through the trees behind the quay area, to the first of two historic wells found in Terryglass. The two wells, St Augh's Well (known locally as the Eye Well) and the Headache Well of St Colmcille supposedly have curative properties. St Augh's Well is the one located behind the quay area, and is named after a ninth-century saint. This is a natural spring well, which is paved and enclosed by modern concrete. The Ordnance Survey Namebooks (1840) describe how 'it is said that persons affected with sore eyes have been cured'. The narrow winding path continues on to the steep road to Terryglass village. At the top of the road, just before the village, a signpost leads to the second of the wells. This one is dedicated to St Colmcille and is supposed to cure headaches. It seems to be more frequently visited than St Augh's as there are some small offerings surrounding the well, which is itself surrounded by a stone wall.

Terryglass is a small, picturesque village on the northeast shore of Lough Derg in north Tipperary, with a population of approximately 450 people. In Irish the town is called Tir-dá-ghlas (the land of the two streams). St Columb (Colum mac Cremthain) founded a monastery here in the sixth century, the remains of which are now part of the north and west walls of the church. By the twelfth century Terryglass had become a centre of learning, and the abbot at that time, Aedh Mac Crimthainn, is associated with the Book of Leinster.

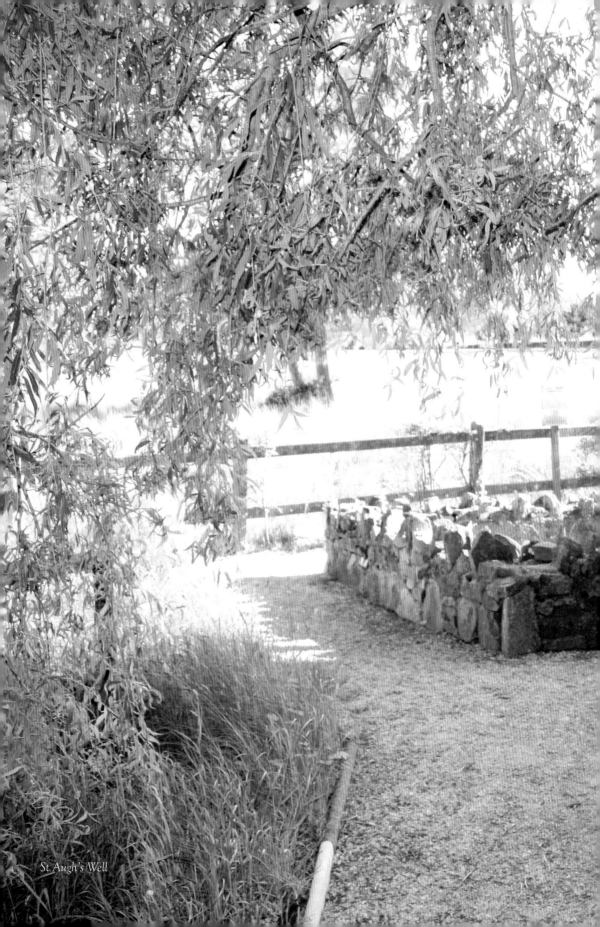

St Augh's Well

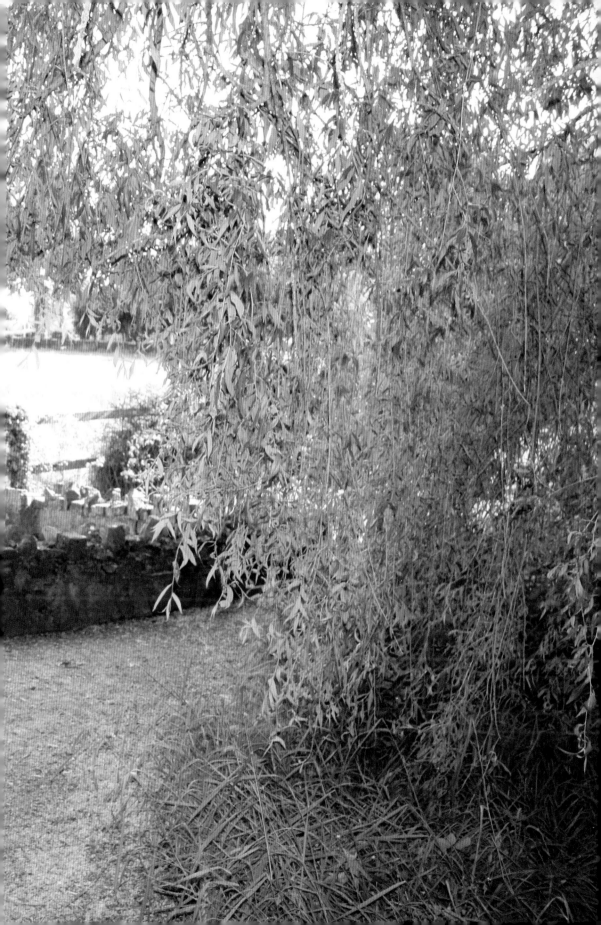

Now housed in Trinity College Dublin, this is the earliest manuscript entirely in Irish. It is a collection of Irish stories, verse and geneaology, and includes a version of An Táin Bó Cuailnge (the Driving of the Bull of Cooley).

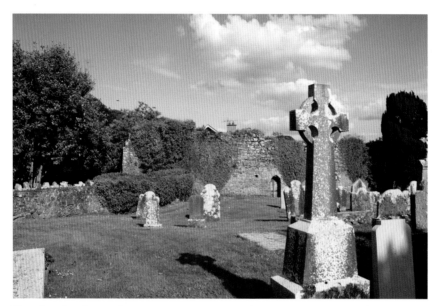

*Terryglass church grounds*

Terryglass lies in an area of Lough Derg that is now the last known Irish home of the protected Irish Fleabane (*Inula salicinia*). This small yellow flower from the daisy family (*Asteraceae*) is widespread in Europe and used to be common around the shores of Lough Derg, but due to habitat loss it is now restricted to a small area around Terryglass. The *Inula* is part of Ireland's Lusitanian flora: plants that are native to Ireland and extend down to Spain, but are not found in Britain. Also known as the Willow-leaved Inula, the fleabane has hairy green leaves and a yellow flower not unlike a dandelion. In the 1930s the famous Irish botanist Robert Lloyd Praeger recorded the flower 'from the head of the lough at Portumna as far S[outh] as the vicinity of the Carrikeen Islands, near Dromineer'. A community-based project is underway in Terryglass to try and save the remaining plants, by establishing new populations around the lake. In conjunction with the National Botanic Gardens and BEC Consultants, the project aims to cultivate a number of plants at the Botanic Gardens and then relocate them to various locations along the Lough Derg shoreline. The volunteers from the local community monitor and tend to the newly planted populations.

On this sunny Sunday in June the town is alive with the hustle and bustle of visitors enjoying the sunshine, and a spot of lunch, outside the two pubs that sit side by side facing a small stream. We make the time to enjoy a pint in the sun outside Paddy's Bar, but we do not linger as we are all keen to get out onto the lake again. We stroll happily down the hill towards the quay to where the *Nieuwe Zorgen* awaits us and before long we are slowly navigating our way out of Terryglass Harbour, heading south towards Mountshannon.

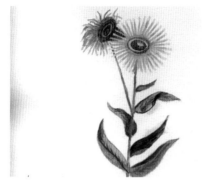

*Irish Fleabane © Michael Kemp*

*And when I put about and steer, back for the walls of Dromineer,*
*Then, far on the horizon's line, the pillar tower of Caimin's shrine*
*From out the water rears on high its finger in the western sky;*
*'Tis thirteen hundred years agone, since thence the sacred lightnings shone*
*Throughout three nights on Shannon's foam to light the course of Colum home,*
*From Inis Cealtra o'er the wave to Tír dhá Ghlas, his chosen grave.*

*(Taken from 'The Place Where I Was Born', by Dermot F. Gleeson)*

Below Terryglass on our way down the lake we pass by Kilgarvan Quay, which was built in the 1820s as a collection point for barley being shipped to the maltings in Banagher. The village of Ballinderry is 2 km inland and home to a substantial group of Black Poplar trees (*Populus nigra*), a tree that is threatened globally with extinction. It is thought that the Black Poplar might be native to Ireland, but has yet to be confirmed. Although there are only around 15 trees in this group, it is the largest group found in Ireland. However, the small numbers and lack of female trees means that the population may be unsustainable. Cuttings from these trees are being collected to maintain the genetic stock and ensure the survival of the species.

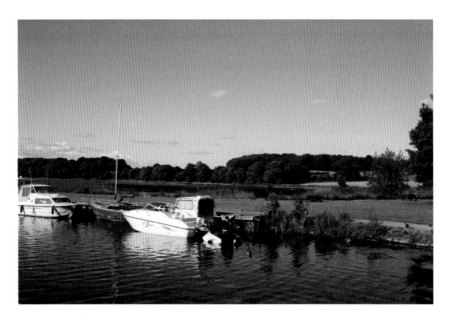

*Leaving Terryglass*

Just below Kilgarvan Quay on the opposite shore of the lake we pass by Rossmore. Conditions are beginning to deteriorate and we are unable to moor here. I am disappointed, as John Feehan describes it in his book, *The Magic of the Shannon*, as a 'shaded haven of beauty and peace'. Instead we continue down the lake, passing Goose Bay on the western side of the lake and navigating our way past Illaumnmore, the largest of the Lough Derg islands at 85 hectares. The remains of an early monastic site, thought to be Franciscan, are found on the island, and there is a standing stone on the south side of the island that reputedly commemorates the departure of the friars to Holy Island. The island was inhabited up until the 1960s and some of the houses are still intact; there is also a large grassy area still used for grazing. We carefully make our way past the dangerous Benjamin Rocks, and head towards Dromineer Bay, our last stop before Mountshannon.

The village of Dromineer, or Droim-inbhir, sits on the shores of the broad and sheltered Dromineer Bay on the east side of Lough Derg. The name translates as 'the ridge of the inver', or river mouth. This is probably because Dromineer is close to where the River Nenagh enters Lough Derg. The weather has changed dramatically since leaving Terryglass, and we are battling lashing rain and howling wind as we arrive into the harbour, and although plenty of boats are moored, there is no sign of life. This was an important station of the Inland Navigation Company in the nineteenth century, and the transit point for most of the traffic on the waterways, including the canal barges. In 1835 the Grand

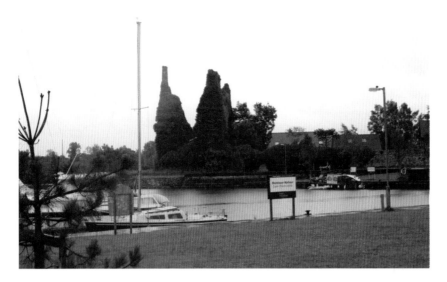

*Dromineer*

Canal Company built a canal store on the quay here, and the bright blue paintwork on the restored building gleams even on this dull day. From there goods were transported by horse to Nenagh and beyond. Goods also came from Nenagh for transport on the water to Limerick and Dublin, and even on to Britain.

I decide to brave the elements to get a closer look at the castle ruins that sit in between the harbour and the famous Lough Derg Yacht Club, which was established in 1835, making it one of the oldest yacht clubs in the world. The Shannon One Design sailboat is a specially designed boat unique to the River Shannon. It is an 18 foot racing dinghy that

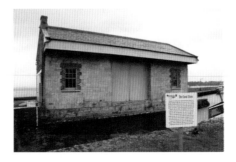

*Dromineer Canal Store*

was introduced in the 1920s to standardise the design of boats used for sailing and racing on the Shannon between the Lough Derg, Lough Ree and North Shannon yacht clubs. The weather is so bad today that no boats are in use, and from the castle I can see them neatly moored in rows outside the yacht club.

The castle was originally a hall house built in the thirteenth or fourteenth century by the Norman followers of Theobald Butler, and later converted into a tower house in the fifteenth or sixteenth century. The ruins are located just behind the harbour at Dromineer, as is the public playground, picnic area, restored navigation trade building (being used as a hostel) and Neddy's thatched cottage. When conditions improve we continue on our way towards Mountshannon, located on the north shore of Scarriff Bay on the western shore of Lough Derg. This journey to Mountshannon will bring us across the widest section of Lough Derg, between Youghal Bay in the east and Scarriff Bay in the west. Before the last glaciation the ancient Shannon entered the sea near Scarriff, but post-glaciation blockages diverted the river down through Castleconnell and Ardnacrusha.

Before long the wind starts to get stronger and the waves bigger. The skipper is shouting orders to the crew to drop the sails, as sheets of rain lash across the deck. Those of us surplus to requirements retire to the cabin and settle in for the bumpy ride to Mountshannon.

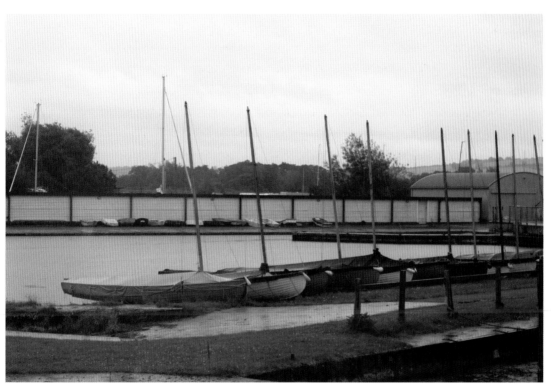

*Lough Derg Yacht Club*

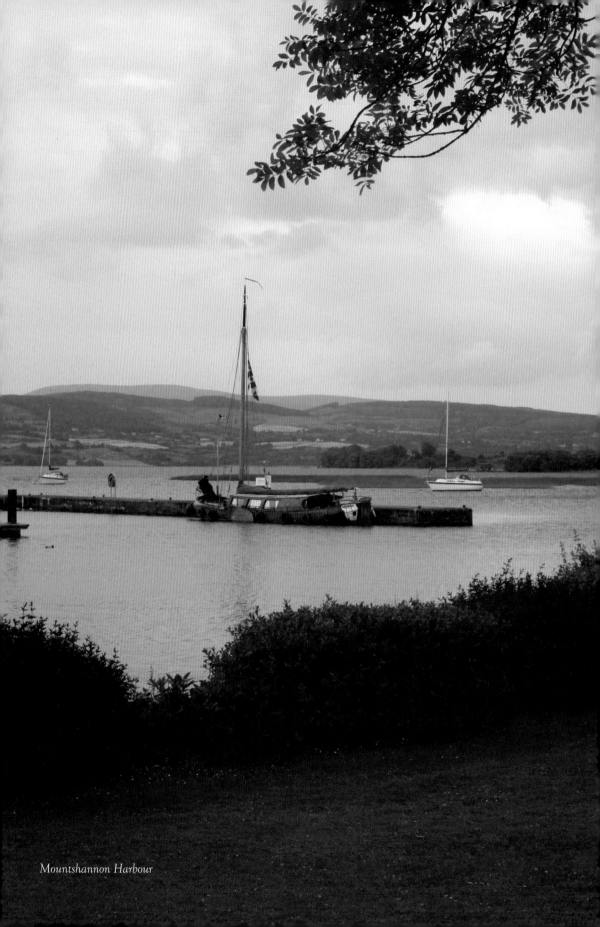

Mountshannon Harbour

# 15: Lough Derg – Mountshannon

It is too shallow for the *Nieuwe Zorgen* to moor off Inis Cealtra, also known as Holy Island, so the skipper slowly manoeuvres her into the large public harbour at Mountshannon. We will approach the island by canoe instead, as it is only a short distance out into Scarriff Bay. We decide to leave our exploration of the island for now, as conditions are still not ideal on the lake. A lunch in Moutshannon calls instead. It is a short, steep walk up to the village from the lakeside, either by road or through the park that lies directly behind the harbour.

Mountshannon has the linen industry to thank for its existence. A linen merchant from Limerick called Alexander Woods leased the land from John Daly in 1738. Included in the lands were the islands of Inis Cealtra (Holy Island), Cooledorragh, Clounty, Coogey, Knockafort and Kilrateera. Under the terms of the lease, which was for the length of the lives of Woods, his sons and his wife Margaret, 50 houses were to be built within four years, which had to be 'fit for tradesmen and manufacturers to dwell in'. Another term was that within four years Woods must build a market house, a school and a slated house for religious worship 'for the use of protestant dissenters commonly called Presbyterians'. Woods intended his town for Protestant settlers only, and hoped to attract conversions from the surrounding Catholic communities when they witnessed the success of his industrious flax-producing Protestant town.

Mountshannon is a pretty and well-kept village of just one street. It is surrounded by tree-covered hills and located in the east of County Clare on the western shore of Lough Derg. The harbour is on the north shore of Scarriff Bay, and it is possible to navigate to Scarriff town up the narrow, winding river of the same name. The Shannon Commissioners dredged the River Scarriff in the mid-nineteenth century, extending the navigation upstream and constructing a harbour. The town then developed into a market town, and in the 1830s a flour mill was established, which was used as a workhouse in the late 1830s. The mill burnt down in 1868 when struck by lightning. The current town stretches uphill from Scariff Bridge to the square.

The park that lies behind Mountshannon Harbour is called Aistear Inis Cealtra, a 4.5 acre community project that was opened in 2000. It is a great example of what a community can achieve when it comes together. There had been a lot of development in the years prior to the project's inception, especially of holiday homes. The local community feared for the future of the last public green area in the village, and so the Aistear Inis Cealtra project was born. The main entrance to the park is under a beautiful stone arch that frames the view of Inis Cealtra from the village. Immediately to the left is a play area for children, but for me the highlight of the park is the maze. The curved stone walls of the maze brings the visitor through seven periods in the evolution of Irish spirituality, from prehistory to present, with various nooks and peaceful corners, complemented by the surrounding plants and shrubs.

It is possible to travel to Inis Cealtra by boat, under the guidance of Mr Gerard Madden, who is a renowned local expert on Inis Cealtra and Mountshannon. Gerard runs the East Clare Heritage Centre in St Cronan's Church in Tuamgraney. It is the oldest church in continuous use in Ireland and its origins can possibly be traced to the tenth century as there is record of a church there in AD 964. Despite many attacks and burnings through the ages, the church has survived to the present day. We are feeling a bit more adventurous and decide to take our trusty touring double canoe for the short journey across the bay. The weather has settled down completely now, and the lake is perfectly still. We launch the canoe from the Blue Flag beach close to the harbour. After a half hour of fairly relaxed paddling, we arrive at a small jetty on the shore of Inis Cealtra, only slightly soggy after a close encounter with the wake of a cruiser. A few steps up from the water bring us to the first remains of the monastic settlement.

Inis Cealtra is around 20 hectares in size and the largest of 14 islands in Scarriff Bay. The monastic remains on the island are well preserved and consist of six churches, a round tower, several bullaun stones, high crosses, an eighth-century cemetery and a holy well. It is thought that the monastery was founded by St Columb of Terryglass in the sixth century, and was also associated with St Caimin. The monastery became so wealthy by the ninth century that it was attacked by the Vikings (Danes) in AD 836 under Turgesius, and again in 922 under Tomran. Brian Boru funded the rebuilding of the monastery and the construction of St Caimin's Church after this last raid, when his brother Marcan was the bishop-abbott of the island. The reform of the church in the twelfth century saw the end of the monastery on Inis Cealtra. St Mary's parish church was then constructed in the thirteenth century, as were various pathways to accommodate the pilgrims who continued to visit the island until the pilgrimage or 'pattern' was suppressed in the nineteenth century. The paths used by these pilgrims were uncovered during archaeological excavations in the 1970s and 1980s.

The first structure we encounter on our way up from the shore is the confessional. The building has been rebuilt a few times and the current remains date to the 1700s. Excavated and rebuilt in the 1970s, it is one of the buildings that would have made up the core of the monastery. (The other core structures are the Church of the Wounded Men, St Caimin's Church, the high cross, the round tower and the Saints' Graveyard). The small rectangular building has no roof, so it is easy to see the upright stone slabs inside. These jambstones are slightly inclined toward each other so from the entrance all I can see is a triangular space at the bottom between the two stones. This inner space or cist may have been used to house sacred relics, but the building was definitely used by pilgrims in the eighteenth and nineteenth centuries as a confessional.

Next we come across the Church of the Wounded Men (teampall na bhfear ngonta), located inside the walls of the Saints' graveyard. This is an early eighteenth-century mortuary chapel of the O'Gradys, whose motto was 'wounded but not vanquished'. St Caimin's Church is just behind the Church of the Wounded Men, and was originally constructed in the tenth century. In the twelfth century a Romanesque doorway was added to the west wall and a chancel was inserted between the antae of the east gable. Through locked metal gates at the Romanesque door, we can see various crosses and grave slabs along the walls. Apparently there was some theft by souvenir hunters in the past, which would explain the gates. To the right is an archway that leads us into the Saints' Graveyard via a nineteenth-

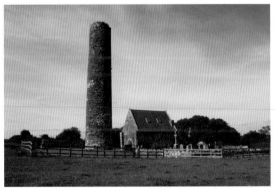

The round tower and St Caimin's Church

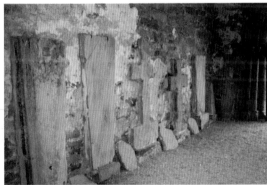

Inside St Caimin's Church

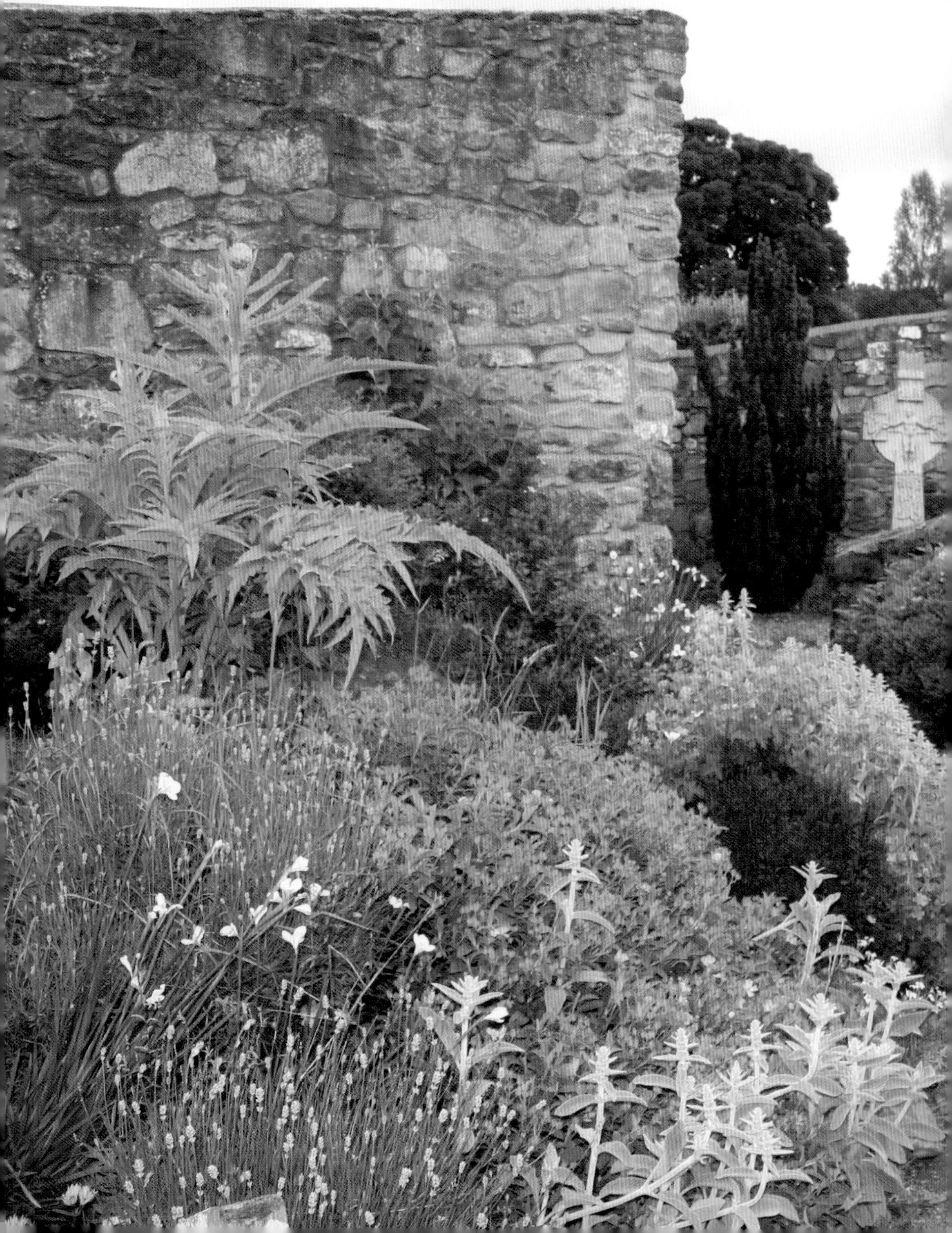

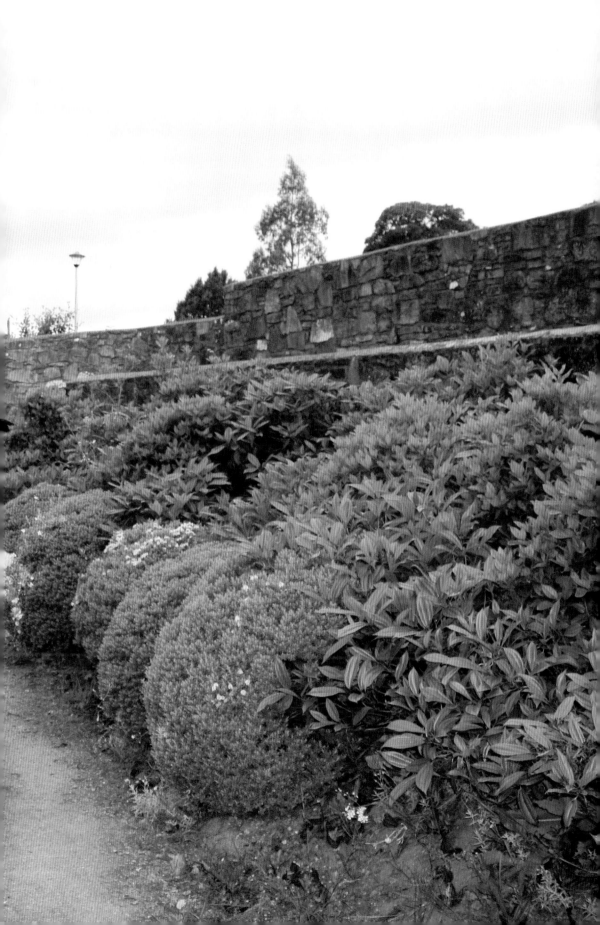

century graveyard. The headstone of Cosrach, 'the miserable one,' who died in 898, is marked with a footprint. There is another grave belonging to the 'the ten men', but it is not known who they were or where they came from.

Passing the incomplete tenth-century round tower, we make our way to the southern shore of the island, away from the monastery core. We come across St Brigid's Church first, which has also been known as the Baptism Church and even as the Piggery. It is a small Romanesque building enclosed by a stone wall. St Mary's Church lies a little farther on, near to the water. It dates to the thirteenth century and is the largest building on Inis Cealtra. In 1210 St Caimin's went out of use and St Mary's became the parish church. By 1615 St Mary's was derelict. The space where the altar once was is occupied by a seventeenth-century box tomb. This had been removed to Whitegate for use as an altar but was returned to the island in 1880. The graveyard in St Mary's Church is still used today and mourners transport the coffins of their loved ones by boat to be buried.

On the highest point of the island lies an earthwork enclosure, which once surrounded a small church. This was marked on an old Ordnance Survey map as 'Garaidh Mhichaeil' or Michael's Garden. It is believed to be a children's burial ground called a cillin, where unbaptised babies were buried in the past. These children were usually premature or born out of wedlock, and the church would not give them a Christian burial. People who committed suicide were often buried in the cillin too. The cillin was usually located in a church ruin, or close to a church or graveyard, and the burials took place secretly at night.

From Michael's Garden I can see out across the still waters of the lake, sparkling in the summer sun. The conditions are just perfect on our return paddle to Mountshannon, so we leave this sad, still place and walk downhill past the main monastery to where our canoe

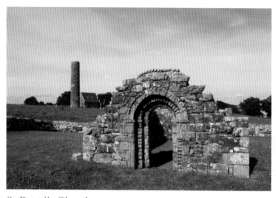
*St Brigid's Church*

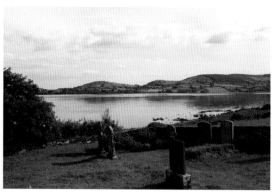
*Graveyard at St Mary's Church*

is waiting. Clear still waters, a light breeze and a blue sky, and the only sound the dip and splash of our paddles as our canoe cuts through the lake – now *this* is the way to appreciate the Shannon. We are looking forward to joining the rest of the crew in the Mountshannon Hotel for dinner and a pint, and to discuss our final leg of the journey to Killaloe.

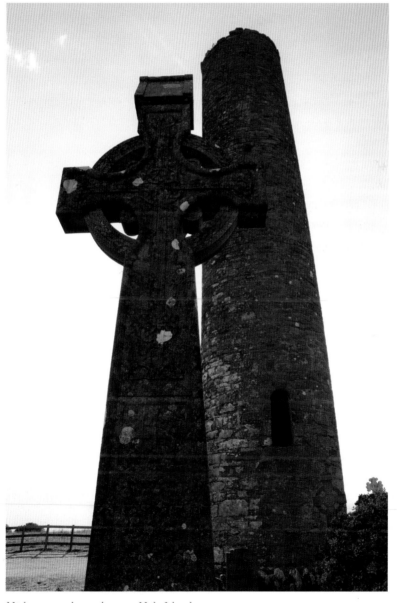

*High cross and round tower, Holy Island*

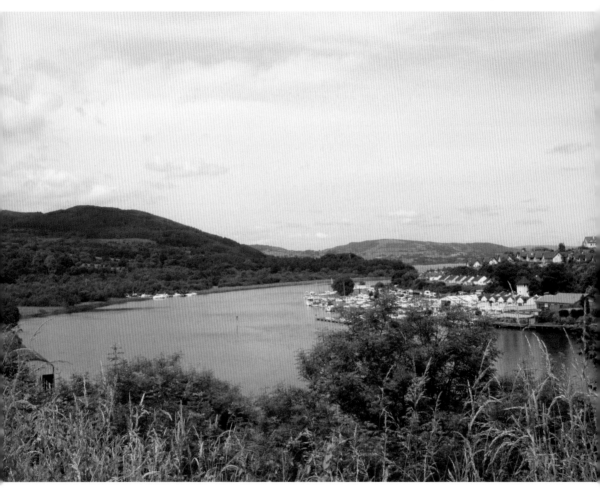

*Approaching Killaloe–Ballina*

# 16: Killaloe–Ballina

Killaloe in County Clare and Ballina in County Tipperary lie on opposite banks of the River Shannon at the southern end of Lough Derg. They are connected by a nineteenth-century bridge that used to have 13 arches, but 4 were removed to insert the navigation section. The settlements developed at an important fording point (now submerged) that has been utilised since the prehistoric period. The approach to these twin towns is spectacular: the lake narrows below Scarriff Bay, and is enclosed by the Slieve Bernagh Mountains to the west and the Arra Mountains to the east. Just before we reach the outskirts of Killaloe–Ballina we pass by the site of the medieval ringfort called Béal Borumha. Although not visible from the water, it is only about 2 km from Killaloe on the R463 and is clearly marked. There is a tree-lined, grassy path leading up to it from the road, bumpy and uneven with tree roots pushing up through the ground. The path opens up to a grassy area enclosed by trees, and a steep-sided mound sits in the centre. There may have been a Norman motte added to the fort in the late medieval period, but all that is visible now is a grassy ring, with a circle of trees on top.

The towns are associated with two early medieval saints, Lua (Molua) and Flannan. The town of Killaloe takes its name from Lua, as it is called Cill Dalua in Irish, or 'The Church of Lua'. St Molua, originally from Clonfert–Mulloe in County Laois, established a church in the area before he died in the seventh century. St Flannan was the first bishop of Killaloe in the seventh century, and the predominantly Romanesque twelfth-century cathedral and oratory located next to the river in Killaloe are dedicated to him. But perhaps the most famous resident of Killaloe was Brian Boru, High King of Ireland from AD 1002 to 1014.

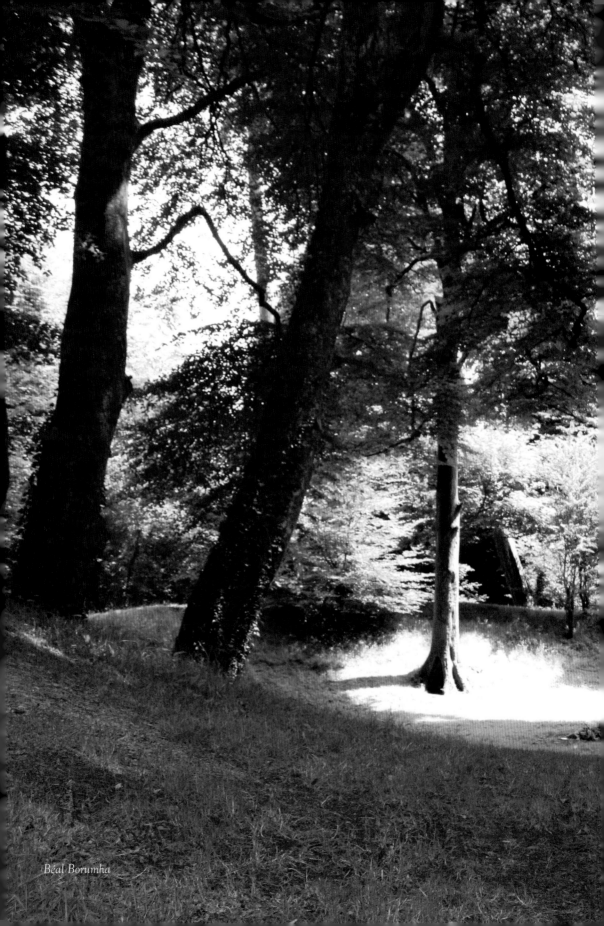

Béal Borumha

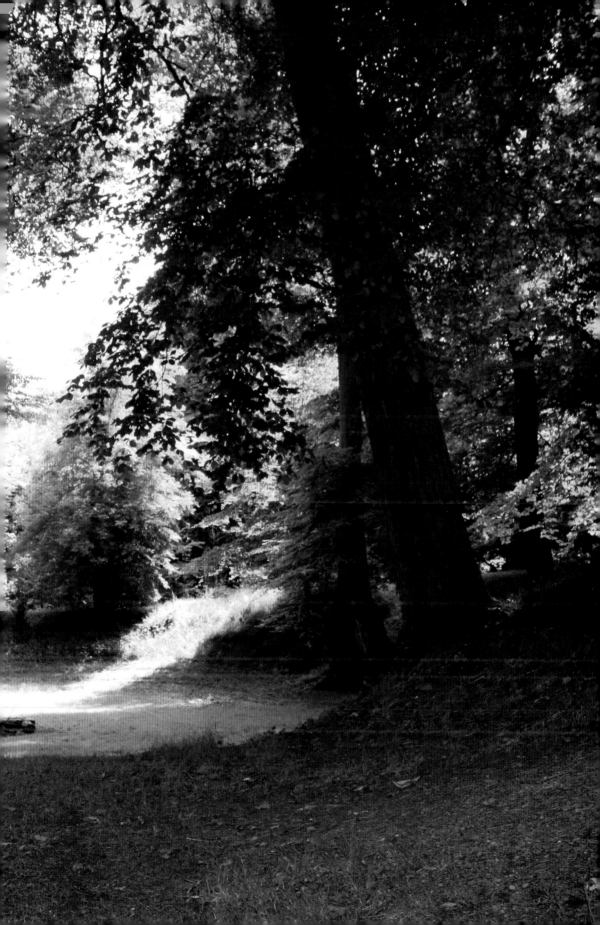

His palace of Kincora, of which no trace remains, stood on the hill in Killaloe where the Roman Catholic church stands today.

Brian Boru was the leader of the Dál gCais sept of County Clare. In Irish he is called Brian Bórumha or Bóirmhe – variations of the word bóraimhe which means 'cattle-tribute'. However, Dáithí Ó hÓgáin's book, *Myth, Legend and Romance*, mentions a poem that refers to Brian Boru as 'Brian from Borumha'. This could be Béal Borumha on the right bank of the Shannon just north of Killaloe. This translates as 'the port of the cattle tribute', and Brian may have grown up there. Brian and his brother Mathghamhain (Mahon) battled constantly against rival septs and the Scandinavian invaders commonly called Vikings (although they referred to themselves as Ostmen). It is the struggle against the Vikings for which Brian Boru is probably best known. Brian became leader of the Dál gCais on the assassination of his brother in 976 and went on to become the High King of Ireland. His reign came to an end in 1014 at the Battle of Clontarf in Dublin.

Brian's power in Ireland had remained unchallenged until a revolt by a combination of Vikings and Leinstermen under Mailmora and Sitric of the Silken Beard (the son of Gormlaith, who had previously been married to Brian Boru). The Vikings enlisted aid from the Western Isles of Scotland and from the Isle of Man, but to no avail as the forces of the elderly Brian Boru and his son Murrogh defeated them at Clontarf on Good Friday 1014. On the night before the battle a lady of the otherworld, called Aoibheall, came to the aged Brian and told him he would be killed the next day. As Brian's forces were beginning to subdue the Leinstermen and their Viking allies, a fleeing Dane called Brodir saw Brian praying in his tent and attacked him. Despite having his leg severed by Brian's sword, Brodir managed to smash Brian's skull with his axe, killing the High King. The descendants of Brian Boru, the O'Briens, held the high kingship of Ireland after Brian's death, but eventually lost it to the O'Connors. The O'Briens remained Kings of Thomond for centuries, until they allied themselves with the English and were granted an Earldom. Brian is described in the Book of Armagh as *Imperator Scotorum*: 'emperor of the Irish'.

Molly's Pub, which sits beside the bridge in Ballina, is a great spot to stop and contemplate the river and Killaloe on the far side of the water. The bridge itself was built between 1825 and 1840, and has a plaque attached to it commemorating four Clare men who lost their lives during the War of Independence (McMahon, Egan, Gildea and Rogers). On the downstream side of the bridge there is a series of metal posts and a metal walkway. This was part of the Killaloe eel fishery, and during the eel-fishing season nets were hung from the posts. The European eel (*Anguilla anguilla*) is the only species of freshwater eel in Europe, and one of only 15 native fish species found in Ireland's freshwaters. The numbers

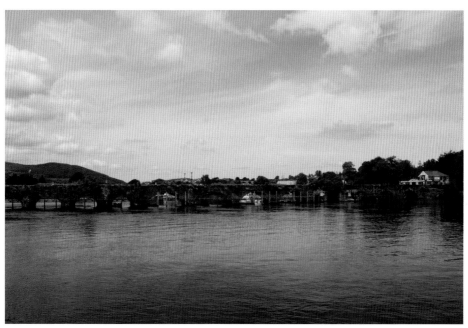

*Killaloe–Ballina Bridge*

of European eel have declined dramatically since the 1980s, but the exact reasons for this decline are not known. Theories include overexploitation, loss of habitat, barriers to migration (i.e. hydroelectric stations), water quality, parasites and oceanic climate change. Here in the Shannon system it has been shown that eel numbers reduced dramatically after the hydroelectric power station at Ardnacrusha began to operate – something I will talk about more when we get to Ardnacrusha.

Scientific research, conducted by the International Council for the Exploration of the Sea (ICES), has indicated that 'the European eel fish stock is so depleted that it is now outside safe biological limits'. There is no evidence to suggest that eels return to the waters or even the countries they were born in, and this makes it extremely important that eel numbers are protected all over Europe. As of 1 January 2010, eel fishing in Ireland is no longer permitted. This move is part of a Europe-wide push to conserve the European eel, under the European Council directive, 'Establishing measures for the recovery of the stock of European eel'. The directive requires all European member states to set up management plans for the conservation of eel stocks.

Although this was devastating news to Ireland's eel fishermen, the government saw the ban as a necessity to save the European eel in Ireland. However, eel fishing has not been banned on Lough Neagh in Northern Ireland, the largest wild eel fishery in Europe, and it continues to operate. The management plan for Lough Neagh found that the fishery there is sustainable due to prudent management of the fishery. The Killaloe eel weir has changed from a commercial fishery in recent years, and the silver eels caught here now are transported overland and released downstream of the power station at Ardnacrusha, free to escape to the Atlantic and return to the Sargasso Sea to reproduce.

The European eel is a mysterious and fascinating creature. Towards the end of their lives the adults journey to breed in the Sargasso Sea, 4,000 km across the Atlantic and the longest migration undertaken by any eel species. The young eels return as leaf-shaped transparent leptocephalus larvae that navigate across the Atlantic to Ireland. They then metamorphose before they can feed in our freshwaters, especially in the lower reaches of our rivers and lakes. There are four more phases in their lifecycle: glass eel, elver, yellow/brown eel and silver eel. The glass eel is the youngest stage that lives in estuarine and inshore waters. They have no pigment in their skin, thus the name. This little eel does not feed, and from December to spring they make their way into our river systems, and travel towards freshwater. When the glass eel develops black skin pigment they become known as elvers. The elver reaches our freshwaters in the spring and begins feeding. When they reach a length of around 9 cm and are more than a year old, the elver stage is over. The next stage – the yellow eel – is where most of the feeding and growing happens.

The yellow eel stage can last between 5 and 25 years. When the yellow eel is big and fat enough it will metamorphose into a non-feeding silver eel, which migrates downstream with the autumn floods on the first leg of its mammoth migration to the Sargasso Sea. The silver eels in the Shannon range between 11 and 15 years old, but eels as old as 25 or more have been recorded too. Christopher Moriarty has studied Irish eels for many years, the yellow eels of Lough Derg in particular. For a more detailed description of this fascinating creature, look for his book, *Eels – A Natural and Unnatural History*.

Leaving the pub and the eel weir behind, we decide that the site of Kincora, or Ceann Coradh (head of the weir), must be our first stop in Killaloe. The Aillebaun walk will lead us up to the top of Killaloe. It starts just across the road and the canal from the tourist office. We were unsure at first, because the start of the walk is not marked and it looks like a front garden, but a helpful local assures us it is the right way. It is a narrow muddy path that winds uphill away from the bridge, but alongside the water. The views across the river and up towards Lough Derg are beautiful. We enviously peer down on the series of fine houses with jetties that sit on the Ballina banks of the river, as we make our way farther uphill. Before long we emerge onto a residential street beside a holiday village, and a little farther along we come to St Lua's Oratory and the present-day church.

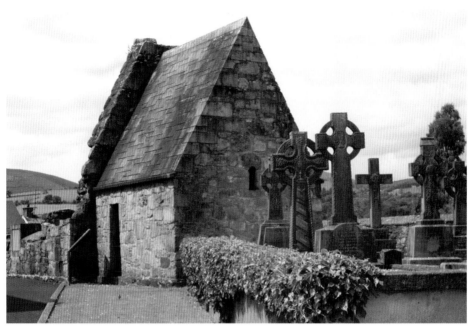

*St Lua's Oratory*

The Oratory, also called St Molua's, was originally located on Inis Lua or Friar's Island downstream of Killaloe. It was dismantled in 1929 when the Shannon Hydroelectric Scheme was established, and rebuilt here to protect it from the rising water levels of the Shannon that would have submerged it. It is ninth or tenth century originally, but not much is known about its history. It is made mostly of yellow sandstone. The oldest part of the present church is the tenth- or eleventh-century nave. The chancel was added later, possibly in the twelfth century, and has a very rare example of a pitched stone roof.

St Flannan's Cathedral lies at the bottom of the hill that is Killaloe Main Street, on the banks of the Killaloe Canal. The cathedral was built in the thirteenth century from purple and yellow sandstone and is cruciform in layout. On entering the churchyard the first building we see is St Flannan's Oratory. It is a well-preserved example of a stone-roofed Romanesque church built in the early twelfth century. This oratory is unusual as it has an intact stone roof. Inside there is a small living space over the vault of the nave.

The entrance to the Church of Ireland Cathedral next to the oratory is through the Gothic western door. Inside there is a Romanesque doorway in the south wall that actually belonged to an earlier church on the site, which was built in the twelfth century, but by the beginning of the thirteenth century it had been destroyed. The doorway is an extraordinary piece of work with beautiful carvings of spirals, leaves, strange animals and pretty flowers.

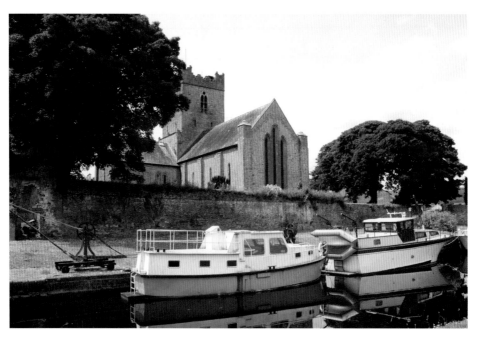

*St Flannan's Cathedral*

On the floor near the Romanesque door sits a very unusual stone. It is part of the shaft of
a cross, and was discovered in 1916 in the graveyard wall by R. A. F. Macalister, Professor of
Celtic Archaeology in University College Dublin (UCD) from 1909 to 1943. What makes
it so unusual is that it is the only known example of a stone with carvings in Ogham and
in Scandinavian Runes. It dates to AD 1000 and is dedicated to a Viking convert called
Thorgrim. The runes read: 'Thorgrim carved this cross.' The Ogham carving on the side
reads: 'A blessing upon Thorgrim.'

There is a memorial in the church to John Grantham, who was responsible for the
introduction of steamers to the River Shannon. Grantham suggested the use of steamboats
for transportation to the Directors General of Inland Navigation in 1820. His proposal
was accepted in 1824 and he was given a plot of land in Limerick to build a store. This
store was to house his steamboat company and the first of his boats, the *Marquis Wellsley*.
Killaloe became the headquarters of the Inland Steam Navigation Company, and in 1833
it introduced the largest of the Shannon steamers, the *Lady Lansdowne*. This company
was actually an amalgamation of Grantham's Shannon Navigation Company and a rival
operator, the Shannon Steam Navigation Company. The latter began operations in 1826
with the *Mountaineer* steamboat. The steamboat era reached its peak in the 1840s, but
fell into decline following the Famine and the coming of the railways. At the end of the

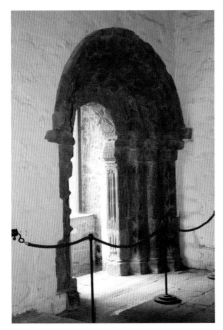

*Romanesque doorway, St Flannan's*

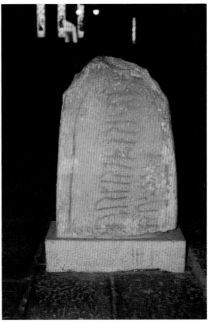

*Ogham stone in St Flannan's*

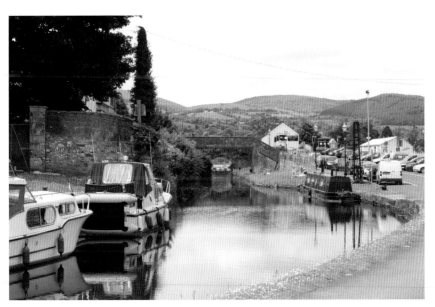

*Killaloe Canal*

nineteenth century, the newly founded Shannon Development Company reintroduced passenger services to the river, and built the Lakeside Hotel at Ballina to accommodate those travelling on the river.

The cathedral backs on to the eighteenth-century Killaloe Canal, which was built to bypass the rapids and eel weirs on the Shannon. The Killaloe Canal is one of three canals built by the Limerick Steamship Company in the eighteenth century. These canals made the river navigable between Killaloe and Limerick. A period of trade on the river began, with Killaloe–Ballina acting as a port for passenger steamers, cargo and turf boats. The canals were no longer necessary after the Shannon Hydroelectric Scheme opened in 1929. The subsequent rise in water levels submerged the rapids below Killaloe, and although the modern navigation now brings river traffic under the bridge on the Ballina side of the river, the Killaloe Canal is still used for mooring.

It is here that we part ways with the *Nieuwe Zorgen*, as she must return north to Shannon Harbour and then to Dublin via the Grand Canal. Our journey onwards, towards Limerick where the River Shannon becomes an estuary, must be by more conventional means. But for now we will follow the river downstream of Killaloe towards one of Ireland's greatest engineering achievements, the Shannon Hydroelectric Scheme at Ardnacrusha.

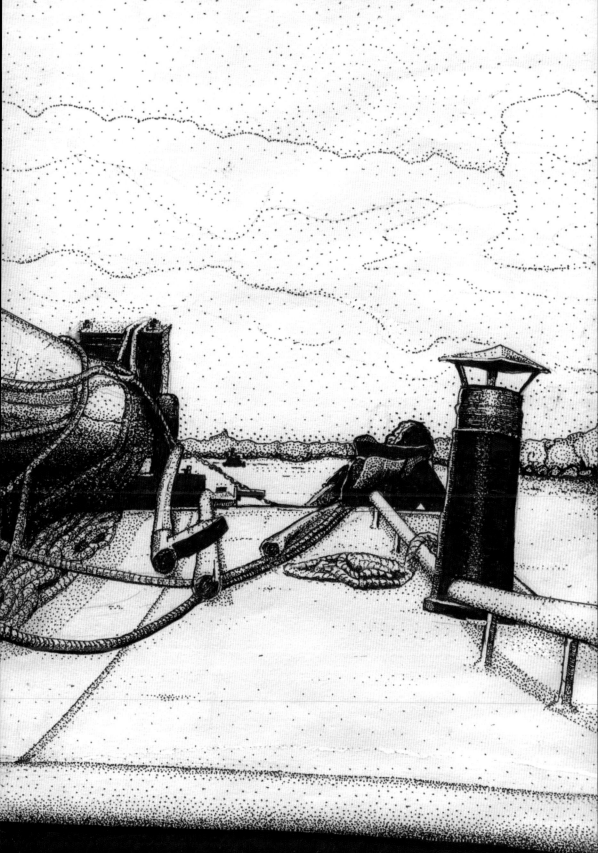

Farewell Nieuwe Zorgen © Eric Kemp

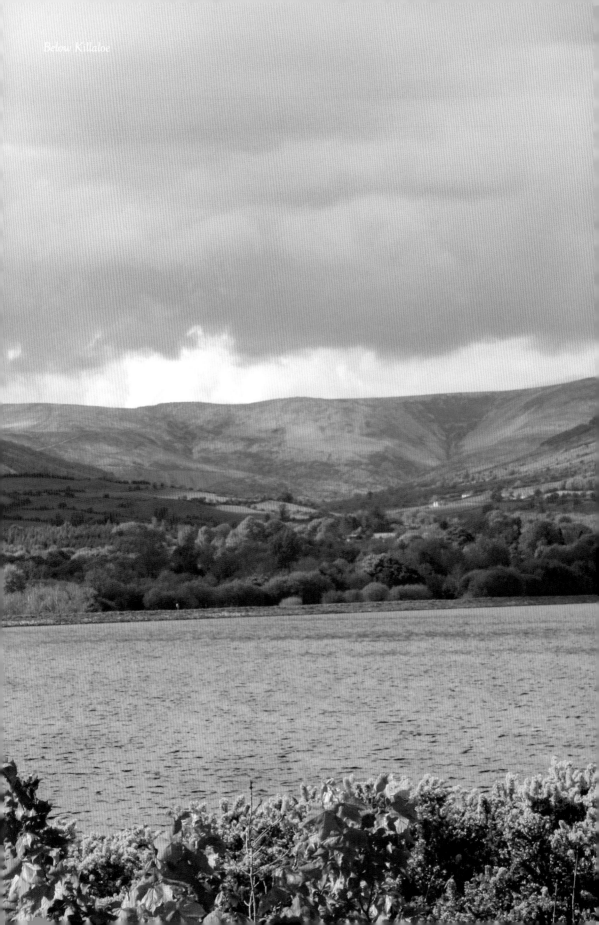

Below Killaloe

# 17: Killaloe to Ardnacrusha

*Oh, were I Homer, that ancient roamer*
*I'd write a poem on a noble theme*
*To sing the story and praise the glory*
*Of that wondrous project the Shannon Scheme*

*In Ballyvalley, midst oak and sally*
*I sat me down and I dreamed a dream*
*Of more employment and more enjoyment*
*And happier homes through the Shannon Scheme.*

*'Twill light our houses, 'twill switch our blouses*
*'Twill milk our cows and 'twill churn the cream*
*'Twill plough and sow Sir, 'twill reap and mow Sir*
*'Twill raise our dough Sir, the Shannon Scheme.*

*On boats and barges as wide and large as*
*The Grecian Argus that ship of fame*
*From famed Portroe Sir and Killaloe Sir*
*The slates will come by the Shannon Scheme.*

*Then fill your glasses, my lads and lasses*
*All creeds and classes of the Irish name*
*And toast the statesmen*
*Those wise and great men*
*Who boldly tackled the Shannon Scheme.*

*(A song by Sylvester Boland, 1927)*

The landscape below Killaloe is not a natural one. Since the 1920s it has been altered on a massive scale by the construction of the Shannon Hydroelectric Scheme. On leaving Killaloe–Ballina the river widens so much that it is almost a lake, and this lake is the result of the Shannon Scheme. The river is dammed up behind a weir downstream at Parteen Villa that diverts most of the river's flow into a headrace canal that feeds the power station. This canal is also the navigation channel for much of the stretch that leads to Limerick. The natural channel winds its way parallel to the canal, until it reaches O'Briensbridge. After this it moves southwards, away from the Shannon Scheme, towards Castleconnell and on to Limerick city. The tailrace canal of the Shannon Scheme brings the diverted waters of the Shannon back to the river in Limerick, just below Parteen, where the river sweeps around St Thomas' Island.

The Shannon Scheme was built to provide electricity to the new Irish Free State, and is considered one of Ireland's greatest infrastructural achievements. The existence of the scheme is largely the brainchild of one Irishman, Dr Thomas Aloysius MacLoughlin, a Drogheda-born scientist and engineer who worked for the German company Siemens-Schuckert in Berlin. It was during his time in Berlin that the UCD graduate started to think about harnessing the power of the Shannon to produce electricity.

It was not the first time that such a project had been considered. There were plans to harness the power of the river as far back as 1844 by the Dublin chemist, Sir Robert Kane. A later proposal, called the 'Frazer Scheme', was not pursued because of the cost, but had been endorsed by the Shannon Water and Electric Power Act (1901). In 1918 the British Board of Trade started to investigate the water power resources of the United Kingdom, including Ireland. Sir John Pursar Griffith was put in charge of an Irish subcommittee to investigate the 'Water Power Resources of Ireland'. The committee's report endorsed the proposal of Theodore Stevens, to develop the Shannon in four steps between Killaloe and Limerick. The first Dáil also established a committee that published a report in 1922, but this was not pursued either.

It was in 1924 that Thomas MacLoughlin approached the Irish government with his proposal for the Shannon. MacLoughlin graduated from UCD in 1918, and went on to University College, Galway (UCG) to earn his PhD. In 1922 he began work with Siemens-Schuckert in Berlin. His enthusiasm for the Shannon project convinced Siemens, and the Irish government was approached. The government appointed an independent commission of experts who vetted the proposal and suggested some changes. The estimated cost of £5.2 million was actually one-fifth of the entire national budget for 1925, so the proposal did meet some opposition. Despite this the Oireachtas passed the Shannon Electricity Act in 1925, making it possible for work on the scheme to commence.

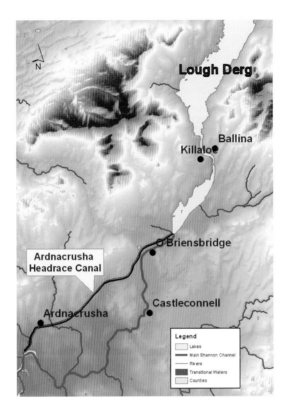

In 1927, Minister Patrick McGilligan established the Electricity Supply Board (ESB), Ireland's first semi-state body, to take over responsibility for the station. When the station was completed in 1929, it was the largest hydroelectric station in the world. This title was short-lived, as soon after the Hoover Dam in the United States would take that honour.

The Shannon Scheme proposed the construction of a weir and intake near Parteen Villa, headrace and tailrace canals spanned by four bridges, and the power station building. Nearly all of the equipment used during the three-and-a-half-year construction period was imported from Germany through the Limerick docks. A standard gauge railway was built from Limerick to Ardnacrusha. Camps for the workers were constructed at Ardnacrusha, Clonlara, O'Briensbridge and, as we saw earlier, at Meelick. The camp at Ardnacrusha housed around 750 workers, some of them German, but mostly Irish. It was a harsh time in Ireland, with little employment and the brutalities of the Civil War still fresh and raw. The 5,000 jobs created by the Shannon Scheme could not have come at a better time for our fledgling Free State.

The Ardnacrusha camp consisted of four large huts and three small huts. The large huts contained three rooms, each of them housing 30 men. There was also a bath-house in the camp, a recreation hall, a 600-seater dining hall, large kitchen, canteen and shop.

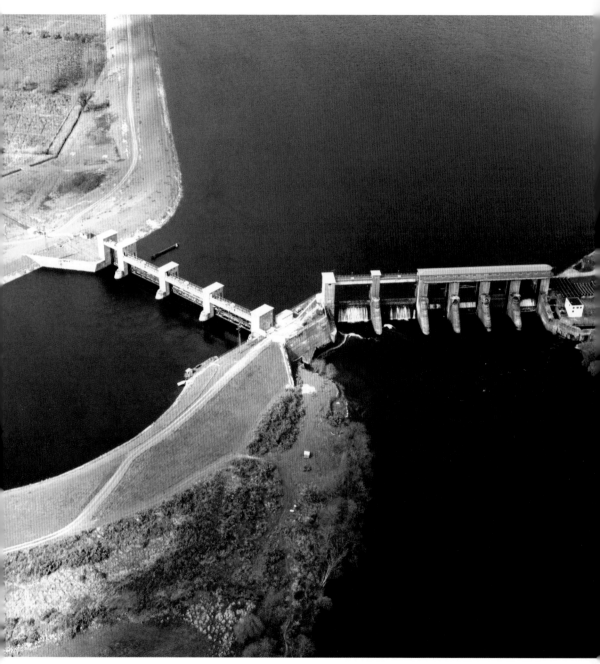

*Parteen Weir © Kevin Dwyer. The Ardnacrusha headrace canal is to the left and the natural course of the Shannon to the right.*

At the weekends there was a cinema and concert performances. However these camps accommodated only one third of the workforce, so the remainder had to find alternative lodgings. One such alternative was provided by a farmer near Blackwater, who rented his farmyard and stables out to 21 families at £1 per family.

For 6.5 km below Killaloe the river is dammed behind the Parteen Villa Weir, which controls the flow of water from Lough Derg into the Shannon Scheme via the headrace canal. The weir also controls the amount of water that enters the natural course of the Shannon. The lake and canal have a very man-made look and feel about them. The embankment on the south side is very obvious and devoid of much vegetation, apart from a well-mown grassy bank. The opposite side looks softer and more natural, but there are very few trees visible. Below the weir there are three separate parallel waterways: the head and tailrace canals, the natural Shannon channel and the Errina Canal. The Errina Canal was built in the eighteenth century to bypass the rapids and series of falls at Doonass, so that boats could navigate between Limerick and Killaloe. The entrance to the canal lies 2 km below O'Briensbridge, and passes through the village of Cloonlara on its way to Plassey Bridge where it joins the Shannon. The canal is no longer in use. The headrace canal feeds the power station with water, and incorporates a massive double lock at Ardnacrusha for water navigation. There are also three reinforced concrete road bridges over the headrace, at O'Briensbridge, Blackwater and Cloonlara.

The natural channel of the Shannon is much smaller than it would have been before the scheme. A large volume of its water is diverted through the weir into the headrace of the scheme. The Shannon winds through the rolling rural landscape of County Limerick, passing through the towns of O'Briensbridge and Castleconnell before it continues on to Limerick city. The construction of the weir raised the water level behind it by 7.55 m to that of Lough Derg, placing a large area of low-lying land next to the river below Killaloe under water. The fall of water between Killaloe and Limerick was now harnessed to drive the turbines of the power station. The embankment we first encountered at Meelick was constructed to prevent flooding above Lough Derg.

Ardnacrusha is Ireland's largest renewable energy generating facility. Although it now provides only 2 per cent of Ireland's electricity, the huge importance of the scheme remains. It is a rapidly available source of renewable energy available at peak demand or for emergency supply. The Shannon Scheme celebrated its 75th anniversary in 2002, with the American Institute of Electrical and Electronics Engineers calling it a 'milestone of twentieth-century engineering'. The American Society of Civil Engineers said that it was an 'international historic engineering landmark'. The scheme is viewed as a statement of

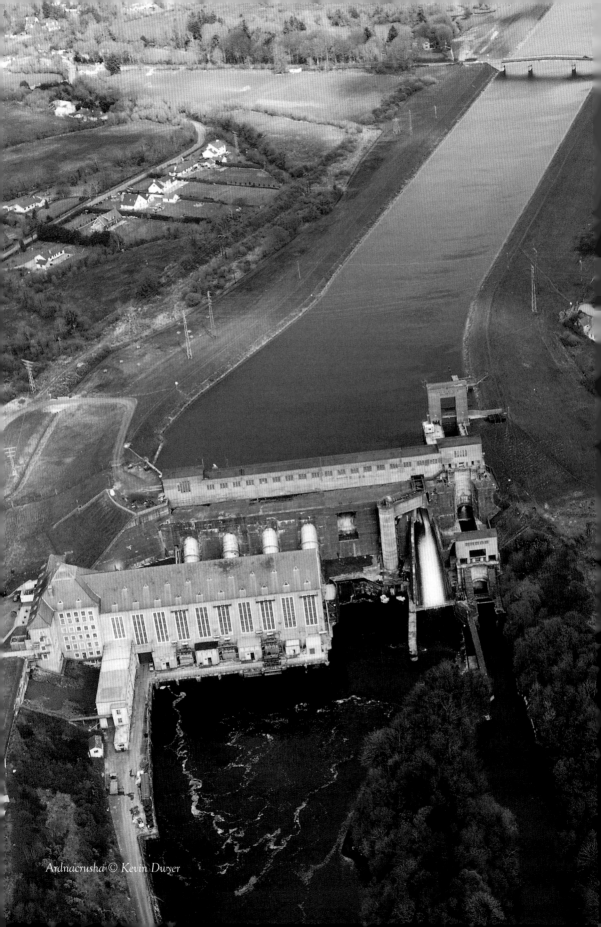

Ardnacrusha © Kevin Dwyer

Ireland's independence and nationhood. After the scheme opened a writer with the *Financial Times*, W. M. Harland, stated that:

> For half a century the country under the British regime toyed with the suggestion
> of harnessing the Shannon. The British are a hardheaded and practical folk, but
> they jibbed at such a venture. Then the Free State came into being, and ardent
> untired administrators, remembering that they had always been accused of being
> dreamers, seized on this chance of showing what they can do ... they have thrown
> on their shoulders the not easy task of breaking what is in reality an enormous
> inferiority complex and the Shannon Scheme is one – and probably the most vital –
> of their methods of doing it.

The construction of the Ardnacrusha hydroelectric power station did not benefit all of the inhabitants of the Shannon region. Two species of migratory fish were adversely affected by the scheme. Both the Atlantic salmon (*Salmo salar*) and our friend from Killaloe, the European eel, suffered greatly. The number of silver eels recorded in 1908 and 1928 was 69 tonnes and 65 tonnes respectively. By the 1940s this number had declined to only 17.8 tonnes. The decline was directly connected to the opening of the Shannon Scheme, and so the ESB, who were responsible for the power station, had to become more involved in the management of the River Shannon Fisheries. The ESB began a major eel-stocking scheme by installing elver traps at Ardnacrusha and Parteen. Since 2000 the ESB has also been trapping and transporting silver eels from Killaloe to sites below Parteen Weir, free to continue their journey across the Atlantic to the Sargasso Sea.

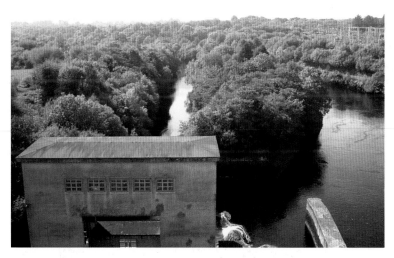

*Downstream of Ardnacrusha*

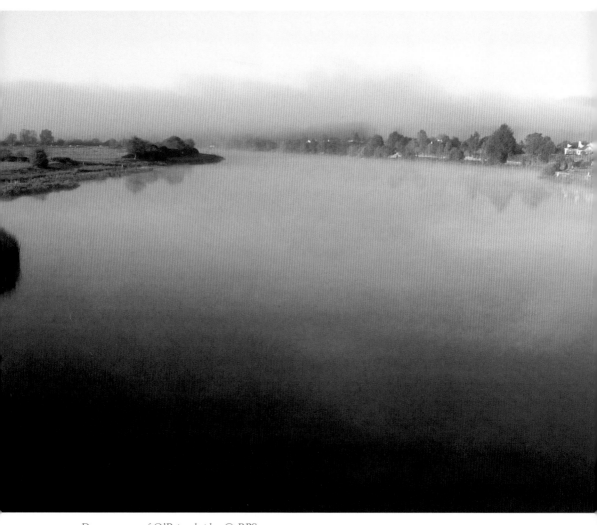

*Downstream of O'Briensbridge © RPS*

# 18: Ardnacrusha to Limerick

Though far from thee, dear Shannon stream,
My lot may be to roam forever,
Thy silver tide and music wild
Shall cease to dwell in mem'ry never!
How often in the days of youth
I stood upon the banks so grassy
And fished from morn till eve
'Neath Castletroy and dear old Plassey
What cared I then for rain or shine,
Provided that the fish were biting?
I knew no better sport than that,
Nor cared for pastime more inviting.

Can I forget my dear Parteen
Where I was born, educated
And lived until I was thirteen
And from the sixth class graduated?
My schoolmates and my boyhood days
I oft recall, when I am sleeping!
Though far away I am today,
In spirit I am vigils keeping!
I romp once more on old Church Hill
Or swim across the lordly Shannon,
Whose waters, roaring at the Weir,
Sound like the boom of distant cannon!

(Taken from 'Recollections', by Clement Garvey – a native of Gortatogher/Firhill)

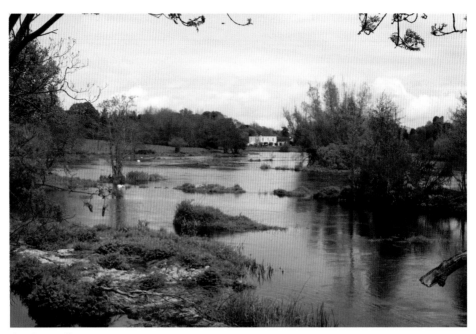

*Castleconnell*

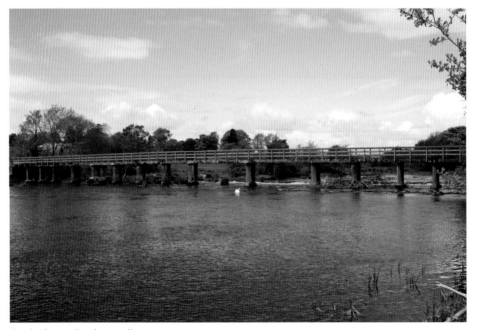

*Footbridge at Castleconnell*

O'Briensbridge in County Clare is named after the 14-arch bridge built there by Turlough and Donal O'Connor in the early sixteenth century. The bridge is unusual because of the variations in arch width and height, and in the materials used. This is a result of the numerous alterations and rebuilds the bridge has undergone over the centuries. Standing downstream of the bridge on the harbour wall these alterations are quite obvious, as halfway along the colour of the stone and shape of the arches are very different.

Like many settlements on the Shannon, Castleconnell sits on a historic fording point on the river. The name derives from Caislean Ó gConaing, after the Ó gConaing clan, an early Gaelic sept who owned part of the lands in the area. Castleconnell passed to William de Burgo (Burke) following the Norman invasion, and one branch of the family had the title of 'Baron of Castleconnell'. Previously the area was called Mur Mic an Duinn or The Fortress of Donn's Son. Donn's son may have been Eogabal, the father of Fi and Áine of Knockainy, who were gods of the Eoghanacht, a clan who dominated the south of the country from the fifth to the twelfth centuries. The castle ruins sit on top of a steep rock outcrop just outside the town. It is on private land now, so it is only possible to view it from the roadside, not that there is much to see apart from the remains of a tower. The castle was destroyed on the orders of General Ginkel in 1691 with 84 barrels of gunpowder.

During the eighteenth and nineteenth centuries, Castleconnell became a popular tourist destination, with visitors from Limerick and farther afield coming to avail of the mineral spa, salmon fishing and to visit the falls at Doonass (Dún Easa, or 'the stronghold of the waterfall or rapids') to the south of the town. The falls ceased to exist after the construction of the Shannon Scheme, but today it is a shady peaceful place, frequented by

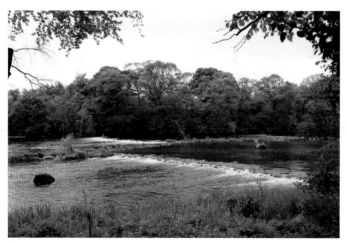

*Doonass*

fishermen and accessed by a footbridge from the riverside walk in Castleconnell. In the past an enormous volume of the Shannon pounded over the falls here, and supposedly it was a spectacular thing to see.

*Have you been to Killarney, the Causeway or Quay,*
*The proud Bay of Dublin, Loophead or Kinsale?*
*The city Cove of Cork seems but shadow or gas*
*When compared to the proud rolling falls of Doonass.*

*And if you're not tired of walking proceed further still,*
*To the right of Massey's mansion, 'tis there you'll get your fill;*
*And when you reach the summit, come fill up your glass*
*Drink health, wealth and honour to the falls of Doonass.*

*Hail Castle Connell! where incessantly*
*The Shannon pours her rapid, foaming*
*Stream, impatient to find out her native Sea.*
*O for a Shenstone's pencil, to describe*
*The spot where peace and health so*
*much abound.*

*Anonymous*

The falls may be gone now, but the river here is still very beautiful and definitely worth a visit. In the hallway of the Castle Oaks Hotel there are photos of some of the famous fishermen who have visited this stretch of the Shannon, including Ireland's adopted Englishman, the former Republic of Ireland football manager Jack Charlton. From the playground just outside the town, or from the grounds of the hotel, it is possible to access a riverside walk that leads down to Powell's Island where there is a fishing beat.

To the north of Castleconnell village there is an area now known as 'World's End'. In his book, *Portrait of Limerick*, Mainchín Seoighe notes that the area was once the location of 'Worral's Inn', so the current name may be a version of this. Below Castleconnell the river weaves around numerous small tree-covered islands and over small weirs. The peace of Doonass continues along this leafy stretch of birdsong and insect hum. Soon the river straightens out on its approach to Limerick city, and as it turns south we are joined by the River Mulkear. Before long we arrive at Castletroy and the suburbs of Limerick city.

The river takes a westerly turn now, and weaves between some more wooded islands before passing by the University of Limerick (UL). There are over 11,000 students at the

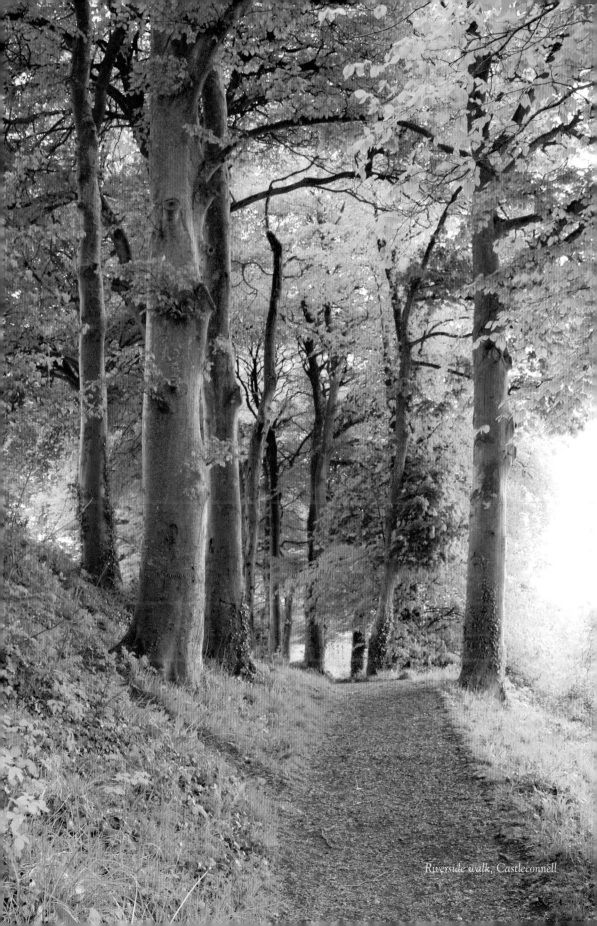

Riverside walk, Castleconnell

university, which spreads over 133 hectares on the banks of the river, including 46 hectares on the Clare side of the Shannon. The two UL campuses are connected by a footbridge over the river, which was built in 2007. The river continues on under the Plassey Bridge and is joined by the River Blackwater from the north and the disused Errina Canal. The river swoops down in a loop and then turns north under Athlunkard Bridge. Along the bank from Plassey to Athlunkard there is a riverside walk, which passes through the Shannon

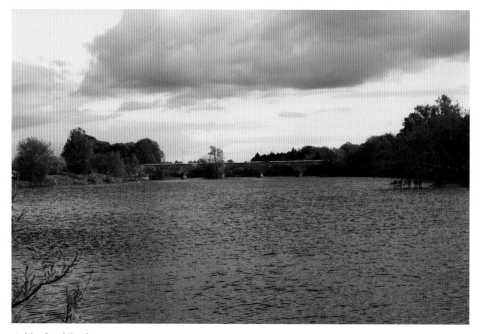

*Athlunkard Bridge*

Fields and eventually leads to the Corbally Baths. The baths are no longer in use, and are home to Arrowhead (*Sagittaria sagittifolia*) and Rigid Hornwort (*Ceratophyllum demersum*).

Athlunkard, or Áth an Longphort in Irish, translates to 'the ford of the ship enclosure or encampment'. The area was originally called Áth Coille (the ford of the woods), until 1301 when the O'Briens changed it to Áth an Longphort. The 'longphort' referred to in the current name was a temporary Viking settlement, and it was probably located in Fairyhill opposite St Thomas' Island near Athlunkard Bridge. A large D-shaped enclosure was discovered there in recent years. This longphort was possibly part of a two-year Viking campaign on the Shannon in the 840s. This area of Limerick is called Corbally or 'Odd Townland' (Cor translates to odd). Here the river is wide, and continues to wind its way around small wooded islands. Beyond the 1830s' bridge at Athlunkard, the Shannon first meets the incoming tide of the estuary, and ceases to be the river we have travelled with until now. The river continues in a northerly direction until it meets St Thomas' Island in the middle of the channel, where its course splits and loops around the island. From here the Shannon swoops southwards together with the waters of the Ardnacrusha tailrace canal, which enter the river from the north just beyond St Thomas' Island.

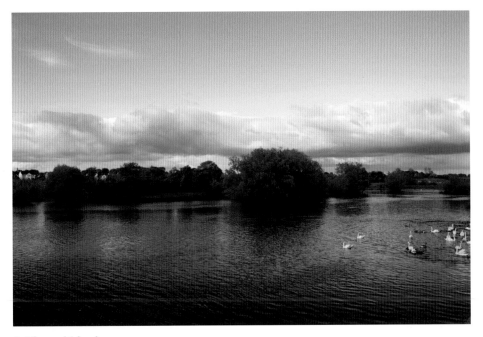

*St Thomas' Island*

Corbally is a quiet and picturesque suburb, with various fishing boats moored behind the houses backing on to the river. A shady path follows a stream parallel to the main river and emerges from the trees close to the now disused Corbally Baths. It is possible to walk out into the river along the now dry walls of the regulating weir, which was built in the nineteenth century as part of works to improve the navigability of the Limerick section of the Shannon. The remains of another weir exits a little farther downstream, at the tail of St Thomas' Island. This is the Lax Weir, built by the Vikings, the oldest feature in Corbally. On this final approach to the Limerick city, the river is shallow, broad and slow, and interspersed with spits and ridges of sand, mud and stone. Leaving Corbally behind, Thomond Bridge looms ahead, one of the oldest man-made structures on the river, and beside it sits King John's Castle. We have arrived in Limerick.

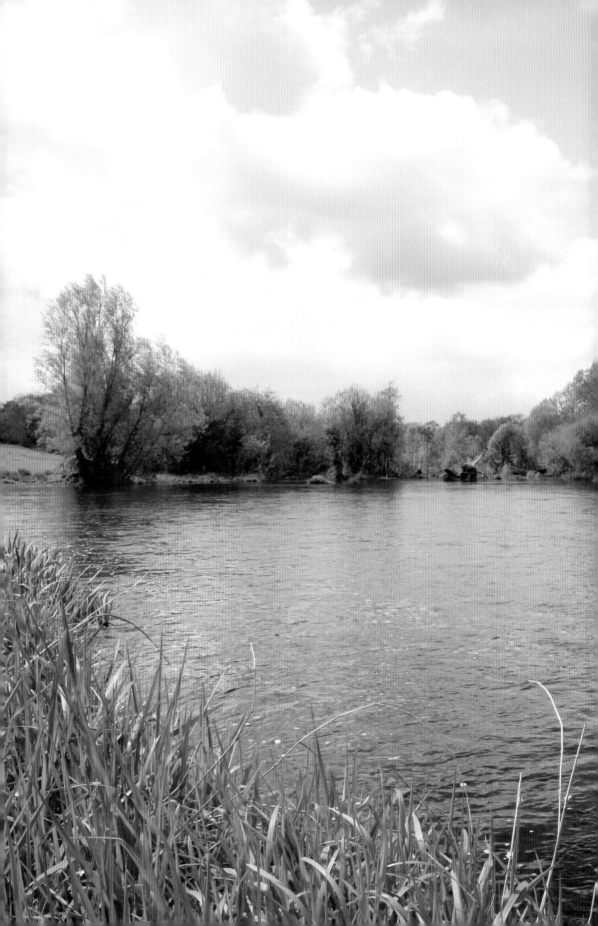

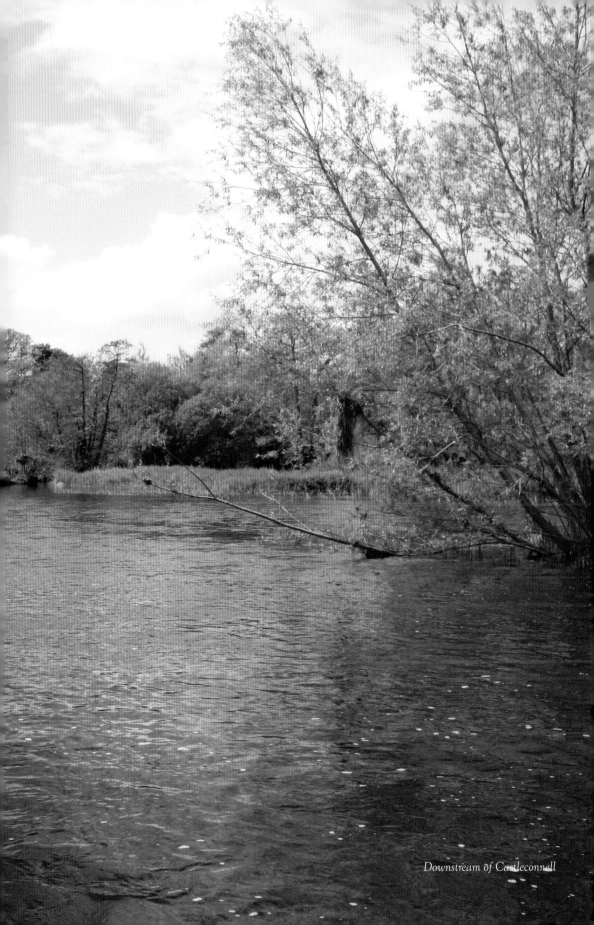

*Downstream of Castleconnell*

*Below Corbally*

*Far over the tumbling billows*
*Of the broad Atlantic sea*
*The thoughts of my heart oft wander*
*To the friends who are dear to me;*
*And I visit well-known places,*
*The scenes by boyhood knew,*
*Where the Shannon by Limerick city*
*Rolls down all his waves of blue.*

*I mark how the lordly current,*
*As it sweeps in its grand career,*
*Gives back like a might mirror*
*Till the eyes of my fancy rest on*
*That bend in the river's course*
*Where the Bridge of Athlunkard*
*spans it,*
*As a rider does his horse.*

*The memory bounding backward*
*Through the long vale of years,*
*Recalleth a sombre vision*
*Of banners and blood-red spears –*
*All red with the blood of out kindred –*
*And enter Limerick town*
*Over Athlunkard's arches*
*And pillars of granite brown.*

*And I anxiously ask – Shall ever*
*Athlunkard's Bridge again*
*Re-echo the measured tramping*
*Of some fierce marauder's men;*
*Of Hessian or maybe Hindoos*
*Let loose on our trampled land*
*To plunder and slay out people,*
*As did once 'Fierce Billy's Band'?*

And a voice within me answers:
'See that palace upon the ridge
That rises in graceful beauty
Close by Athlunkard Bridge?
There dwells in that lordly palace
One fitted like king to reign,
And to watch o'er his faithful people
As a chief o'er his broad domain.

'And as long as that noble prelate
In his hand the crozier wields,
No ill can befall his people,
No marauders waste their fields.
Athlunkard Bridge may have echoed
The foreign foes' tramp of old,
But whilst Butler guards the approaches
'The pass can ne'er be sold.'

As again upon Fancy's pinion
I fly from Athlunkard Bridge,
From its old historic approaches
And the palace upon the ridge,
There rises within my bosom
This sentiment fond and true–
'Would each pass in our brave old
island
Were sentinelled safe as you!'

(John F. McGrath, 'Athlunkard Bridge, Corbally')

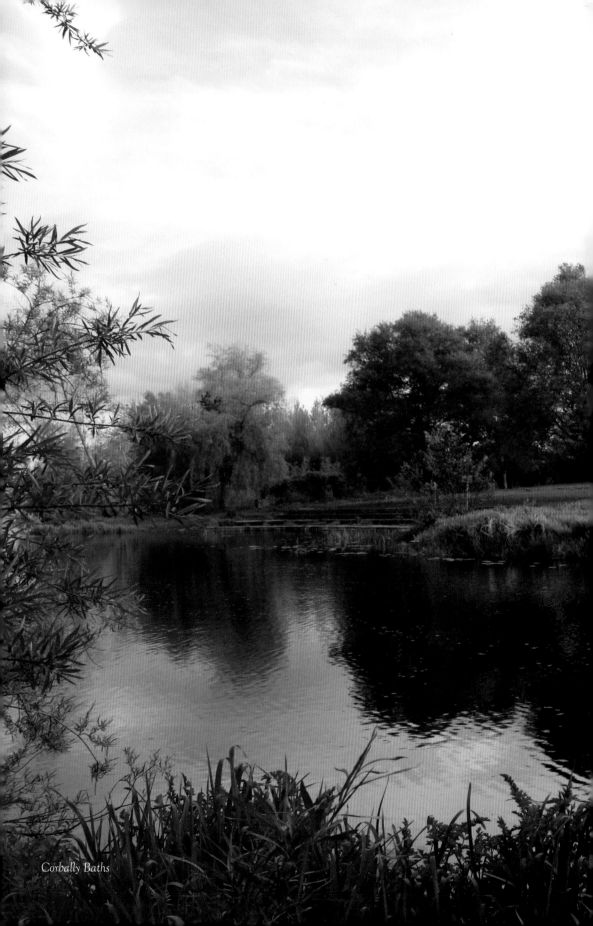

Corbally Baths

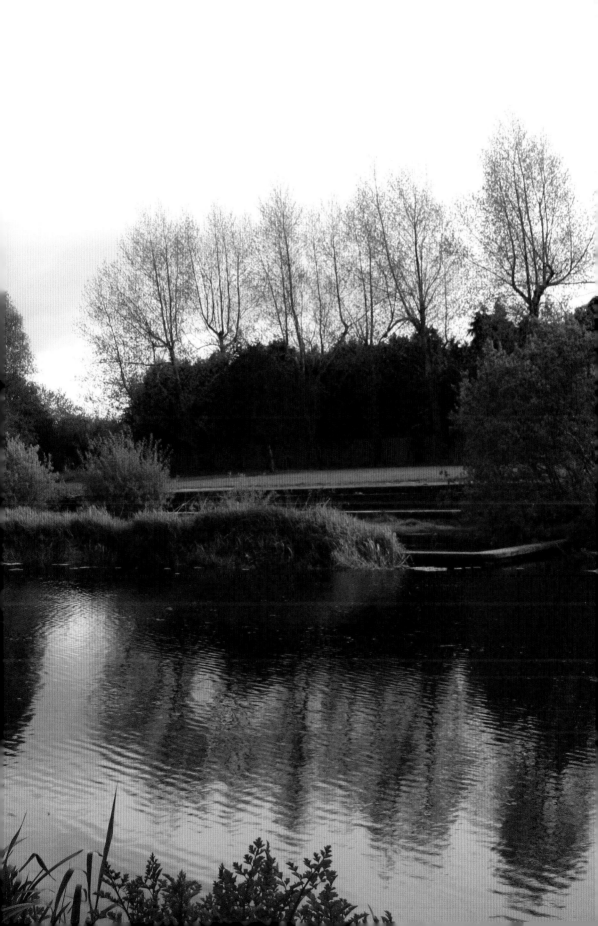

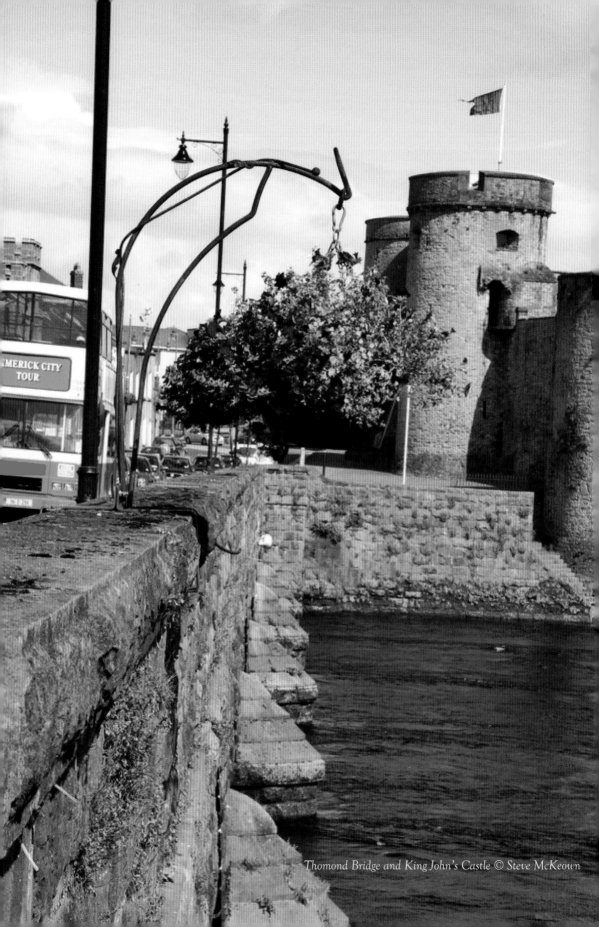

*Thomond Bridge and King John's Castle © Steve McKeown*

# 19: Limerick

The modern city of Limerick is home to just over 52,000 people, but this figure rises to over 90,000 if you include the immediate surroundings of the city too. The story of modern Limerick is a complex one, but I do not wish to focus on negatives here. Some consider Limerick to be a city of two tales, and it is the tale of community and progress that deserves attention. Where this spirit is most evident to me is in the support of Munster rugby. It seems to transcend all boundaries, and unites the people of Limerick in a way I do not think is seen in any other city in the country. The fluttering bunting of red Munster flags are a permanent fixture across O'Connell Street, continuously displaying the city's pride in their team. The Munster team is probably most famous for its defeat of the All Blacks 12-0 in 1978. They were the first (and so far the only) Irish team to beat the famous New Zealand side, which they did in their home ground of Thomond Park. Before Ireland entered the current recession, Limerick was undergoing a process of regeneration, a large element of which was the refocusing of the city on to the river.

According to P. W. Joyce, author of the 1870 book *Irish Local Names Explained*, Limerick is a corruption of the Irish form Luimneach. Opinions differ on the exact meaning of Luimneach. Some say that it means 'a bare spot of land', while another version says that the name derives from Lom na nEach, meaning 'the place bared by the horses', referring to a story about two warring leaders, one of whom camped out on a grassy area that his cavalry's horses grazed bare in 24 hours. The version in Maurice Lenihan's 1866 *History of Limerick* tells the story of how the King of Munster and the King of Connaught and their followers met in what is now Limerick to settle a dispute. A crowd gathered to watch the two kings' champions battle, and because it was so warm the spectators removed their cloaks and

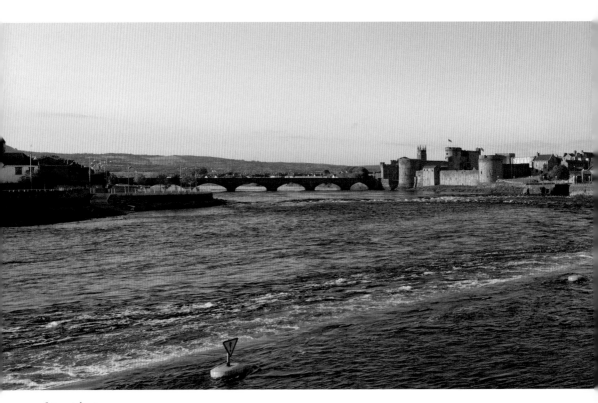

*Limerick city*

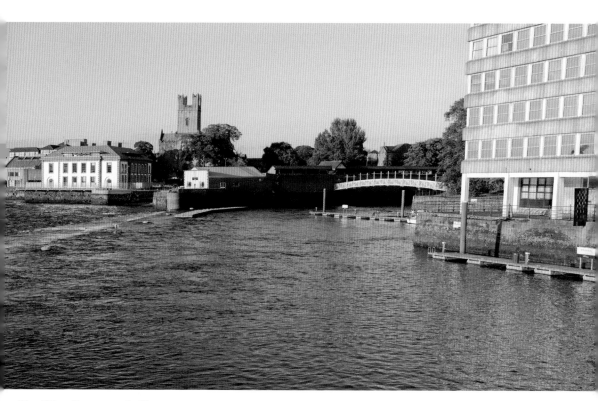

*The Abbey River joins the Shannon*

threw them on to the strand. The battle commenced, and the crowd were so enthralled that they did not notice the waters of the Shannon rising to sweep their cloaks away. These grey-green cloaks were called luimin, and so when one of the crowd noticed the cloaks float away, she called out 'Is Luiminochola in t-Inbear anossa', or 'cloakful is the river now'.

The Vikings first arrived in Ireland in AD 795, to the shores of Lambay Island off the coast of Dublin. By 922 they had established themselves permanently in Limerick on Inis Sibhtonn, King's Island, under Thormador Helgason or Tamar. From this island, surrounded by the Shannon on one side and the Abbey River on the other, Tamar used his immense fleet to control the centre of Ireland, while handling Norse trade coming in from the Atlantic. Tamar's fleet plundered nearly all of the major monasteries along the Shannon, including Inis Cealtra and Clonmacnoise. The Vikings dominated the region until their eventual defeat by the Dál gCais kings under Mathgamain in 967.

The most notable remnant of the Vikings in Limerick is the abundance of surnames of Norse origin. These names include Harold (whose two brothers and father were slain by Brian Ború), Godfrey/Mac Caffrey, Cotter (from Mac Oitir, son of Oitir who was Oitir the Black) and Costelloe. Other names were Irish descriptions of the 'foreigners', such as Fennell, which derives from Fionn Gaill or 'Fair Strangers', and Doyle, from Dubh Gaill or 'Black Strangers'. The only place name that remains from the Viking settlement is that of the Lax Weir at Corbally. The word 'lax' is the Scandinavian word for salmon.

Following the defeat of the Vikings, Limerick spent a short spell under Norman control, until the city was attacked by Dónal Mór O'Brien, and became the seat of the O'Brien Kings of Thomond until Dónal's death in 1194. The Normans then became the rulers of the whole county of Limerick. Under Norman control Limerick began its evolution to city when, in the late twelfth century, it was granted a charter. (Dublin and London did not have charters at this time.) Limerick started to develop as a large medieval town, with two main districts divided by the river: Englishtown, which included the Norse settlement on King's Island, and Irishtown on the mainland to the southeast. The two areas are connected by Baal's Bridge over the Abbey River, which was probably first constructed as a four-arch bridge in 1340, but replaced in 1831 by the single-arch bridge that remains today. Baal might be derived from the word 'bald', as the bridge did not have any battlements on it and was called An Droicheda Maol in Irish, 'the bald bridge'.

The Normans built the first bridge over the Shannon, Thomond Bridge, in the thirteenth century, which was followed by King John's Castle. The modern seven-arched limestone bridge replaced the original between 1836 and 1839. The castle sits at a strategic point, overlooking Thomond Bridge. This is because the Thomond, or Clare, side of the

Shannon was home to the Gaelic septs, including the O'Briens. The earliest bridge that is still standing in Limerick is Sarsfield Bridge, which dates to between 1824 and 1831. It is a five-arched bridge designed by Alexander Nimmo, and was called Wellesley Bridge until 1882.

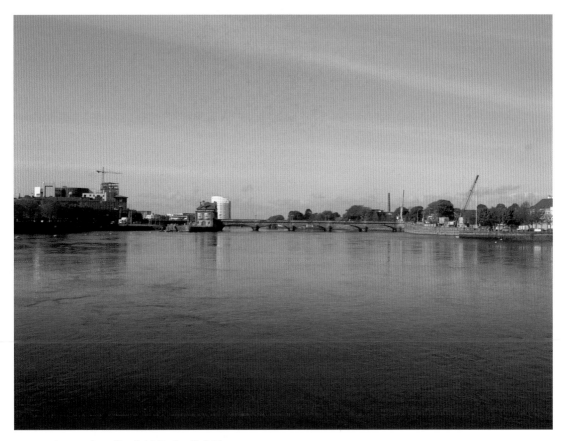

*Approaching Sarsfield Bridge © RPS*

At the northern end of Sarsfield Bridge there is a small island originally called Wellesley Pier, but now known as Shannon Island. This tiny island is home to the clubhouse of the Shannon Rowing Club, founded in 1868. Between the club and the shore is a navigation lock for boat traffic coming off the Abbey River and travelling out towards the estuary. Downstream of the lock on the other side of the bridge is a small grassy area that juts out into the river. This is known locally as the poor man's Kilkee, as it is where local people who did not have the means to travel to Kilkee for the day came to picnic, sunbathe and swim. I do not know if that is still the case, but the area is still very popular on our rare sunny days.

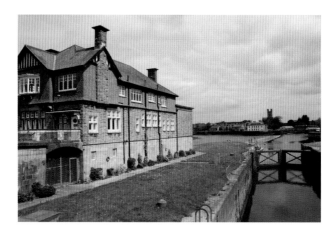

*Shannon Rowing Club*

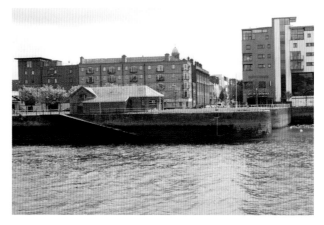

*Shannon Island*

Another medieval building of note in Limerick is St Mary's Cathedral, built by Dónal Mór O'Brien in the late twelfth century. The cathedral is one of the oldest surviving cathedrals in Ireland, and the official name is actually the Cathedral of St Mary Blessed Virgin. It was originally founded in 1168 on the site of Dónal Mór O'Brien's palace, and the stone lid of his coffin is on display in the Lady Chapel. It is thought that parts of O'Brien's palace were incorporated into the cathedral structure. The palace, in turn, had been built on the site of a Viking meeting house or Thing-mote. The twelfth-century Romanesque Transitional church was cruciform in shape and had aisles, a chancel and transepts. There have been many additions and alterations over the centuries, and even some wanton destruction during the Cromwellian siege of 1650. The Cromwellian soldiers supposedly stabled their horses in the Lady Chapel, and sharpened their swords on the Romanesque door that faces the river. The marks made by their swords in the stone arch are still visible.

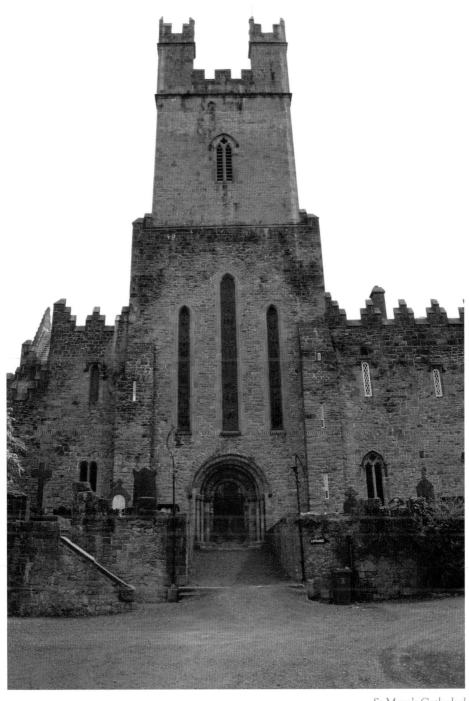

*St Mary's Cathedral*

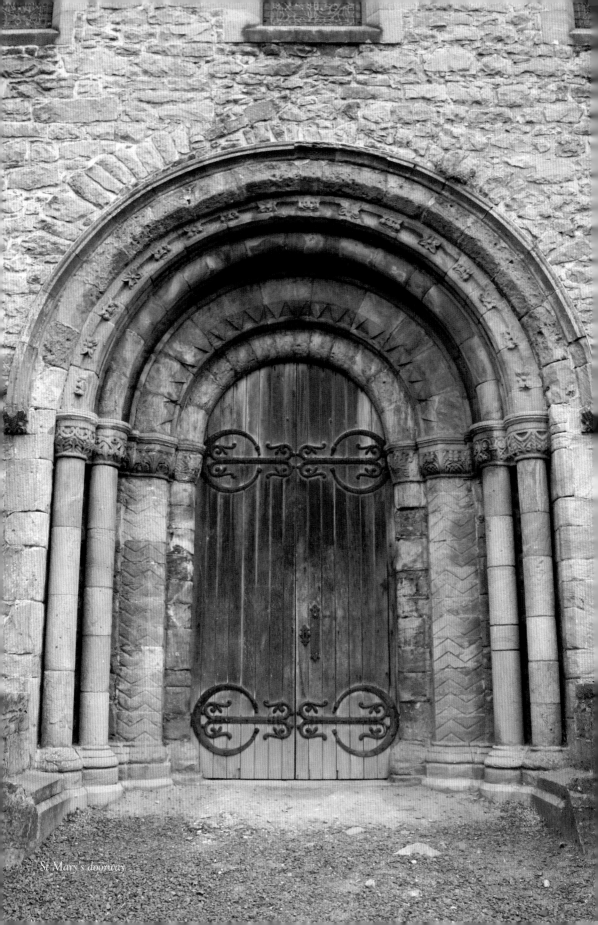

St Mary's doorway

The chapel next to the baptistry was the burial place of Lord Inchiquin, Murrogh O Brien. Murrogh is better known as Murchadh na dTóiteán or Murrogh the Burner, as he joined the Cromwellians and was involved in burning churches and monasteries. It is said that his body was dug up after his burial in 1673 and thrown into the River Shannon.

The city suffered three separate sieges during the seventeenth century, which is no surprise given that the motto of Limerick city translates to 'An ancient City well versed in the art of War'. The first siege took place in 1650 when Cromwellian forces captured the city. The second siege happened in 1690 when the army of King William of Orange was temporarily held off, before returning for the third, and probably best-known, siege in 1691.

For the 1690 attack, General Ginkel's army was made up of German, Dutch, Swedish, English and Scottish soldiers, as well as 2,500 Ulstermen and a hired troop from the King of Denmark. The 30,000-strong force took up key positions outside the city on 9 August 1690. The opposing Jacobite army was composed of the Clare Dragoons, Scottish Celts, English Catholics and a large number of French forces. The army numbered 20,000 and was based near Ardnacrusha. Patrick Sarsfield and 500 of his best horsemen undertook a daring raid on 10 August, when they intercepted and destroyed a Williamite siege train in Ballyneety, County Limerick. But the attack on Limerick city proceeded as planned. The battle took place around King John's Square and the Good Shepherd Laundry. In his song 'The Walls of Garryowen', Willie O'Connell describes the heroism of the Irishwomen during this battle, as they stood side by side with their menfolk on the ramparts.

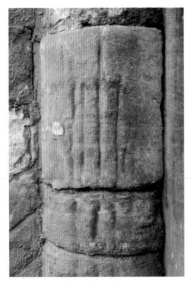

*Sword marks*

*King William's hirelings trembled when Sarsfield's troops assembled,*

*The women on the ramparts kept the Hession foe at bay*

*'Til their Gaelic blood ran red on the bosom of the Shannon*

*A land that bred such heroines will never know decay.*

*And Limerick's sons and daughters at home or o'er the water,*

*Will keep the ancient struggle on till Gráinne gets her own,*

*Until freedom's booming cannon resounds along the Shannon,*

*And reveals that ancient sunburst on the Walls of Garryowen.*

The Williamite forces lost 5,000 men, while only 500 from the Irish side died. The Williamites fled back to England, before returning a year later to commence a new campaign against the Jacobite forces. Sarsfield felt there was little chance of repelling the Williamites a second time and called for a truce. The Treaty of Limerick was signed at Páirc an Champa in Shannabooly on 3 October 1691. This treaty, which promised civil and religious liberty to Irish Catholics, is known as the broken treaty, and it is said that it was broken before the ink with which it was written was dry. The Treaty Stone now stands on the west side of Thomond Bridge at Clancy Strand.

In the eighteenth century the town defences were nearly all demolished, and a new section of city was planned and built outside the walls. This area, Newtown Pery, with its elegant Georgian terraces, lies to the southwest of Irishtown, and is the current commercial centre of Limerick. Newtown Pery gets its name from the landowner of the area, Edward Sexton Pery.

There is a long tradition of water sports in Limerick city. In the early nineteenth and twentieth centuries a number of boat and rowing clubs were set up along the riverbanks: the Limerick Boat Club, the Shannon Rowing Club, St Michael's and Athlunkard. This is more rowing clubs than any other Irish city. Perhaps the best-known club is the Shannon Rowing Club, whose clubhouse, we have seen, sits on Sarsfield Bridge and is a significant landmark in Limerick today. Rowing is still hugely popular in Limerick, but the rowers now share the Shannon's waters with more modern water sports such as kayaking. The Curragour Falls in the city centre, close to the mouth of the Abbey River, are home to the highest standing wave in the British Isles. Nearly every time I pass through Limerick city, I see these kayakers playing in the waves, under the shadow of King John's Castle.

The almost freshwater tidal muds of Limerick have a special assemblage of plants. These include the dense willow thickets, with patches of Summer Snowflake (*Leucojum aestivum*), and extensive reedbeds of Common Reed (*Phragmites australis*) and Club-rushes

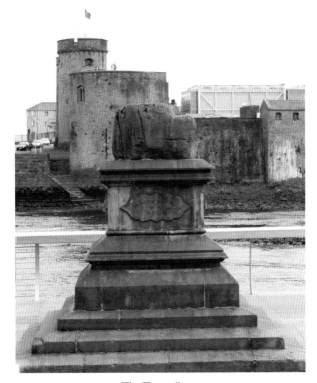

*The Treaty Stone*

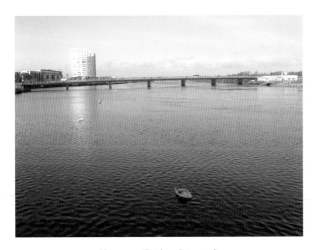

*Shannon Bridge, Limerick*

(*Schoenoplectus lacustris* and *S. tabernaemontani*) fringed on the lowest side by the rare and protected Triangular Club-rush (*Schoenoplectus triqueter*). The reedbeds are easily seen from Barrington's Pier at Westfields on the north side of the estuary, not far from Coonagh. The reeds are collected for thatching, and bundles can be seen on the Dock Road where it crosses Ballinacurra Creek. Most parts of the upper estuary are now controlled by embankments, also extending for miles inland up the River Maigue.

Farther out towards the Shannon Estuary, along the north shore at Rineanna, sits Shannon Airport. In between the airport and the estuary there is a lagoon that, like the Shannon Callows, was created by human intervention. In the 1930s work began on the construction of an airport at Rineanna, beside Shannon town. A seawall was built out into the estuary between Dernish Island and the mainland, to protect the airport from high-tide flooding of the estuary. Rainwater draining from the airport towards the Shannon was trapped between the wall and the shore, and the area became a lagoon.

The lagoon is brackish, with reedbeds of Phragmites (the Common Reed), Rush, Willows and Alder. Over 250 plant species have been identified so far, including the protected Pondweed (*Groenlandia densa*), Ragged Robin and Marsh Orchid. The lagoon is also home to the Annex II-listed otter, and is an important stopover for wading birds and wildfowl. Other birds found on the site include Water Rail, Black-tailed Godwit, Redshank, Dunlin, Gadwall, Wigeon and Teal.

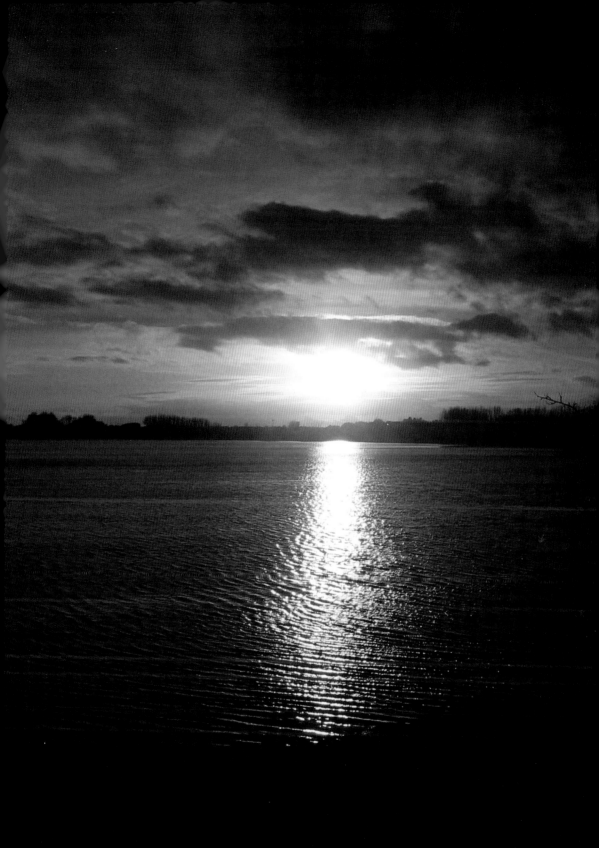

*Estuary at Shannon Airport* © *RPS*

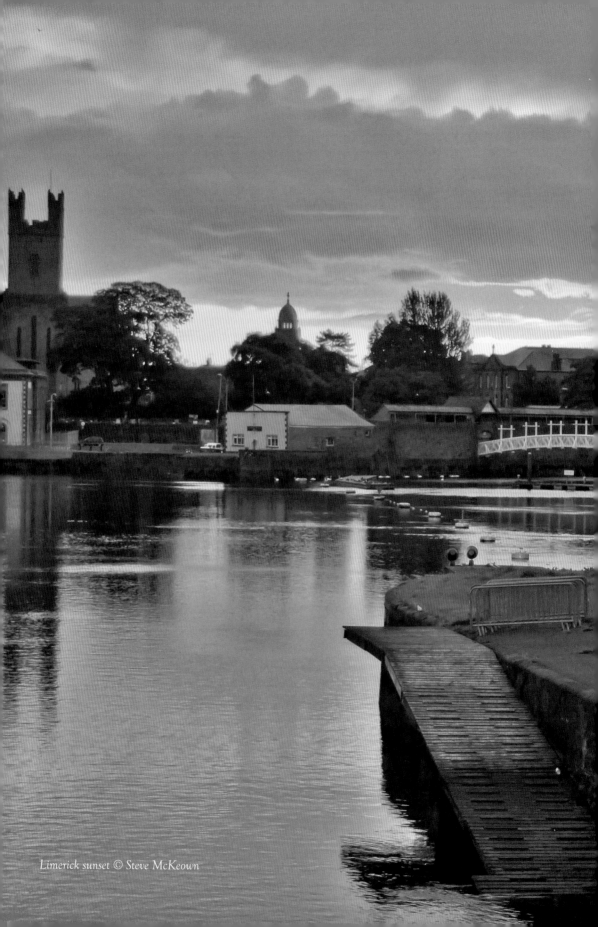

*Limerick sunset* © Steve McKeown

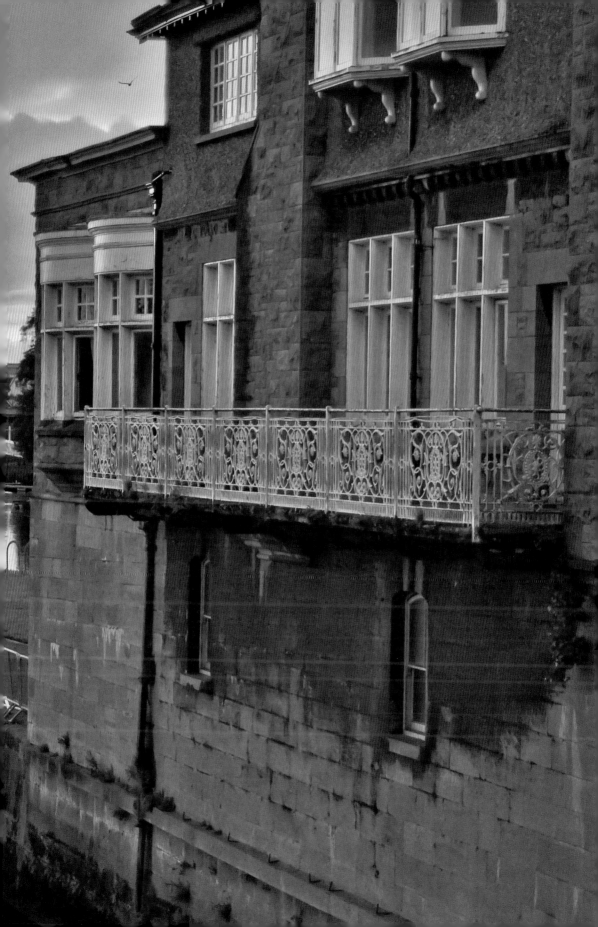

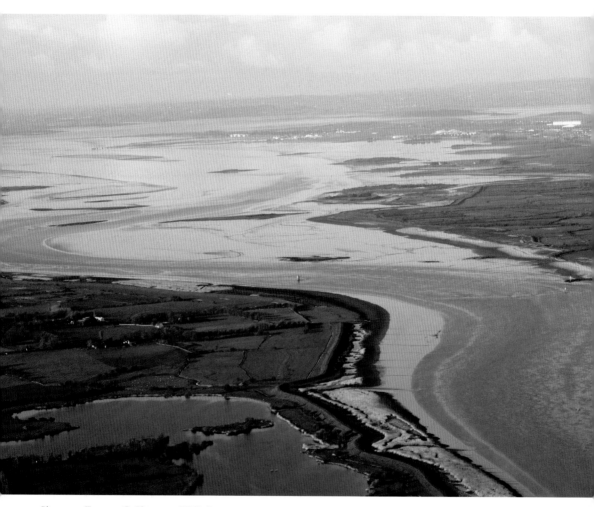

*Shannon Estuary © Shannon RBD Project*

# 20: The Shannon–Fergus Estuary

The rain lashes against our faces and the wind whips the breath from our lungs as it howls up from the Atlantic Ocean. It is summer on the Shannon Estuary, and we are crossing the estuary from Tarbert in County Kerry to Killimer in County Clare on board the *Shannon Breeze* car ferry. Our mission here is to see the Shannon dolphins. They are well known along the ferry route and farther out into the estuary towards Loop Head in County Clare. We are booked in with a dolphin-watching tour that leaves from Kilrush marina, but as the weather worsens I have a bad feeling that our trip will not be going ahead. As I peer into the dark, choppy waters of the estuary, hoping to spot a dorsal fin or two, I cannot help thinking back to the beginning of this voyage. It feels like a lifetime ago that I stood beside a small pool in the Cuilcagh Mountains, County Cavan, watching the infant Shannon emerging from the earth, while the rain lashed against my face, and the wind whipped the breath from my lungs as it howled down the mountain. That was winter at the source of the Shannon.

It has been a long and leisurely journey south for the Shannon, from the source to the sea. It has made its way towards the Atlantic through Cavan, Leitrim, Roscommon, Galway, Westmeath, Tipperary, Limerick, Kerry and Clare, widening at various points along the way into lakes – Allen, Ree and Derg being the largest. Other rivers joined the journey and become part of the Shannon as their waters met – Boyle, Little Brosna, Suck and Fergus to name just a few. This gives the Shannon a catchment area of 15,000 sq. km or one-fifth of Ireland's land mass. The river passes through many towns and cities on this journey south – Leitrim, Lanesborough, Carrick, Athlone, Banagher, Portumna, Killaloe, and eventually Limerick,

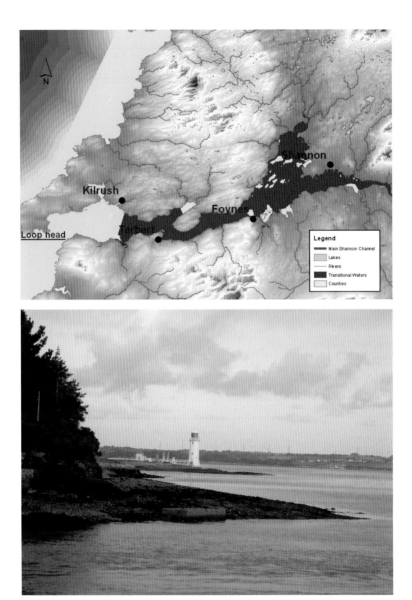

*Tarbert © RPS*

where the river becomes estuary and journeys on to meet the Atlantic at Loop Head.

My own journey down the river, across the lakes, up tributaries and over islands is nearly over too. The Shannon was almost a stranger to me at the beginning of this journey. I am a Liffey girl, reared near the banks of Anna Livia in County Kildare, where the river is fast-flowing and powerful. We would struggle upstream against the flow in our canoe and jump overboard into the freezing water, only recently arrived from the Wicklow Mountains. The flow carried us downstream towards the weir at Templemills, and we would hang on to the wall and peep over the top watching the water cascade down over the weir. The slow-flowing, wide expanse of the Shannon was not what I expected a river to be. And now, finally, here I am looking out to the Atlantic Ocean. The River Shannon ceases to be, as its waters mix with the Atlantic tide at Coonagh to form the Shannon Estuary.

From Killaloe to Loop Head, the River Shannon and the estuary are designated as cSAC (candidate Special Area of Conservation) under the EU Habitats Directive. It is known as the Lower River Shannon cSAC, and is a very large site that includes the lower freshwater reaches of the Cloon, Fergus, Kilmastulla and Mulkear rivers, and the Shannon-Fergus Estuary SPA and Loop Head SPA. The reasons for this designation are the presence of protected habitats including tidal mudflats, salt meadows, sea cliffs and lagoons, and species such as the Bottlenose dolphin, three Lamprey species (*Lampetra planeri, Lampetra fluviatilis* and *Petromyzon marinus*), Atlantic salmon and otter. A result of the variety of habitats found in the estuary is the presence of more wintering wildfowl and waders than any other site in Ireland. These wintering birds like to nest in the saltmarsh vegetation that fringes the vast expanse of intertidal mudflats. This vegetation includes Common Saltmarsh Grass (*Pucinellia maritima*), Sea Aster (*Aster tripolium*), Sea-milkwort (*Glaux maritima*) and Red Fescue (*Festuca rubra*).

Birds of international importance found here include the Dunlin (*Calidris alpina*), Black-tailed Godwit (*Limosa limosa*) and Redshank (*Tringa totanus*). The birds are also partial to the invertebrates living in the mudflats, and they have a tasty selection to dine on from cockles to lugworms. Birds found on the estuary in numbers of national significance include Cormorant (*Phalacrocorax carbo*), Whooper Swan (*Cygnus cygnus*), Curlew (*Numenius arquata*), Greenshank (*Tringa nebularia*), Wigeon (*Anas penelope*), Teal (*Anas crecca*) and Golden Plover (*Pluvialis apricaria*).

The Shannon Estuary is the largest estuary in Ireland, and is actually called an estuarine complex because the River Fergus enters the sea through this estuary also. The estuary stretches for 100 km from the upper tidal limits at Athlunkard Bridge to the mouth between Kerry Head and Loop Head, and covers an area of 50,000 hectares. It is made up of a variety of habitats, each one home to its own distinct assemblage of plants and animals, yet each one dependent on the other for survival.

The tide must be out, because I can see the mudflats exposed at the edges of the channel. The mud almost looks good enough to eat, like the smooth glaze of icing on a chocolate cake. The briny smell of the estuary is less appetising, but still alluring in a special way. It speaks to me of the sea, and indeed I can see patches of seaweed on the shore. There has been extensive reclamation of these mudflats in the last 200 years, and around 6,500 hectares have been lost to reclamation.

I am standing on the bank at Foynes in Limerick, where we have stopped off on our trip along the south side of the estuary to the ferry at Tarbert. As I look out across the estuary towards Foynes Island, I am trying to picture the rich and famous passengers of the flying boats that used to land here during the years of Second World War. The name Foynes probably derives from the Irish word 'Faing' meaning raven, which may refer to Fiang Inis or Raven Island, an island in the harbour.

According to the Flying Boat Museum, from 1939 to 1945 Foynes was the centre of the aviation world. In 1939 Pan Am's luxury flying boat the 'Yankee Clipper' was the first of its kind to land at Foynes. It was not only the famous and the privileged that utilised this service. As you might expect during this period, lots of the passengers were military personnel on active duty during the Second World War. The famous Irish actress Maureen O'Hara was married to one of the pilots, Charlie Blair, and she still comes to Foynes for the annual Irish Coffee Festival (the Irish Coffee was invented by the chef Joe Sheridan in Foynes Airport in 1942). Captain Blair made the first non-stop passenger crossing from Foynes to New York in 25 hours and 40 minutes. It is hard to imagine it all now, with the tide out and the mudflats exposed. Foynes is now the home of the Foynes Shipping Company, and a huge vessel is docked upstream of where I stand. Its deep waters allow ships of over 22,000 tonnes to moor here. Across the estuary I can see the massive aluminium extraction plant at Aughinish.

The reason for our current visit to the estuary is to see perhaps the best-known inhabitants of the estuary, the Bottlenose dolphin (*Tursiops truncates*). This is the species

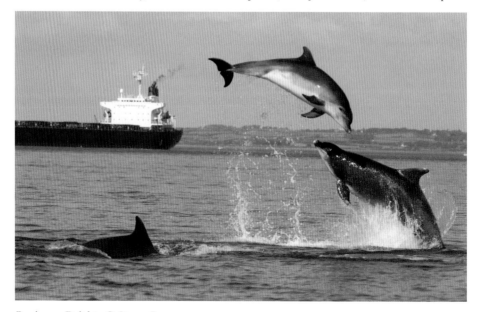

*Bottlenose Dolphin © Simon Berrow*

of dolphin Irish people are probably most familiar with, as they are widespread around Ireland's west coast. What Irish person has not heard of Fungi the Bottlenose dolphin in Dingle, County Kerry? Bottlenose dolphins are found in temperate and tropical seas around the world. They are named after their short and stubby beak, which can be up to 4.2 m long and have an average weight of around 200 kg. They are usually a grey colour with a lighter underside, and have an elongated jaw that bears a characteristic 'smile', which is apt as they are known for their inquisitive and playful nature.

All trips with the Discover Dolphins tour operators have been cancelled for the weekend, and we are disappointed. The wind is too strong and the water is too rough. The only Shannon dolphins we will see on this trip are the fake ones in the water outside the Shannon Dolphin and Wildlife Foundation offices in Kilrush Creek Marina. There has been a resident population of Bottlenose dolphins at the mouth of the estuary for at least several hundred years, and there are recorded sightings dating to 1849.

There is an ancient legend of a sea-monster, the Cathach, which lived on Scattery Island in the estuary at Kilrush. The old Irish name for Scattery Island was Inis Cathaigh, after the Cathach – the legendary beast or Péist which inhabited Scattery, terrorising anyone who dared set foot on the island and even attacking boats in the estuary. According to the legend, St Senan cast out the monster from the island and established the first monastery in the sixth century. Early descriptions of the monster – 'A nondescript creature with spiked back, scales, fishtail, nose curling up spirally, and clawed forefeet' – have some Dolphin-like characteristics, so perhaps the monster was in fact a Bottlenose dolphin? If so, then

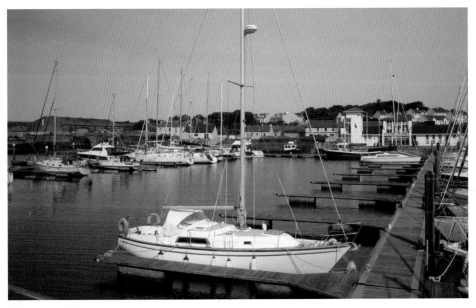

*Kilrush © RPS*

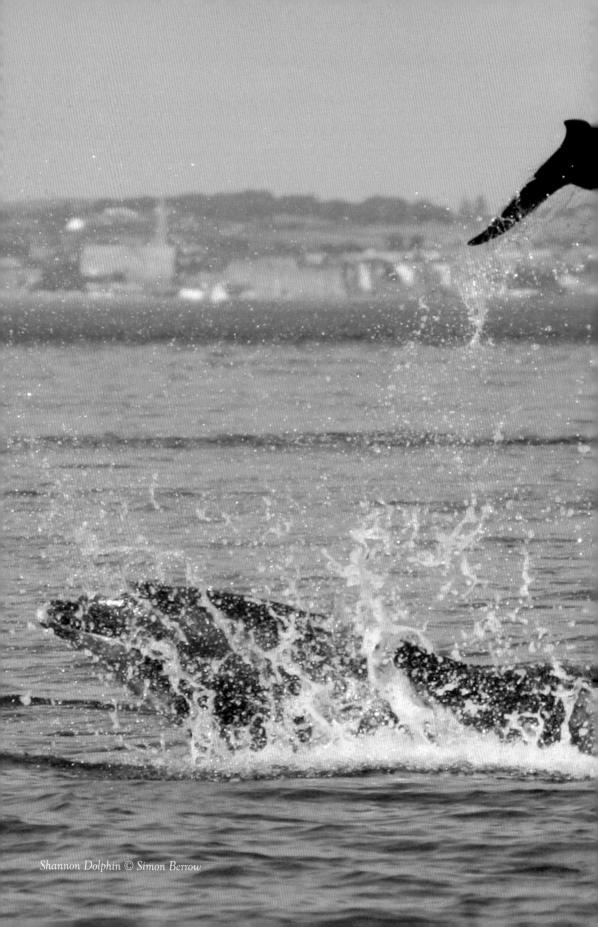

Shannon Dolphin © Simon Berrow

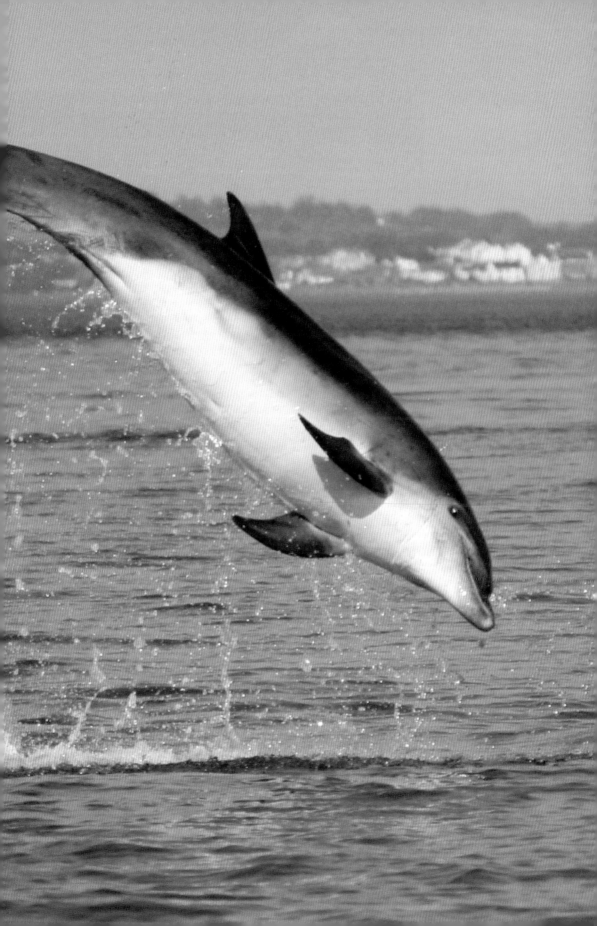

Aughinish © Conor Cahill

dolphins have been living in the Shannon for over 1,000 years.

According to the Irish Whale and Dolphin Group, the estuary is home to around 30–40 dolphins who are there for most of the year, with other dolphins only using the estuary periodically during the summer. In fact, even though the estuary dolphins have been studied since 1993, there is still a lot to learn about their ecology and behaviour. This group is the only resident population in Ireland, and one of only four known resident populations in Europe. The Shannon Estuary dolphins reside there all year round and give birth to their pale-coloured calves between May and September. The dolphins are known to favour two areas within the estuary – along the ferry crossing route between Tarbert and Killimer, and during the summer off Kilcredaun Head near Carrigaholt.

Despite the protection the cSAC designation gives to the Shannon Estuary Bottlenose dolphins, they are still vulnerable to disturbance from humans. Threats to their habitats include pollution from industry and agriculture; disturbance from marine industrial activities; accidental entanglement in fishing gear; physical and acoustic disturbance from shipping; and disturbance from dolphin-watching boat traffic. The Shannon region is a major centre of industry, including the alumina refinery at Aughinish and electricity generation with coal-fired and oil-fired stations located at Moneypoint and Tarbert in the outer estuary. The Shannon catchment also includes large areas of farmland and several tributary rivers, all providing potential sources of contamination of the estuary. The fact that the estuary is designated cSAC for the protection of the dolphins means that strict controls are placed on any activity that might disturb them. This includes dolphin-watching boat tours, so operators must get permission from the National Parks and Wildlife Service in order to provide dolphin-watching tours in the estuary.

In 2000 an accreditation scheme was set up for dolphin-watching boats on the Shannon Estuary called 'Saoirse na Sionna' (Freedom of the Shannon) to encourage sustainable dolphin-watching. Any boats accredited under this scheme fly the 'dolphin-friendly' flag and follow special codes of conduct that include: speed limits for boats; restrictions on the number of boats watching a particular pod of dolphins at one time; limiting the time spent with one group to 30 minutes; steering a parallel course to the dolphins rather than approaching them head on; and no swimming with the dolphins. To guarantee that dolphin-watching tours are following best practice and minimising their impact on the estuary dolphins, it is vitally important that visitors to the estuary only go dolphin-watching on boats that fly the 'Saoirse na Sionna' flag. For a list of accredited operators see the Shannon Dolphin and Wildlife Foundation website at www.shannondolphins.ie.

The ecological importance of the estuary is reflected in the high number of EU designations for habitats and species, and it is important that everything is done to protect the estuary. The Saoirse na Sionne scheme is one that should be emulated. The government is working with experts and local people to encourage an activity that attracts visitors to an area increasingly reliant on tourism for the economy. The scheme is ensuring that dolphin-watching is carried out in a sustainable manner that will benefit the local economy while minimising the impact on the estuary dolphins.

Our final destination on this long journey is Loop Head Lighthouse, which stands at the tip of the Loop Head Peninsula in County Clare. We are staying in the lighthouse keeper's cottage, which has been restored by the Irish Landmark Trust and is available for holiday rental. Kilbaha is the nearest village to the lighthouse, and the sun is setting as we pass through the village, with only 5 km left until we reach the Atlantic Ocean. The lighthouse sits on a clifftop, surrounded by water on all sides except the approach. Massive waves crash against the cliffs on one side of the peninsula, but it is the estuary side that draws our attention. This is the mouth of the Shannon Estuary, and it is here that we say goodbye to the Shannon as the river disappears into the ocean between Loop Head and Kerry Head.

My journey on the Shannon has come to an end. The story of the river has meandered much as the river has done along the way, from Vikings at Clonmacnoise to farming practices on the Callows, prehistoric settlements around Lough Derg, tales of tyrannical landlords during the Famine and fortifications built by the British to defend against the French. From the work of the Shannon Commission in the 1800s to the plight of the Red squirrel and the threat of invasive species to our native biodiversity, the stories have varied as much as the landscapes the river passes through, from mountains to valleys, lakes to rivers, rivers to canals and, finally, estuary to ocean. But I do not think my own story with the river will end here. Although my first journey on the river has ended, I know it will not be my last. Many of the people I spoke to along the way come back to the Shannon year after year for the scenery, the peace and the craic. I know I will be back too. Sionna has drawn me in, slowly and subtly, as I have followed her from source to sea.

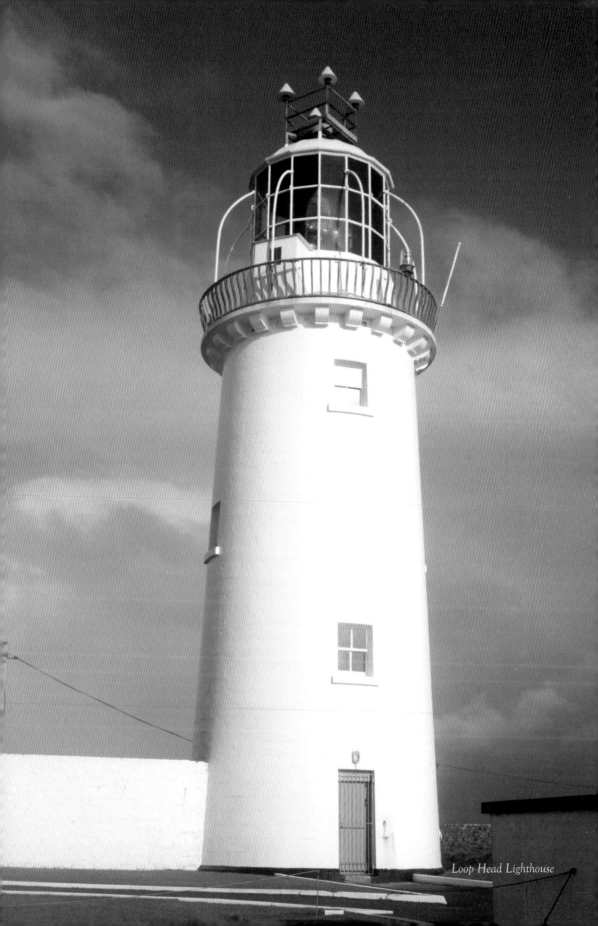

*Loop Head Lighthouse*

Though my feet are planted in a far-off land,
There is somewhere they would rather be,
Shure 'tis firmly planted in the dark brown sand
Where the Shannon River meets the sea.
My heart is e'er returning to my darling
Whose blue eyes mean all the world to me,
Shure 'tis heaven, and someone placed an angel there,
Where the Shannon River meets the sea.

Though my father told me other lands were fair,
I'm afraid with him I can't agree,
For I always long to breathe the scented air
Where the Shannon River meets the sea.
There are no lips so sweet and beguiling
As those lips which sure belong to me,
Though I keep on roaming shure my heart is set
Where the Shannon River meets the sea.

Anon.

# References

<small>BOOKS AND ARTICLES</small>

Berrow, S. D., McHugh, B., Glynn, D., McGovern, E., Parsons, K. M., Baird, R. W. and
    Hooker, S. J. 2002. 'Organochloride concentrations in resident bottlenose dolphins
    (*Tursiops truncates*) in the Shannon estuary, Ireland.' *Marine Pollution Bulletin*, 44, pp.
    1296–1313.

Breen, C. and O'Sullivan, A. 2002. 'Underwater Archaeology in the Republic of Ireland.'
    In: Ruppé, C. and Barstad, J. (Eds.) *International Handbook of Underwater Archaeology.*
    *New York: Springer.*

Browne, A. 2004. 'Waterways Corridor Study: Shannonbridge to Lanesborough and the
    River Suck to Ballinasloe – Natural Heritage.' In: Colin Buchanan & Partners
    *Waterways Corridor Study: A study of the area surrounding Lanesborough to Shannonbridge.*
    Kilkenny: The Heritage Council.

Browne, J. 2005. *Ireland's Mammals.* Kilcullen: Browne Books.

Cabot, D. 2004. *Irish Birds.* London: Harper Collins.

Clyne, M. 2005. 'Archaeological excavations at Holy Trinity Abbey, Lough Key, Co.
    Roscommon.' *Proceedings of the Royal Irish Academy*, 105, 2, pp. 23–98.

Crowe, E. 2005. *Ireland's Wetlands and their Waterbirds: status and distribution.* Wicklow:
    BirdWatch Ireland.

Cunnane Stratton Reynolds. 2006. *Waterways Corridor Study: A study of the area surrounding*
    *the Lower Shannon Navigation including Lough Derg, from Meelick, Co. Galway to Limerick*
    *City.* Kilkenny: The Heritage Council.

Delany, R. 1987. *By Shannon Shores: an exploration of the river.* Dublin: Gill & Macmillan.

Delany, R. and Kidney, P. 1993. *Shell Guide to the Shannon.* Dublin: Imray, Laurie, Norie
    & Wilson.

Delany, R. 2008. *The Shannon Navigation.* Dublin: The Lilliput Press.

Dowd, James. 1990. *Dowd's History of Limerick.* Dublin: The O'Brien Press.

Duane, O. B. 1998. *Celtic Myths & Legends.* London: Brockhampton Press.

Duffy, P. 1990. *Ardnacrusha – Birthplace of the ESB.* Dublin: ESB.

    Englund, A., Ingram, S. and Rogan, E. 2007. 'Population status report for bottlenose
    dolphins using the Lower River Shannon SAC, 2006–2007.' Dublin: NPWS.

Feehan, J. 1980. *The Magic of the Shannon*. Cork: Mercier Press.

Finney, K. 2009. 'Wading through the Shannon Callows.' *Heritage Outlook*, Summer/ Autumn 2009, pp. 28-31.

Fossitt, J. 2000. *A Guide to Habitats in Ireland*. Kilkenny: The Heritage Council.

Ginna, R. E. 2006. *The Irish Way: A walk through Ireland's past and present*. New York: Random House.

Gunn, J. 1996. 'Source of the River Shannon, Ireland.' *Environmental Geology*, 27, 2, pp. 110-112.

Hayward, R. 1940. *Where the River Shannon Flows*. London: Harap.

Heery, S. 1993. *The Shannon Floodlands: A natural history*. Galway: Tir Eolas.

Henry, M. 1996. *The River Shannon*. Dublin: The Conna Press.

Heritage Council. 2002. *Waterways Corridor Study of the Shannon from Shannonbridge to Meelick, and the Grand Canal from Ballycommon to Shannon Harbour*. Kilkenny: The Heritage Council.

Joyce, P. W. 1984. *Irish Place Names*. Belfast: Appletree Press.

Kierse, S. 1983. *Historic Killaloe: a guide to its antiquities*. Killaloe: Boru Books.

King, H. A. 1994. *Clonmacnoise Studies: Volume 1*. Dublin: Department of Environment, Heritage and Local Government.

King, H. A. 1998. *Clonmacnoise Studies: Volume 2*. Dublin: Department of Environment, Heritage and Local Government.

Lee, D. 1997. *Remembering Limerick: Historical essays celebrating the 800th anniversary of Limerick's first Charter granted in 1197*. Limerick: Limerick Civic Trust Press.

MacMahon, M. 2000. *Portumna Castle and its Lords*. Clare: Kincora Books.

McCarthy, T. K., Frankiewicz, P., Cullen, P., Blaszkowski, M. and Doherty, D. 2008. 'Long-term effects of hydropower installations and associated river regulation on River Shannon eel populations: mitigation and management.' Hydrobiologia, 609, pp. 109– 124.

Madden, G. 1993. *For God or King: the history of Mountshannon, Co. Clare, 1742–1992*. Clare: East Clare Heritage.

Manning, C. 1998. *Clonmacnoise*. Dublin: Office of Public Works.

Minchin, D., Lucy, F. and Sullivan, M. 2002. 'Monitoring of zebra mussels in the Shannon–Boyle navigation, other navigable regions and principal Irish lakes, 2000 & 2001.' *Marine Environment and Health Series*, 5, pp. 1-3.

Mitchell, G. F. 1990. *The Way that I Followed: A naturalist's journey around Ireland*. Dublin: Country House.

Mitchell, F. and Ryan, M. 1997. *Reading the Irish landscape.* Dublin: Townhouse.

Moriarty, C. 1999. 'Strategy for the development of the eel fishery in Ireland.' *Fisheries Bulletin*, 19, pp. 7–10.

Murphy, J. 2003. 'The Shannon Airport Lagoon.' *Wild Ireland*, 4, pp. 25–27.

Murtagh, H. 1991. 'Old Athlone.' In: Keaney, M. and O'Brien, G. (eds.) *Athlone: Bridging the Centuries.* Westmeath: Westmeath County Council.

Murtagh, H. 2000. *Athlone: history and settlement to 1800.* Athlone: Athlone Old Society.

O'Brien, D. 2003. *Athlone: A Visitors Guide.* Athlone: O'Brien Books.

O'Flynn, C. *Beautiful Limerick – the legends and traditions, songs and poems, trials and tribulations of an ancient city.* Dublin: Obelisk Books.

Ó hÓgáin, D. 1990. *Myth, Legend and Romance. An encyclopaedia of the Irish folk tradition.* London: Ryan Publishing.

Ó Riain, D. and Ó Cinnéide, S. 1999. *The History and Folklore of Parteen and Meelick.* Parteen: Ó Riain Books.

Office of Public Works. *Portumna Castle Visitor's Guide.* Dublin: Office of Public Works.

Praeger, R. L. 1937. *The Way that I Went: An Irishman in Ireland.* Dublin: Hodges Figgis.

Rice, H. J. 1975. *Thanks for the Memory.* Dublin: Inland Waterways Association of Ireland.

Roscommon County Council. *Lough Key Local Area Action Plan 2009–2015.* Roscommon: Roscommon County Council.

Shannon River Basin Management Project. 2003. *Current Management of Water Levels – River Shannon.* Shannon RBD.

Sterry, P. 2004. *Complete Irish Wildlife.* London: Harper Collins.

Trodd, V. 1985. *Banagher on the Shannon: A historical guide to the town.* Banagher: Trodd Books.

Tubridy, M. and Jeffrey, D. J. 1987. *The Heritage of Clonmacnoise.* Dublin: Environmental Science Unit, Trinity College Dublin.

Warner, D. 2007. *The Liffey.* Donaghadee: Cottage Publications.

White Young and Green. 2006. *Waterways Corridor Study 2006: River Shannon and Errina and Park Canals: Final Ecology Report to the Heritage Council.* Kilkenny: The Heritage Council.

Wyse Jackson, R. 1973. *The Story of Limerick.* Cork: Mercier Press.

INTERNET

The website of the National Parks and Wildlife Service – www.npws.ie – contains a wealth of valuable information, including documents to download, on species and locations discussed in this book.

The website for the Database of Irish Excavation Reports – www.excavations.ie – contains a detailed report by Aidan O'Sullivan and Donal Boland on the early medieval bridge in Clonmacnoise.

The website of the Offaly Historical and Archaeological Society – www.offalyhistory. com – contains an article by Michael Byrne on Charlotte Brontë and her connections with Banagher.

Other websites consulted were:

www.birdwatchireland.ie

www.birdlife.org

www.buildingsofireland.ie (National Inventory of Architectural Heritage)

www.cfb.ie (Central Fisheries Board)

www.clarelibrary.ie

www.environ.ie (Department of the Environment, Heritage and Local Government)

www.habitas.org.uk (National Museums of Northern Ireland)

www.iwdg.ie (Irish Whale and Dolphin Group)

www.nationalarchives.ie

www.opw.ie (Office of Public Works)

# Index

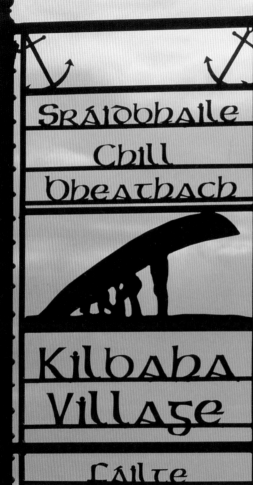

Sráidbhaile
Chill
bheathach

Kilbaha
Village

fáilte
Welcome

*Sunset at Kilbaha © Conor Cahill*